Legacies of Incarceration

Legacies of Incarceration

The World War II Experience of Hawai'i's Japanese

Kelli Y. Nakamura

University of Hawai'i Press
Honolulu

Printed in the United States of America

First printed, 2025

Library of Congress Cataloging-in-Publication Data

Names: Nakamura, Kelli Y. author
Title: Legacies of incarceration : the World War II experience of Hawaiʻi's Japanese / Kelli Y. Nakamura.
Description: Honolulu : University of Hawaiʻi Press, 2025. | Includes bibliographical references and index.
Identifiers: LCCN 2025004000 (print) | LCCN 2025004001 (ebook) | ISBN 9798880700974 hardback | ISBN 9798880700981 trade paperback | ISBN 9798880701001 epub | ISBN 9798880701018 kindle edition | ISBN 9798880700998 pdf
Subjects: LCSH: Japanese Americans—Hawaii—History—20th century | Japanese Americans—Hawaii—Attitudes | Imprisonment—Social aspects—Hawaii—History—20th century | World War, 1939-1945—Hawaii | Japanese Americans—Forced removal and internment, 1942-1945 | World War, 1939-1945—Japanese Americans | World War, 1939-1945—Participation, Japanese American
Classification: LCC DU624.7.J3 N35 2025 (print) | LCC DU624.7.J3 (ebook) | DDC 940.53/17969—dc23/eng/20250513
LC record available at https://lccn.loc.gov/2025004000
LC ebook record available at https://lccn.loc.gov/2025004001

Cover photograph: "Honouliuli Internment & POW Camp—barracks and tents." Japanese Cultural Center of Hawaiʻi, R. H. Lodge photographer, #910. AR 19 Archival Collection.

University of Hawaiʻi Press books are printed on acid-free paper and meet the guidelines for permanence and durability of the Council on Library Resources.

Contents

Preface

This project began many years ago when I was an undergraduate looking for a historical research project for my senior thesis. By chance, I found stories of Hawai'i incarceration during World War II in Hamilton Library's Hawaiian Collection at the University of Hawai'i at Mānoa. I was immediately drawn to stories of individuals incarcerated without cause, separated from their families and communities for years, and forced to undergo humiliating strip searches at the direction of military officials. None of this had been mentioned in my classes on Hawaiian history, and what little I did know about World War II history was centered on the triumphalist narratives of the experiences of Nisei veterans of the 100th Infantry Battalion and the 442nd Regimental Combat Team.

This question about the divergent fates of the Japanese during World War II would take me to Hiroshima, Japan, to learn more about Japanese repatriates and Japanese families with Hawai'i connections whom the war had impacted. Through the generous support of Dr. Fumiko Kaya and the Goto of Hiroshima Foundation, I was fortunate to interview several of them who had become atomic bomb victims or *hibakusha*, after participating in the Hiroshima Peace Memorial Ceremony held annually on August 6. I also made numerous trips to the National Archives in Maryland, Washington, DC, and San Bruno, California, to obtain military documents, inmate records, and State Department files. I have only cited a handful of the hundreds of pages of materials to provide important context for the events that would unfold before, during, and after the war. However, subsequent visits to existing incarceration sites, archives, libraries, personal collections on O'ahu and the neighbor islands, and interviews with inmate family members and residents brought their stories to life. On Moloka'i, I met residents over breakfast at Kanemitsu Bakery in downtown Kaunakakai, who shared old photographs of the local jail and information about the local courthouse that was now deteriorating at Mālama Park. On nearby Lāna'i, I visited the restored historic Lāna'i Jail, located at the corner of 8th Street and Gay Street around Dole Park. I saw the cramped conditions inmates endured before being transferred to Maui or O'ahu and understood the humiliation they must have experienced with their public arrest. On Maui and Kaua'i, I interviewed individuals at the local veterans' center and pored through manuscripts and jail records at historical societies to identify the individuals incarcerated on each island. My research also took me to Hawai'i Island, where the staff at Hawai'i Volcanoes National Park Archives were unfailingly generous with their time and insight in locating photographs and historical records. On O'ahu, the Hawaiian Collection and Archives at Hamilton Library became a second home. I spent hours in the microfiche room reading articles in Japanese and English newspapers to learn more about these inmates and the prewar Japanese community. Winter and spring breaks were spent at the Japanese Cultural Center of Hawai'i, Bishop Museum, and the Hawai'i State Archives for photographs, documents produced by the Military Governor, and even business records, as many of these inmates occupied prominent positions within the prewar Japanese community. Evidence of these sites and information about these inmates were scattered throughout the islands, but slowly and surely, these pieces began to come together.

As most inmates had passed on before my research, I began searching for oral histories, diaries, newspaper interviews, songs, and poetry in Japanese and English to gain critical insights into their experiences. It soon became clear that the civil and military fears that led to the removal of Japanese from their families and communities throughout the Islands had originated as early as the mid-nineteenth century with the emergence of plantations. As white elites sought to control what they perceived to be a growing Japanese threat both on the plantations and in urban areas, they became increasingly aligned with military officials who considered the Japanese a threat to national security. Martial law, which some scholars believe to be a more enlightened alternative to the mass incarceration of Japanese on the mainland, culminated in these racist fears that justified an unprecedented extension of military authority with targeted policies to control the Japanese within and outside incarceration centers. While all Hawai'i residents were subject to martial regulations and experienced the suspension of their civil liberties, only the Japanese had been targeted and investigated by civil and military authorities before and during the war due to their alleged racial threat. However, military control was never uniformly implemented, particularly on the neighbor islands, where residents of predominantly rural plantation communities witnessed the extraordinary mobilization of their communities and the arrest and incarceration of Japanese residents.

Although neighbor island incarceration is often presented as a preliminary step before inmates were transferred to O'ahu and mainland incarceration centers, the diverse experiences these inmates endured highlight the varying influences of both the military and the plantations that shaped the evolution of incarceration policies that were never static or uniformly enforced.

Thus, my study examines residents' experiences on Hawai'i Island, Maui, Moloka'i, Lāna'i, and Kaua'i, expanding beyond an O'ahu-centric, urban focus to highlight the community impact of incarceration as authorities often held inmates in public facilities within rural plantation towns. These inmates would demonstrate the power wielded by military and plantation officials that extended to areas removed from Pearl Harbor and the Military Governor, as many of these early inmates would be some of the first to be sent to mainland incarceration centers as the construction of Honouliuli would not be completed until March 1943. Additionally, I endeavor to address the implementation and evolution of incarceration policies throughout the war as authorities continued to utilize incarceration as a method of control. With this specific focus, essential stories such as the experience of Japanese Americans from Hawai'i who were sent directly to War Relocation Authority concentration camps such as Jerome, Arkansas, and Topaz, Utah, from November 1942 to March 1943 still demand scholarly analysis as they represent nearly half of the inmates from Hawai'i. Further, the story of Nikkei who were excluded from their homes and businesses in the Islands following the Pearl Harbor attack, is also not covered as they will comprise a future study. Instead, this collective approach to understanding the incarceration of Hawai'i's Japanese residents seeks to provide a holistic understanding of the incarceration experience throughout the various islands to highlight the factors that shaped incarceration on each island before, during, and after the war to illustrate the uniqueness of Hawai'i's incarceration story.

Subsequently, Hawai'i incarceration was informed by community dynamics, military, civil interests, racist fears, and even generational differences within Japanese communities that contributed to various experiences during and even after World War II among Hawai'i residents. Within this analysis, it is essential to recognize that while the balance of power often favored whites, not all whites contributed to the atmosphere of fear and repression. Some whites supported Japanese resistance against discriminatory policies, challenging racist notions about the Japanese. Additionally, many Japanese effectively resisted the destruction of their identity and their community. Some Japanese even benefited from their wartime experiences, aligning themselves with Americanization efforts or informing other Japanese officials to prevent incarceration.

While this study ends with the economic, political, and social ascension of the Nisei within the Democratic Revolution of 1954 that witnessed democratic majorities in both the House and Senate, it highlights the divergent fates of Nisei veterans and former inmates. It also invites further research and critique of the outsized impact Japanese residents in Hawai'i continue to wield that has raised issues of Asian settler colonialism. While this project initially started as a personal journey to learn more about my history as a resident of Hawai'i, it has come to encapsulate some of the enduring legacies of war that continue to reverberate in various communities within the Islands and beyond, highlighting the vulnerabilities of minorities to racist fears in times of war.

Acknowledgments

It has been said that acknowledgments can be categorized into two types: gratitude to those who assisted in countless ways during the writing and publication process and appreciation of those who gave you the space and allowed you to be absent in their lives (and sometimes yours) as you slogged through countless drafts, revisions, and rejections. To the former, I need first to recognize my late graduate chair, Margot "Mimi" Henriksen, who bravely took on a clueless graduate student and tried to teach her how to creatively and analytically approach history through her irreverent wit and stellar editing. While I did not embark upon a post-doctorate, I often consider the teaching and insight that I received working with Brian Niiya and Densho an invaluable education that increased my awareness and understanding of the minutiae and significant events and individuals in Japanese American history. I still regard myself a student of Brian's and thank him for his kindness and the knowledge that he generously shares with others. I am also profoundly indebted to librarians and staff in the numerous archives and libraries that became my second home. Jodie Mattos, Dore Minatodani, Sherman Seki, and Dawn Sueoka have been unfailingly kind and helpful. While I know that they probably dread my emails with obscure questions and numerous requests for materials, they have yet to turn me out (and they should!). I am particularly indebted to Jodie, who has guided me from an undergraduate student to a professor in my research and scholarly endeavors with countless invaluable suggestions and recommendations.

At Kapiʻolani Community College and the University of Hawaiʻi at Mānoa, I have been blessed with incredible colleagues and friends who have often served as sounding boards, editors, and occasionally co-authors on different projects. They include Sarah Bremser, Brandon Marc Higa, Martin Holzgang, Shaun Kiyabu, Davin Kubota, Cheryl Miyahara, Dawn Oshiro, Catherine Mau Primavera, Julie Rancilio, and Michelle Shin. Brandon and Julie, in particular, should be acknowledged for their unfailing support of my projects, no matter how ridiculous or impossible they may seem. Additionally, this project greatly benefited from the guidance and critical feedback provided by two excellent editors: Mike Baccam of University of Washington Press and Emma Ching of University of Hawaiʻi Press. Despite my ignorance of book publishing, they were consistently professional and helped to shepherd this project through multiple revisions and iterations. Finally, this research was made possible by a Mellon/ACLS Community College Faculty Fellowship from the American Council of Learned Societies. This fellowship allowed me to devote critical time and resources to bring this project to fruition.

As this project has been decades in the making, I am forever indebted to my family, who have kept the home front running in my absence. They have sustained and supported me in countless ways. To my brothers Marc, Reid, and Taylor, thank you for your generosity and encouragement. The past few years have been particularly challenging, and I have always benefited from your gestures of assistance, both small and big, which are often unasked but recognized and appreciated. I have also been the recipient of the kindness and support of Randy Shimanuki and his family, Eriko Moriyama Hufen and her family, as well as my ʻĀina Hina family, Melissa Chee, and her parents, Hon Ping and Leatrice Chee. I have been the grateful recipient of their hospitality and thoughtfulness for decades, and they have become a second family. Finally, I need to thank my beautiful daughter, Ella, for her patience and understanding as I dragged her to libraries, archives, and countless lectures during her holidays and breaks. I recognize that no elementary school student willingly attends college classes or should be familiar with university libraries and archives. Yet she was always in positive spirits and had the good sense to extort extra playtime, trips to McDonald's, or shave ice and musubi afterward from her mother.

In closing, this book is dedicated to the two most important people who have always supported me: my parents, Wesley and Liane Nakamura. Their countless sacrifices and selflessness made this project and many more possible. Thank you from the bottom of my heart.

Introduction

This boss would make us stand in the rain, practically naked, in our undershirts and underpants. It was because of this that we who left Kauai had our first casualty.[1]

Kaetsu Furuya, a former Japanese language schoolteacher on the island of Kaua'i, describes in this story a gripping memory of the incarceration he and over 2,000 Japanese on the Islands experienced on O'ahu during World War II. Furuya's testimony offers a brief glimpse into the humiliating and devastating ordeal of incarceration in Hawai'i that had two fundamental purposes. First, it was to destroy the lives of the individuals who represented the leadership of the Japanese community in Hawai'i. Second, the threat of incarceration instilled fear in others who suspected they might be subject to a similar fate. The attack on Pearl Harbor on December 7, 1941, not only launched America's entry into World War II but also began America's war against a specific ethnic group within its shores: Japanese and Japanese Americans. Both terms will be used in this study to highlight the broad experiences of the Japanese community but also to delineate events specific to the Issei (who were denied American citizenship until 1952) and their Nisei children, who were American citizens by birth. While the Japanese were not the only workers on the plantations—other groups included Chinese, Portuguese, Koreans, and Filipinos—they soon became the largest ethnic group on the plantations. They also had a contentious history with white plantation owners who soon recognized them as a potential economic, political, and social threat.

Although scholars have extensively documented the story of Japanese incarceration on the mainland, little attention has been given to incarceration throughout Hawai'i, where martial law gave military officials unprecedented power and authority. Like their mainland counterparts, select individuals from Hawai'i's Japanese community were arrested, incarcerated, and treated like criminals. Many would not return until the war had ended. Isolated from the larger Japanese community and subjected to arbitrary punishments that included interrogations and strip searches, these inmates became victims of racist fears and suspicions. Further, the military used those incarcerated as "examples" to control the rest of the Japanese population in Hawai'i, who feared sharing a similar fate. A study on the effects of incarceration on Hawai'i's Japanese community during the war confirmed that "an extreme degree of fear was present" due to the loss of traditional leaders and religious institutions.[2] Although incarceration could be seen as a product of wartime hysteria, its long history of planning and its carefully conceived goal of weakening and controlling the Japanese community undermines this argument. With lessons learned from over fifty years of experience dealing with the Japanese, territorial authorities and military officials sought complete control of the Japanese community through extralegal means under the exigencies of war.

Incarceration was thus the culmination of long-standing racist fears by white elites and military officials. Consequently, the experiences of Hawai'i's Japanese challenge the assumption that Hawai'i's Japanese had a more benign wartime experience than their mainland counterparts due to a tolerant racial environment. Further, as legal scholars Harry N. Scheiber and Jane L. Scheiber note, this portrayal of Hawai'i's wartime experience as more respectful of the constitutional rights of its residents distorts the fact that government officials suspended the liberties of the entire civilian population. In place of civil authority, the army imposed a comprehensive, restrictive, and essentially "arbitrary and capricious" military regime that set aside most of the liberties guaranteed in the Bill of Rights and Constitution. As a result, military officials could exercise absolute authority over the civilian population while targeting Japanese residents.[3] A critical context that is missing is the understanding of the impact of the plantations and the racial fears of the Japanese held by white elites that had developed over seventy years with the beginning of large-scale migration in 1868. Before and after the Pearl Harbor attack, military officials and plantation owners collaborated to control the Japanese population in the Islands, who they believed posed an economic, political, and social threat to their interests within Hawai'i. As migrants, Japanese workers were legally Japanese citizens, yet subject to the laws of the Kingdom of Hawai'i (1795–1893) and later the Territorial Period of Hawai'i (1900–1959). As such, civil officials often assisted plantation owners with the enforcement of labor contracts as they had shared economic and political interests. The arrest and incarceration of Japanese leaders on December 7, 1941, had clear precedents on the plantations where authorities routinely arrested recalcitrant workers and strike leaders. White officials also criminalized labor movements and enacted policies to control entire communities due to the alleged racial threat of the Japanese.

(Re)Examining Incarceration in Hawai'i

This study examines the implementation of martial law and the incarceration of select individuals in Hawai'i during World War II, which was the result of prewar fears by the military and white elites. I highlight the evolution of incarceration and martial law policies through the incorporation of multiple voices and experiences within this narrative. The stories that emerge reflect the unprecedented collusion between military and plantation officials to control the perceived Japanese "threat," particularly on the neighbor islands, which lacked a strong federal presence before the war. As noted by the Scheibers, who traced the development of martial law by army officials who were "willing to invoke the specter of subversion and disloyalty as a justification for the martial law regime," incarceration similarly evolved according to circumstances and the need to maintain army control.[4] Thus, before formal military facilities were constructed, authorities often utilized community structures across the Hawaiian Islands to incarcerate residents. The military use of jails, schools, and even a gymnasium to house prisoners highlights a stark contrast in their planning and the actual logistics of incarcerating individuals.

This research also highlights the distinctiveness of Hawai'i incarceration. Unlike the mainland, where authorities forcibly removed entire communities, officials arrested and incarcerated specific individuals in confinement sites on Hawai'i Island, Maui, Moloka'i, Lāna'i, Kaua'i, and O'ahu. It expands upon previous research that predominately focused on the experience of O'ahu's inmates and sites to encompass all of the major Hawaiian Islands and the experience of inmates throughout the war.[5] Thus, this study explores the scope and scale of martial law in Hawai'i's communities. It focuses on the diversity of experiences endured by Japanese inmates, particularly on the neighbor islands where incarceration was often a localized event within tight-knit plantation communities. These individuals were often the first prisoners to be sent to mainland incarceration centers in February 1942, before the opening of Honouliuli in March 1943. As a result, this dislocation was often more profound as authorities sent them to multiple sites.

Regardless of their island of origin, a defining feature often shared among the inmates was the impact of their selective arrests and imprisonment as authorities utilized incarceration to control other Japanese who feared a similar fate. Although some have argued that these selective numbers and targeted incarceration were reflective of efforts by the army to distinguish between loyal and suspect individuals rather than prejudicing an entire population based on race, the impact of incarceration extended beyond the inmates. It resonated throughout Japanese communities across Hawai'i as residents understood they could be targeted due to racial fears. Thus, military officials could successfully defend their control over civilian life by claiming to promote racial unity both before and during the war in pro-American campaigns. In the meantime, they could also identify individuals for incarceration based on race whose arrests further inspired others to prove their loyalty in response to the perceived guilt of the inmates. Many Japanese residents responded with public demonstrations of patriotism that included military service. These actions highlighted the contradiction of swearing allegiance and demonstrating loyalty to the same country that unilaterally imposed martial law and imprisoned individuals without due process. Numerous scholars have extensively documented Hawai'i residents' demonstrations of Americanization and loyalty to the United States, as well as efforts to promote interracial unity before and during the war. This study also recognizes those who embodied more complicated loyalties, such as the Issei, who were denied American citizenship until 1952.[6] I also examine the disillusionment and hardship experienced by those who had been arrested and incarcerated without due process, as well as the impact of their incarceration on their families and the larger community. Thus, during World War II, two divergent narratives of oppression (for those incarcerated) and empowerment (for those who demonstrated their loyalty during World War II and beyond) began to define the war experience of Hawai'i's Japanese. While the latter interpretation has characterized most World War II Hawai'i accounts, stories of resistance and resilience—both within and outside the confinement sites—highlight individuals' agency in their struggle for equality in Hawai'i and beyond.

Prewar Plantation Tensions

From the outset of Japanese migration, the Japanese community in the Islands experienced violence and mayhem on the part of whites and Japanese. Workers fought for authority and autonomy on the "contested terrain" of the plantations, while planters sought to extract as much effort from laborers as possible.[7] As migrants, Japanese workers were legally Japanese citizens. Yet, they were also subject to the laws of the kingdom and later Territory of Hawai'i and obligated to fulfill the conditions of their labor contracts. These overlapping and sometimes conflicting responsibilities often seemed contrary to the personal aspirations that initially compelled them to leave Japan, to seek new opportunities and a better life. In this nebulous legal context, the Japanese encountered a dual system of justice that subjected migrants to social, legal, and economic discrimination. Within this biased system, authorities often prosecuted Japanese to the fullest extent of the law, whether they had committed the alleged crime or not. At the same time, whites charged with similar offenses were often never arrested or avoided full punishment for their crimes. Scholars such as Edward Beechert, Ronald Takaki, and Gary Okihiro have extensively detailed the vast hardships experienced by these workers. Japanese migrants were essentially indentured servants who worked for little pay, labored under harsh working conditions, and had little legal recourse to protest such discriminatory policies, unfair treatment, and abuse.[8]

The Japanese did not passively accept this treatment and, throughout the early years of the twentieth century, engaged in strikes, various forms of protest, and even criminal activity and violence against planters and their collaborators.[9] As they did so, tensions slowly escalated between whites and Japanese, who engaged in physical confrontations on and off the plantations, verbal debates in newspapers, and legal battles in the courtroom. For example, owing to their involvement in labor struggles and other perceived anti-American activities, Japanese language schools became the target of territorial legislation designed to weaken their influence. They were considered "centers of an influence which, if not distinctly anti-American, is certainly un-American."[10] Ironically, the planters established and subsidized Japanese language schools as they saw them as incentives to keep the laborers on the plantations. Planters also initially welcomed Buddhist missionaries because they believed they fostered cultural differences that prevented worker solidarity and deepened ethnic divides. According to scholar Noriko Asato, "Buddhist priests and planters saw each other serving mutual interests. Buddhist priests initially stood on the side of the planters and reconciled troubles between Japanese workers and their plantation managers in exchange for planters' support for their ministries."[11] By the 1920s, however, many whites alleged that the language schools were "under the control of reactionary Buddhist priests" who undermined the efforts of "genuine Americanization."[12] Some supported these assimilationist efforts, including eliminating Japanese language schools and Americanizing public schools. However, as scholar Eileen Tamura points out, "while Nisei acculturated into American middle-class society, they also retained aspects of their Japanese cultural heritage" as an alternative path to "absorption" and "differentiation."[13] These scholars highlight critical events within Hawai'i's prewar history of targeted attempts by civil officials to control the Japanese population in the Islands. This study connects these events to similar efforts by military officials to control the Japanese in the prewar period and with the outbreak of war even as the Japanese continued to resist discriminatory treatment.

Despite these efforts to assuage white fears, acts of resistance continued against white paternalism and white authority, and by extension, the dual system of justice in Hawai'i, which granted whites select privileges at the expense of minority rights. These actions led to growing fears of the Japanese population and to demands for extralegal restrictions and regulations designed to control and suppress the unruly Japanese once and for all. Incidences like Myles Fukunaga's 1928 kidnapping and murder of Gil Jamieson, the son of a wealthy white family, and the 1932 Massie Case, when Navy wife Thalia Massie accused a group of local men, who included Japanese, of a brutal rape further contributed to tensions between Japanese and whites over perceptions of Japanese violence and criminality.[14] Media representations of individual Japanese and the Japanese community were hotly debated in the Japanese newspapers and, in general, proved of particular concern during this period as many in Hawai'i already questioned the loyalty of the Japanese—well in advance of World War II.[15] Ultimately, negative perceptions of the Japanese held by political elites and by the U.S. military in Hawai'i became one of the factors leading to the institution of martial law during World War II and to the incarceration of those individuals within the Japanese community who were considered particularly disloyal or threatening.

A closer look at these events and others throughout this period reveals a much more complex and nuanced view that challenges the underlying theme of Japanese victimhood in the face of absolute white authority. It highlights Japanese resistance and agency as well as cooperation and collaboration with white authorities and other ethnic groups on and off the plantations. This study expands upon the past scholarship of Hawai'i's plantation history, tracing Japanese exploitation and resistance from the beginning of the immigration period to the outbreak of war and beyond. It bridges Hawai'i's agricultural past with the islands' growing importance as a strategic outpost in the Pacific for U.S. military forces before World War II. Shared racial fears of the Japanese held by civil and military officials resulted in unprecedented extralegal measures to control a perceived danger to white interests. These fears eventually culminated in martial law with the outbreak of war. This study incorporates labor, social, economic, political, legal, and even military history to highlight the complex circumstances, events, and even individuals who would shape the experiences of the Japanese before, during, and after World War II. While some residents and their families suffered during the war following their family members' arrest, others in Hawai'i benefited from their wartime experiences. The impact of their divergent postwar fates continues to resonate today.

Within the unique environment of Hawai'i, populated by a diversity of ethnicities, however, it is essential to note that these migrants were given tantalizing opportunities within the recently established legal, economic, and social institutions of the Islands to challenge their oppression and exploitation. Taking a cue from their white oppressors, they resorted to extralegal means of justice, such as beatings of white sympathizers and attacks against plantation authorities, demonstrating this legal system's weakness. Thus, the dual system of justice was never wholly established to the satisfaction of whites as migrants were never entirely disenfranchised, nor were whites free from prosecution for their crimes. Additionally, tensions existed within and between different ethnic communities that highlighted the complexity of race relations, extending beyond whites and Japanese. They encompassed the myriad groups who resided in Hawai'i and occasionally collaborated with the Japanese over their collective oppression. However, acts of resistance collectively spurred repeated calls for American military intervention to protect white interests in Hawai'i as civilian and military elites increasingly aligned with one another over shared interests and growing concerns about the Japanese population.

Prewar Military Concerns about Japanese "Undesirables"

Years before Japanese planes flew over Pearl Harbor, preparation for the incarceration of the Japanese had begun. As early as 1935, the Army established the Army Service Command, creating a partnership between "civil control forces" and the military to prevent sabotage and local uprisings.[16] The Army's plan for civilian warfare in Hawai'i also led to the creation of a paramilitary organization called the Provisional Police in July 1940. Led by plantation manager T.G.S. Walker, its mission was to prevent and suppress any insurgency, such as "sudden and unpredicted overt acts by disloyal inhabitants."[17] Through the efforts of the Army, the Honolulu mayor, the chief of police, and plantation managers on O'ahu, the Provisional Police was established to allow civilians to defend Hawai'i against possible attack. Throughout the fall and winter of 1940, plantation employees, members of the American Legion, and utility workers trained in guard duty around the island. By April 1941, some 1,500 guards were ready for action; by May, more than one-third had participated in Army maneuvers.[18] The idea was to free the regular militia from guard duty by utilizing plantation laborers who were familiar with local faces and terrain and who could be efficiently managed and mobilized through Hawai'i's existing plantation hierarchy.

Federal Bureau of Investigation (FBI) Surveillance

In addition to the Army, the Federal Bureau of Investigation (FBI) was interested in exposing subversives within Hawai'i's Japanese community. In August 1939, just before war broke out in Europe, the FBI reopened its Honolulu office, which had closed years earlier. FBI agents joined the efforts of Army and Navy intelligence staffs, which had been compiling lists of anti-American suspects, mainly those of Japanese ancestry. Together, they attempted to gather more detailed information about the Japanese population in the Islands. They focused surveillance on 35,000 older aliens and 120,000 younger Japanese Americans. Of the 119,316 Nisei in Hawai'i in 1940, 73,281 held dual citizenship. Prior to 1924, government officials in Tokyo regarded all children born to Japanese fathers in any part of the world as Japanese citizens according to the principle of *jus sanguinis* (their parents' citizenship determines a child's citizenship).[19] Although Japanese citizenship had been passively awarded along with American citizenship by virtue of their birth in American territory, military officials regarded it as an indication of their inherent loyalty to Japan and, consequently, disloyalty to America.

The FBI was also assisted by the Honolulu Police Department, which formed an espionage bureau at the FBI's request. This entity became active in December 1940, following the approval of Police Chief William A. Gabrielson, the mayor, and the Board of Supervisors. The police bureau employed a Japanese, Korean, and "Hapa-Haole" (Japanese-White) officer, who all spoke Japanese, to investigate matters for the FBI and to engage in undercover activities within Hawai'i's Japanese community. Police Captain John Burns—later governor of Hawai'i—was the liaison with certain Japanese and advised the U.S. military and civilian intelligence bureaus on Japanese activities.

Counter Intelligence Corps (CIC) and Army Investigations

The main impetus behind the investigation of suspicious Japanese activity was the Counter Intelligence Corps (CIC), not the FBI, as some scholars believe.[20] According to an Army document, its mission was to "contribute to the successful operations of the Army of the United States through the detection of treason, sedition, subversive activity, and disaffection, and the detection and prevention of enemy espionage and sabotage."[21] In Honolulu, the CIC was activated in January 1942 and assigned the title G-2 Headquarters, Hawaiian Department. On the initial day of its existence, the local CIC detachment had twelve officers and eighteen special agents. Most of the officers and agents came from the military intelligence agency, the Corps of Intelligence Police (CIP), organized during World War I. Until early 1941, there were fifteen men in the CIP, four assigned to O'ahu. Locally, the CIP expanded on April 5, 1941, and after the CIC's formation, the CIP personnel joined this unit. By January 27, 1942, there were twenty-seven agents; a month later, six more agents were added to bolster the investigations. One year after the outbreak of war, there had been a dramatic increase in personnel as eighty-one agents conducted studies on the Japanese. Two years later, the force's strength peaked at ninety-seven agents.[22]

In the years prior to the war, the CIP was essentially an information-gathering organization. Among its many functions was the preparation of a pick-up list of individuals posing a potential threat to the United States in the event of war. The list included Buddhist and Shintō priests, consular agents, language school officials, commercial fishermen, and Kibei.[23] Suspects classified as "1-A" were to be apprehended immediately upon the start of hostilities. Others listed as "1-B" were to be put under surveillance, their activities curtailed until they no longer posed a threat. There were approximately three hundred persons listed in each group. The vast majority of those investigated were Japanese.[24]

Loyalty Campaigns within the Prewar Japanese Community

In 1941, the Army compiled a list of individuals for detention or surveillance in the event of war. Investigators added and removed names and rehearsed identifying, arresting, and transporting suspects to incarceration centers. While agents were covertly conducting investigations of the Japanese, intelligence officials began a public program stressing Japanese loyalty to America and interracial unity in Hawai'i. Two advisory groups of Americans of Japanese Ancestry (AJA) met with the FBI at least weekly after the spring of 1940 to discuss plans for controlling subversive elements and provided valuable assistance. Chinese residents established the Committee of Interracial Unity to minimize friction among Chinese, Japanese, and Filipinos. The Oahu Citizens Committee for Home Defense—an outgrowth of one of the advisory groups with a broader range of membership of AJA—also contributed to the loyalty program as members committed "to work with the constituted authorities in the continuing task of evaluating what went on in the Japanese community" to bring "out more positively the inherent loyalty of the Americans of Japanese Ancestry toward the United States."[25] Morale and Emergency Service Committees within the Japanese community were also formed with the approval of Army, Navy, and FBI authorities to "promote the interracial good will which had been built up in Hawai'i."[26] Unless the Japanese were accepted into Hawaiian society and acknowledged as part of the citizenry, many believed they would be "a burden, even a danger, to our security."[27]

Army and FBI officials took every opportunity to promote cooperation with the local Japanese and to celebrate interracial unity by speaking before club luncheons, school assemblies, and special meetings organized by the advisory groups. In a patriotic rally for two thousand Japanese sponsored by the Oahu Citizens Committee for Home Defense in June 1941, a representative of the Army's commanding general promised fair treatment to the Japanese as long as they showed no disloyalty to the United States. He predicted that "the fire of this period of national emergency and any war—even a Pacific war—will weld our Japanese into the structure of American unity."[28] However, even as military officials promoted the loyalty of the Japanese, war clouds over Hawai'i darkened, and the tension between the desire to exclude the Japanese or encourage their participation in the war effort reflected the complexity of Hawaiian race relations.

The Implementation of Martial Law in Wartime Hawai'i

The Japanese air attack on Pearl Harbor on December 7, 1941, had only been over for a few hours when the Territorial Governor Joseph Poindexter declared martial law and suspended the privilege of the writ of habeas corpus in the Hawaiian Territory, citing the 1900 Organic Act.[29] Martial law resulted in the total suspension of constitutional liberties as civilian courts were closed, all government functions—federal, territorial, and municipal—were placed under Army control, and Army officials established a military regime. The commanding general, Delos Emmons, declared himself the "military governor" of Hawai'i and controlled the entire civilian population with absolute discretionary powers. At the outbreak of war, a reluctant governor, Joseph Poindexter, enacted martial law at the insistence of General Walter Short. Poindexter was only persuaded to do so after being convinced that martial law would be lifted "within a reasonable time."[30] A proclamation was issued declaring martial law and relinquishing the entire civilian governmental authority to the Army. The territorial governor and some leading members of the Hawaii Bar Association informed Army officials directly that they had gone too far in suspending ordinary liberties, even in such an emergency. One of the most outspoken critics in Hawai'i was J. Garner Anthony, former president of the Bar Association of Hawai'i and later Hawai'i Constitutional Convention delegate. As the territorial attorney general, Anthony continued to work for the return of civil government to Hawai'i, highlighting that not all whites in the Islands supported martial law or the military's targeted racist policies. In a talk before the University of Hawai'i graduating class of 1943, Anthony was critical of suggestions made soon after the start of World War II that persons of Japanese descent be removed from the Islands, stating, "Those suggestions, which fortunately are no longer current, savor of fascism in one of its ugliest forms, the mass condemnation of people simply because of the accident of birth—their racial ancestry."[31] In late 1943, Anthony resigned as attorney general and was involved in a case to challenge the legality of civilian convictions by military courts.

At the outbreak of war, there was little concern over the implications of martial law in either Hawai'i or in official circles in Washington, as many believed Army control was necessary due to the exigencies of war.[32] Some thought that the civilian courts would be reopened and criminal jurisdiction returned to the territorial government once the threat of imminent invasion had passed. However, it was not until March 1943, more than fifteen months later, that military officials who had ruled Hawai'i with virtually no restrictions lifted the suspension of constitutional guarantees, including the right to a jury trial in criminal cases and the privilege of the writ of habeas corpus.[33] Martial law was not fully lifted until October 24, 1944, more than two years after the Battle of Midway.

The institution of martial law in Hawai'i was unique in its lack of precedence in any U.S. Territory, as well as its scope, duration, and lack of justification, even with the "exigencies of war." In October 1941, the territorial legislature, anticipating a war emergency, enacted the Hawaii Defense Act. This act authorized the civilian governor to exercise sweeping executive powers in any war emergency but with enforcement left in the civilian courts and due process for any individual accused of violations. Military officials considered this statute on December 7, 1941, but authorities ignored civilian rights and constitutional law in favor of martial law, which had been advocated as early as 1928. The Defense Act became essential for discussing whether Army rule was necessary. Many civilian leaders in Hawai'i contended that the act gave the governor ample powers over security in the civilian community, with no need for Army courts to enforce laws. In the early months of 1942, however, the Defense Act was rendered irrelevant by the preemptive effect of martial law.[34]

Military Rule in Wartime Hawai'i

Lt. Col. Thomas H. Green, an Army adjunct who was the chief legal officer for the military command in Hawai'i, led the Army's eagerness to take over every facet of government in Hawai'i only hours after the Pearl Harbor attack. He had spent the better part of 1941 planning the details of martial law, and thus, a bevy of "general orders" were in his files and ready for promulgation long before the Pearl Harbor attack.[35] During military rule in Hawai'i, commencing with the institution of martial law on December 7, 1941, and in effect to late October 1944, Commanding General Delos Emmons and Colonel Green, the latter named "Executive, Office of the Military Governor," issued 181 general orders. Under that title—and operating from the Office of the Territorial Attorney General at 'Iolani Palace, which the Army had appropriated for its military governor's functions—Green controlled much of civilian life and criminal law enforcement in Hawai'i until mid-1943.[36]

General Delos Emmons took command of the Army in Hawai'i in January 1942 and succeeded to the appropriate title of Military Governor. He authorized Green to extend Army control to the full range of federal administrative functions. These eventually included all the wartime powers exercised by the Office of Price Administration, the War Production Board, the War Labor Board, and other "alphabet industries." The Army's general orders in Hawai'i also controlled wartime wages and working conditions. The military regulated the allocation of labor on the plantations. It included "sweetheart deals" with the sugar and pineapple plantation companies by keeping their labor force in place but contracting their workers to the Army's military construction projects. The Army won over powerful employer interests and thus gained political influence within the civilian community by criminalizing job switching and workforce absenteeism. Under martial law, employees were required to obtain employer permission to leave a job. It was an offense to be absent from a job without permission. Organized business groups, therefore, provided enthusiastic support for Army rule. At one point late in 1942, an officer of the Honolulu Chamber of Commerce told the Territory's attorney general that the organization wanted martial law to continue as it "was not interested in the courts or the rights of civilians, but was only interested in the obtaining of priorities and the freezing of labor."[37] While this was only one man's view and not necessarily an accurate reflection of the prevailing view within the Chamber of Commerce, that organization did become a mainstay of white elite political support for the Army when civilian officials in Washington moved to reduce the military's authority in Hawai'i. Although martial law would last nearly three years, it is essential to note that military rule was heavily contested, first by civilian authorities in the Islands and by the Department of the Interior, who negotiated a partial return to civilian rule by 1943, and later by the federal courts in cases brought by non-Japanese imprisoned by military tribunals.[38] These challenges would eventually culminate in the 1946 landmark U.S. Supreme Court case *Duncan v. Kahanamoku,* which ruled that provost court justice and the military control of the civil government was illegal. This ruling would be of little comfort to those who would experience the impact of military authority for the duration of the war.

Pickup Lists: The Arrest and Incarceration of Japanese Suspects

As on the mainland, the Army and the FBI quickly rounded up aliens and other individuals in the Japanese community who had been investigated earlier and were suspected of being disloyal or perceived to be a threat during a war. With the assistance of the FBI, the Office of Naval Intelligence (ONI), and Honolulu Police Department reservists, the CIP immediately began the apprehension of those individuals on the "1-A" list. Authorities began arresting individuals at about 11:00 a.m. on December 7, 1941, while Japanese planes were still in the air. Working steadily around the clock, CIP personnel continued to pick up individuals they considered potentially dangerous. By December 10, 400 individuals were in temporary detention at the Honolulu Immigration Station.[39] Eventually, 2,270 Japanese would be incarcerated on suspicion of disloyalty creating "extreme insecurity" in many communities.[40]

Hawai'i incarceration was unique as it took place within the Islands compared to the mass removal of mainland Japanese to sometimes remote, uninhabited regions where inmates were disconnected from their former homes and lives. This collective upheaval created an extensive body of work by former inmates, government officials, and scholars who documented, analyzed, and debated the experiences, meaning, and legacy of mainland incarceration even as the centers were operating.[41] Yet, analysis of Hawai'i incarceration failed to occur in the postwar period, partly due to the relatively small numbers of Japanese incarcerated compared to the rest of the Japanese community, who numbered about 158,000 or more than one-third of the Territory's total population. News about the incarceration of residents was unreported under military censorship during martial law, and this community silence lasted long after the end of martial law on October 24, 1944. Members of the Japanese community shunned returning inmates and their families as their experiences of suspicion, discrimination, and even arrests were contrary to widespread wartime Americanization efforts in the Islands and demonstrations of patriotism to counter accusations of disloyalty and long-standing anti-Japanese sentiment. The beginning of the Cold War, the continued militarization of the Islands, and the celebrated return of Nisei veterans also promoted a historical narrative of Japanese American wartime sacrifice, valor, and bravery that excluded stories of incarcerated Japanese. While the Democratic Revolution of 1954 was a watershed event in Hawai'i's history that witnessed the election of Nisei politicians and the ascension of the Democratic party, the emergence of the Nisei and decline of the Issei had started years earlier with the Pearl Harbor attack. The war accelerated the generational role reversal of Issei and the Nisei. It resulted in the "retiring" of the Issei within the public sphere, the physical erasure of Japanese culture in public and private areas, and the replacement of Japanese with English as part of "speak American" campaigns.[42]

Thus, oral and written accounts by Hawai'i Issei of their incarceration experiences became limited to an increasingly smaller audience of Japanese speakers and readers. Later generations, including the Sansei, Yonsei, Gosei, and others, were further removed from a language once prohibited by military censors. The closure of Japanese language schools and the arrests of teachers during the war increased the linguistic divide between generations. It contributed to the absence of understanding of the experiences of Issei inmates.

The Postwar Silence on Incarceration

For many years, Hawai'i incarceration was a section within the general histories of Japanese Americans in the Islands or a footnote in broad wartime histories.[43] Finally, in 1998, a local news station called the Japanese Cultural Center of Hawai'i (JCCH) seeking information about local incarceration to broadcast before the airing of *Schindler's List*. Unable to provide many answers, the staff at the JCCH began researching the history of Honouliuli over fifty years after its closure. Eventually, community efforts led to the "rediscovery" of Honouliuli in 2002, resulting in studies by the National Park Service, culminating in President Barack Obama announcing the designation of Honouliuli as a National Historic Site on February 19, 2015.[44] Since that initial inquiry, there has been a proliferation of Hawai'i incarceration narratives, beginning with firsthand accounts from individuals such as Japanese-language newspaper editor Yasutaro Soga (2008), Japanese language schoolteacher Otokichi Muin Ozaki (2012), Hawai'i Island resident George Hoshida (2015), and the translation of a compilation of a series of Suikei Furuya's Japanese-language incarceration memoir, *Haisho Tenten* (2017).[45] Similar to these personal memoirs are other accounts that examine the lasting impact of incarceration on subsequent generations who reflect upon the experiences endured by family members during World War II.[46] While these studies provide critical insight into the unique circumstances endured by these individuals, this project seeks to provide a comparative or holistic understanding of incarceration across the Islands to capture the breadth and diversity of experiences that emerged throughout the war.

This book builds upon previous scholarship by examining prewar anti-Japanese sentiments that originated on the plantations, which military officials similarly held and who began to expand their presence in Hawai'i. It connects events like plantation strikes, infamous court cases like the Fukunaga kidnapping and Massie case, restrictions against Japanese language schools, and Americanization campaigns, with growing fears of Japanese that in part justified the imposition of martial law. Although all Hawai'i residents were subject to martial law restrictions, prewar fears and investigations of the Japanese influenced specific policies, such as the arrest and incarceration of Japanese residents, designed to instill fear and encourage the cooperation of remaining community members. While tracing the contentious and complicated history of the Japanese in Hawai'i, this study will highlight Japanese agency, resistance, and even collaboration with authorities. It also recognizes the diversity of experiences across islands and even within the same community as military and civil authority was never complete. Subsequent chapters focus on the institution of martial law and the wartime and postwar impact of incarceration on the communities in which imprisonment occurred, detailing inmates' experiences within the context of the wartime mobilization of the Islands and the postwar transformation of Hawai'i. The extensive investigations and advanced preparations that preceded the actual incarceration of individuals challenge assertions of wartime necessity. They also highlight the long-standing racist fears that would influence the treatment and experiences of the Japanese during the war. Events in wartime Hawai'i would profoundly affect those whom authorities had arrested and those who remained free under martial law as even they remained subject to the continuous threat of incarceration. By analyzing incarceration as a strategy of control that evolved throughout the war, this project will connect the stories of those initially arrested and sent to mainland incarceration centers with later inmates transferred to Honouliuli. Finally, it will examine the legacies of the wartime experience of Hawai'i's Japanese to highlight the uniqueness of their experiences and the impact of these events still today.

Chapter Overview

Chapter 1 examines how martial law and incarceration had clear precedence in the extralegal forms of justice on Hawai'i's plantations as military officials and white elites aligned to control the Japanese population who sought to exert autonomy and control over their lives. Their growing numbers and questions about their loyalty made them an economic threat to planters. They were also a national security concern to military officials, particularly as tensions with Japan escalated in the prewar period.

Chapter 2 details the events following the Pearl Harbor attack as racism against the Japanese in Hawai'i motivated not just demonstrations of loyalty by the Japanese but also heightened surveillance and extralegal actions against remaining community members authorities sanctioned under martial law. While most Japanese in Hawai'i remained free, many were affected by military and civil policies targeting the Japanese.

Despite efforts by the Japanese to assuage fears and accusations of disloyalty, military officials began the systematic arrest and confinement of individuals throughout Hawai'i, which is the focus of chapters 3 and 4. On the mainland, authorities sent inmates to incarceration sites that included Assembly Centers, Department of Justice Camps, Federal Bureau of Prisons, U.S. Army Internment Camps, War Relocation Authority Camps, and War Relocation Authority Citizen Isolation Centers. In Hawai'i, most were U.S. Army Internment Camps consistent with military control under martial law.[47] The role of U.S. military officials in Japanese incarceration further highlights the militarization of the Islands following the Pearl Harbor attack and the mobilization of U.S. armed forces on the Pacific front of the war. Imprisonment served as a strategy to control the Japanese with the selective removal of its leadership while maintaining a needed labor force critical in the mobilization of war.[48] While stories of inmate resistance and creativity exist, officials intended to control the Japanese population by exerting absolute control over the lives of its former leaders. The experience of Japanese inmates thus highlights the extent of military authority under martial law and efforts to destroy the lives of once prominent individuals.

This study concludes with the end of martial law, the closure of the sites, and the lifting of military regulations. Yet the impact of war and incarceration would reverberate throughout the community. Those incarcerated often experienced isolation within their community, while some were susceptible to postwar rumors. Others, however, clearly benefited from their wartime participation and patriotism, which became a defining feature of Japanese American identity in Hawai'i. Thus, the postwar era witnessed the Nisei's dramatic social, economic, and political rise. Many had embraced Americanization efforts and wartime patriotism to challenge prewar fears and suspicions. However, understanding the experience of incarcerated individuals is essential in bridging the historical gap between prewar concerns of the Japanese on the plantations and their postwar celebratory status as patriotic Americans. These fears became the basis for martial law and deliberate efforts by the Japanese to counter these racist claims through military enlistment, personal sacrifice, and community service. Recognizing the wartime experience of Hawai'i's Japanese thus illuminates the often uneven path toward inclusion and equality of minorities in both Hawai'i and America. These inmates serve as a reminder of the fragility of civil rights, particularly during times of war. Kaetsu Furuya, forced to stand nearly naked in the rain by his white captors as his incarceration began, survived to offer just some of the testimony that collectively provides a greater understanding of the legacies of Hawai'i's incarceration history and the wartime experiences of its people.

1 Deconstructing Hawai‘i's Racial Paradise

Ethnic Discrimination in the Law and a Dual System of Justice

Within this plantation community are many camps of either Filipino, Japanese, and Portuguese mixed with other racial groups. Many years back the camps were mainly designated as "Jap camp" or Filipino camp and when a family from a different ethnic group moved into the area, they were disregarded by the rest. Nobody would make them feel at home and welcomed in that section. There was this feeling of mistrust between ethnic groups.[1]

This account by a Japanese woman from Hawai‘i Island describes her upbringing in a plantation community where, according to planter policy, individuals were segregated by ethnicity to reinforce hostility and increase suspicion among different groups. By segregating workers, encouraging competition, and promoting cultural diversity, planters hoped to eliminate the possibility of a united labor force weakening the economy by strike or riot. Using this strategy known as "divide and rule," white planters, who constituted a minority in Hawai‘i, ensured they maintained a dominant position in society by pitting different groups against one another.[2] Competition and hostility from this strategy resulted in tensions between other ethnic groups that remained even after workers left the plantations. The racist attitudes among various groups promulgated and reinforced on the plantations ultimately influenced their experiences and histories in Hawai‘i, particularly during World War II.

Race and racism thus played essential parts in the perception and subsequent treatment of the Japanese in Hawai‘i. They were subjected to institutional and individual discrimination before and after the bombing of Pearl Harbor, as well as individual and community policing reminiscent of the plantations. As a result of widespread community hostility that drew upon long-standing tensions between different groups, the Japanese in Hawai‘i were forced to prove their American citizenship and loyalty as they faced pressure from other ethnic groups and the military. However, it was only the military, aligned with certain white elites in the Islands, which was able to enforce official control over the Japanese in Hawai‘i under martial law that culminated in the incarceration of over two thousand people of Japanese ancestry. Thus, martial law and incarceration originated in the racial tensions and extralegal forms of justice created on the plantations in response to Japanese activism against efforts to control their lives. Both planters and military officials who had extensively investigated prewar Japanese communities in Hawai'i became convinced of the inherent danger and disloyalty of the Japanese. However, these assumptions did not account for the diversity within the various Japanese communities. Nor did they address the complexity of the issues of loyalty and allegiance for the Issei and Nisei. Nevertheless, questions surrounding the citizenship, loyalty, and allegiance of the Japanese during successive decades of Japanese migration only grew with the increasing number of Japanese. Thousands of immigrants arrived to fill the labor needs in the Islands and were willing to challenge their economic exploitation and political disenfranchisement.

Subsequently, plantations were fraught with violence committed both by plantation owners and overseers as well as by the workers who engaged in both overt and subtle actions of resistance, such as arson, malingering, drug and alcohol usage, desertion, and even strikes. In response to Japanese activism and challenges to white authority both on the plantations and in urban centers in proximity to military bases and personnel, military and plantation officials became aligned in a shared goal to control the Japanese population and their perceived threat. This perception grew in importance as tensions between Japan and America increased, resulting in increased surveillance of the Japanese by military officials that was seemingly validated with the outbreak of war.

The Arrival of Japanese and the Creation of Prewar Communities

At the beginning of Japanese immigration, it would be difficult to imagine that less than seventy-five years later, widespread racial fears and hostilities would be directed at a group that initially had a tenuous presence in Hawai'i. As the "gathering place" of Hawai'i, O'ahu would be the site of the arrival of the first Japanese immigrants. In 1868, or "Meiji One," the British ship *Scioto* set sail out of Yokohama on May 17. On board were 153 Japanese, including 146 men, 5 women, and 2 teenagers. These "first-year men," called *Gannenmono*, represented the initial effort to determine the feasibility of further Japanese labor migration. The experiment had an auspicious start, and the laborers received a warm reception upon arriving on June 19, 1868, at Honolulu Harbor. They went ashore immediately without medical inspection and received salted fish as a gift from the king of Hawai'i. Fifty-one immigrants remained on O'ahu while the rest departed to Kaua'i, Maui, and Lāna'i. However, unaccustomed to agricultural work, resentful of taking orders from non-Japanese, and routinely beaten by *lunas* assigned by the plantation owners to monitor their progress, Japanese laborers quickly became disillusioned with plantation work. Many quit working in the cane fields and headed to Honolulu for other employment. Complaints about their treatment and letters of appeal for help soon reached Japan, and authorities recalled the *Gannenmono* from Hawai'i.

Eventually, immigration in Japan would resume; during the government-sponsored immigration period between 1885 and 1894, twenty-six ships carrying Japanese immigrants landed in Honolulu, bringing approximately 29,000 Japanese to Hawai'i's shores and transforming traditional racial dynamics.[3] After arriving in Honolulu, many left for alternative employment opportunities on the other islands, where they established distinct farming communities throughout Hawai'i. In Kona, immigrants primarily from the Kumamoto prefecture dominated the coffee industry beginning in the twentieth century. Their shared background helped to create a unique cultural enclave that became the focus of study for University of Hawai'i sociologists in the prewar period.[4] By the 1930s, over 90 percent of the eight hundred coffee farmers in Kona were Japanese and had organized cooperating groups called *kumi* or *kumiai*.[5] The Japanese in Kona established more than fifty *kumi* in the prewar period. At the same time, Hilo was home to organizations such as the Upper Wainaku Japanese Community Club and the Kyū Pahoa Kumiai due to the large number of Japanese laborers employed on the sugar plantations in the surrounding areas such as Waiākea.[6] Large Japanese communities emerged across the Islands, attracting attention for their often insular character and regional nature that heightened the perception of their foreign character.

Japanese immigrants often retained aspects of their home culture that many regarded as antithetical to American culture. Hawai'i Island, for example, was home to at least twenty-seven Buddhist temples in the prewar period, only one fewer than what existed on O'ahu, and thus had the most significant number of Buddhist temples per capita. By 1940, Hawai'i Island could claim the highest number of Japanese outside of O'ahu, with 23,268 Japanese out of 157,905, the total number of Japanese in Hawai'i. The large number of Japanese who comprised over one-third of the total population in Hawai'i greatly alarmed both civil and military officials, as plantation owners sought to create a tractable, predictable labor force. In contrast, military officials focused on the large number of foreign-born residents who potentially posed a military threat.

Maui, Lāna'i, and Moloka'i also witnessed the arrival of large numbers of Asian laborers with the growth of plantations that, to some, demonstrated the growing influence of foreign workers. During the 1820s, two Chinese immigrants named Ahung and Atai and a Spaniard called Antone Catalina established the first sugar operations on Maui in Wailuku and Waikapū.[7] Although these early ventures were unsuccessful, by 1862, four plantations on Maui at Makawao, Kaluanui, Ha'ikū, and

'Ulupalakua produced 650 tons of sugar, which comprised nearly 50 percent of Hawai'i's total output. That same year, three more plantations at Waikapū, Hāna, and Lahaina harvested their first crop. Following the Reciprocity Treat of 1876, allowing Hawaiian sugar to enter the United States duty-free, entrepreneurs established plantations at Kīhei, Huelo, Nāhiku, Olowalu, Pā'ia, Hāmoa, Spreckelsville, Kīpahulu, Hāmākuapoko, Keāhua, Kahului, Pu'unēnē, Waihe'e, Kū'au, and Wailuku. Eventually, many of these plantations failed or were consolidated; by 1929, six major sugar plantations operated on Maui. Pineapple cultivation also flourished on Maui after its introduction in 1890 at Grove Ranch in Ha'ikū. Maui Pineapple Company would eventually become a major employer of Maui's Japanese community. While the number of companies decreased, sugar production expanded on Maui. Hawaiian Commercial & Sugar Company (HC&S), the largest and most profitable sugar operation in Hawai'i for decades, produced 75,000 tons of sugar in 1929 and cultivated 7,600 acres.

O'ahu and Kaua'i similarly experienced the growth of Japanese communities with the emergence of cash crop agriculture. In 1825, Englishman John Wilkinson established the first plantation in O'ahu's Mānoa valley after making arrangements with Boki, governor of O'ahu. Although Wilkinson was an agriculturalist with experience in the West Indies, he became ill and died a year later with more than one hundred acres of sugarcane under cultivation.[8] Nearly ten years later, William Hooper, Peter Allen Brinsmade, and William Ladd arrived in Kōloa in the southern part of Kaua'i, drawn to the Garden Isle's temperate climate, fertile soil, and ample rainfall. After establishing a mercantile business called Ladd & Company, the three men would lease from the king and local chiefs approximately one thousand acres of land for silk and sugar culture, mainly in Weliweli Ahupua'a, for fifty years at $300 a year.[9] However, due to their lack of experience and difficulty convincing Native Hawaiians to labor for them, they failed in their endeavor.

Nevertheless, as Kaua'i's first plantation town, Kōloa would mark the beginnings of cash crop agriculture on Kaua'i, which would influence the social, economic, and political life of the Garden Isle until World War II. There were at least eleven major sugar plantations active on Kaua'i in the prewar period—Olokele Sugar Company, McBryde Sugar Company, Koloa Plantation, Hawaiian Sugar Mill Company, Grove Farm Plantation, Lihue Plantation Co., Kekaha Sugar Co., Waimea Sugar Mill Co., Gay & Robinson, Hawaiian Sugar Co., and Kilauea Co.—that flourished in the pre–World War II period on Kaua'i.[10] The majority of these workers would ultimately be from Japan.

Eventually, 10,621 Japanese would settle on Kaua'i and Ni'ihau in the prewar period, comprising over 43 percent of the population on these two islands, the highest percentage for any island in the Territory.[11] Over half of Kaua'i's people resided in Kōloa and Waimea districts. On the island's west side, Waimea was the most populous district, with 10,852 residents, while Hanalei, located in the north, had only 2,065 residents. The largest towns were Līhu'e, with 4,254 residents; Kapa'a claimed 2,828 residents; and Kekaha had 2,536 residents.[12] Nearly 55 percent of workers on Kaua'i worked for the sugar plantations, compared to 37 percent on Maui and 23 percent for the Territory. As author Tim Klass notes, "during this period plantations functioned largely as self-contained economic, social and political units," controlling various parts of the Islands and dictating the economic, political, and social life on Kaua'i.[13] Thus, the plantations were particularly influential on the Garden Isle, with most Japanese dispersed across the various plantations on Kaua'i in rural areas.

The growth of plantations across Hawai'i brought thousands of workers from Japan who soon dramatically outnumbered whites. In response, planters were organized under the Hawaiian Sugar Planters Association (HSPA) in 1895 to promote the sugar industry in the Islands and protect their financial, political, and social interests. The HSPA conducted scientific research on improved seed, fertilization, and irrigation practices and centralized management information and decision-making among the various plantations as it became a repository for knowledge of the sugar industry in Hawai'i. Planters focused on developing labor control methods and regulating wages to maximize profits. Many of its members were influenced by notions of plantation paternalism and developed sophisticated labor regulations to control workers, including many Japanese.

Planter Paternalism

Recognizing the importance of controlling a potentially unruly population of uprooted laborers, many planters attempted to cultivate the loyalty and discipline of the workers through planter paternalism. Shortly after the 1920 strike, the HSPA summed up the essential purpose of this strategy: "That the plantations have a humanitarian interest in their employees is self-evident. Money and time have been spent liberally by the plantations to cater to the physical, mental and moral welfare of the laborers. The planters find that humanity in industry pays."[14] While the paternalism of the plantation managers sometimes emerged from a sincere concern for their workers, planters realized that it played an essential role in production and profit making.[15] David Bowman, director of the Industrial Service Bureau of the HSPA, recommended that planters place their Filipino laborers in boardinghouses as it was "good business" to have them "properly fed." It "paid" to make such housing arrangements, "the results being a well-fed, contented lot of laborers."[16]

Thus, the plantations were home to organized communities of workers living in camps and facilities that plantation owners established to control the growing labor force. In 1916, Consul R. Mori encouraged Japanese workers to appreciate the accommodations that the plantations provided:

> Japanese laborers working at Puunene and at Paia are treated by the company like one's member of the family. . . . At Puunene there are several clubhouses established by the plantation for the laborers, for amusement after work, furnished with books and magazines. There are day nurseries to take care of babies for the wives of laborers who wish to work in the field. . . . All sick Japanese laborers are treated in a modern hospital. At Paia I was told that the plantation supplies hot water for the laborers for their bathing. . . . At Wailuku, Puunene, Paia, Lahaina and Kipahulu plantations I asked all the Japanese laborers I met if there were any complaints and all said there was none.[17]

In advising Japanese workers "to stay where they are now and be satisfied," Mori was hardly an impartial voice for the Japanese government that sought to encourage Japanese employment abroad to reduce the unemployment rate during the Meiji reforms. By the 1920s and 1930s, HC&S housed seven thousand workers and their families and built four public schools, three Japanese language schools, a hospital, a dozen day nurseries, three theaters, ten churches, a gymnasium, and a swimming pool, all existing within the plantation. The company also maintained general stores, a dairy, and a meat market. James Higuchi, a resident of Puʻukoliʻi Camp run by the Pioneer Mill Company, recalled how the camps became autonomous economic and social units contained on the plantation:

> In the Puʻukoliʻi Camp, we used to make a border that split the community. One end we used to call 'em "Pigpen Avenue." From the reservoir, they get this waterway that takes the water to the fields. Where the water ran, everybody used to build a pigpen. So they wash down the pen and the [runoff went] into the waterway. So that place we used to call Pigpen Avenue from that certain road. [On the other side], we had a tailor, restaurants, stores, everything. We used to call 'em "Broadway."[18]

Higuchi's recollections capture the utilitarian organization of these plantation camps designed to regulate workers' lives. His observations also highlight the irony of naming a plantation road likely lined by primitive wooden structures after a well-known New York street. However, the proximity of stores, businesses, places of worship, and living accommodations for workers and their families helped to foster community connections and even individual camp identities that still resonate today with older generations in the Islands.

Puʻunēnē's, one of the world's largest plantations, was owned by HC&S and was home to twenty-six camps with colorful names like "Mill Camp," "McGerrow Camp," "Alabama Camp," "Spanish Camp," "Green Camp," and "Ah Fong Camp," all of which separated racial groups and housed rows and rows of plantation workers. According to planter policy, individuals were segregated by ethnicity to reinforce hostility and increase suspicion among different groups. One author noted that this segregation and the self-contained society on the plantations helped to foster a "paternalistic attitude that bordered on feudalism: workers and their families depended on the plantation for almost everything."[19] Both strategies were designed to keep workers on the plantation in a state of dependency that limited their efforts to collaborate for better pay and living conditions. Yet, even as planters could expand cash crop agriculture across most islands and meet their labor needs by importing Asian laborers, the large number of Japanese became a growing concern. Consequently, planters sought to solidify their economic, political, and social control within the Islands, both on and off the plantations, by means of social policies. Formal laws that controlled laborers through their systematic disenfranchisement and denial of legal rights would be echoed in martial law, where military law would replace civil authority, and all Hawai'i residents would experience the suspension of their civil liberties. However, civil and military authorities would subject only the Japanese population to discriminatory treatment before and during the war.

The Exploitation of Immigrants Within Hawai'i's Dual-System of Justice

Before the outbreak of war, a "dual-system of justice" in Hawai'i's legal system was promulgated with varying degrees of success to control the Japanese by privileging whites at the expense of minorities.[20] However, it was a system that developed over time and was tied to the fortunes of white settlers who were instrumental in overthrowing the Hawaiian monarchy. During the Kingdom of Hawai'i, some foreigners, including Japanese and Chinese migrants, became naturalized citizens and enjoyed unprecedented rights and legal protections.[21] Throughout this period, universal male suffrage was often extended to both native-born and naturalized subjects of Hawai'i who met property and age requirements, allowing Japanese and other migrants the opportunity to exercise some political power and be granted some political representation.

Drafted by Lorrin A. Thurston and other Westerners who led a coup against the monarchy, the 1887 Constitution of the Kingdom of Hawai'i represented the most dramatic change to voting and citizenship rights. It not only stripped the Hawaiian monarchy of much of its authority but disenfranchised all Asians as "discrimination became openly a matter of race."[22] Only male "Residents" of American, European, and Hawaiian ancestry who met property and income qualifications were granted full voting privileges and, by extension, legal rights.[23] Alien Asians were no longer allowed to participate in the political process, even if they had become naturalized citizens. Henceforth, citizenship was denied to all Japanese migrants based on race until 1952. Only Asian males deemed of "Hawaiian" birth under the language of the 1887 Constitution could vote. However, they still had to establish that they could read a newspaper in Hawaiian, English, or another European language. These new restrictions emerged as Asians constituted a sizable portion of the population. Japanese and Chinese comprised nearly 33 percent of Hawai'i's population, compared to whites, who constituted only 21 percent. White elites expressed alarm over the "peril" posed by this alien, unassimilable population, and planter William Alexander warned that when the Japanese constituted a numerical majority, Hawai'i would become a virtual "Japanese colony."[24] To counter this perceived "yellow threat," the writers of the 1887 Constitution sought to protect the "established order" and consequently barred Asians from the franchise. Chinese and Japanese migrants residing in Hawai'i, Native Hawaiians, and the Japanese government actively opposed these additional requirements as these changes "gave to the haoles as a group a greatly increased power in the government" and reduced Hawaiians and migrant workers to "apparent and, for a while, actual inferiority in the political life of the country."[25] Asian workers were particularly outraged as they could not vote and influence police policies, yet they were still taxed and essentially financed the law enforcement needs of the plantations.[26]

The passage of the 1887 Constitution marked the erosion of the power of the Hawaiian monarchy and rights granted to migrants in a precedent that foreshadowed the suspension of civil liberties under martial law. On January 17, 1893, the last Hawaiian monarch, Queen Lili'uokalani, was deposed in a coup d'état led by primarily local American and European residents. The Republic of Hawai'i was declared in 1894 after President Grover Cleveland, a friend of Lili'uokalani's, prevented the immediate annexation of the Islands. Eventually, Hawai'i became a Territory of the United States on July 7, 1898, following the passage of the Newlands Resolution in Congress. In 1900, Hawai'i was granted self-governance, and although several attempts were made to achieve statehood, Hawai'i remained a Territory for sixty years. Plantation owners, including the Big Five, found territorial status convenient. It enabled them to continue importing cheap foreign labor while consolidating their political influence through a legal system that attempted to reaffirm their authority in the islands.[27] As historian Gary Okihiro noted, American annexation specifically served planter interests as it "was a way of avoiding being swamped by the 'yellow wave' or by a coalition of Asians and Hawaiians against whites."[28] White anxieties of Asian domination in Hawai'i that were linked to yellow peril fears and anti-Asian movements sweeping through America during the late nineteenth and early twentieth centuries were also articulated in Thomas C. Hobson's 1898 article entitled "Japan's 'Peaceful Invasion.'"[29] Hobson claimed that a large number of Japanese migrants were part of a strategy by the Japanese government to "strike terror in the breasts of every lover of republican principles and American institutions" through an "invasion" of Hawaiʻi. The annexation of Hawaiʻi to the United States subverted this threat by decisively closing the political process to Asian migrants. The United States Naturalization Law of 1790 limited naturalized citizenship to "whites." After systematically disenfranchising plantation laborers, planters were able to utilize the police power of the state to protect their vested interests.[30]

Yet even within this biased legal system, planters could never exert absolute control over migrants as there were continual challenges to their authority that emerged from other sectors of the population in the Islands, including from other whites. Legal scholars Peter J. Nelligan and Harry V. Ball noted that during this period, juries in Hawaiʻi were recognized for their low conviction rate, suggesting that "Northern European" or "*haole*-Hawaiian" jurors—the two most prominent jury groups—did not necessarily agree with the policies of the new government run by a small cohort of whites.[31] However, the murky citizenship status occupied by Japanese migrants—who retained their Japanese citizenship and were denied American citizenship but were bound by their labor contracts—complicated their legal standing. Japanese laborers often found themselves at the mercy of various groups: Hawaiʻi planters, who sought to maximize the returns on their investments by instituting harsh labor controls; the Japanese government, who, out of a need to find employment for its depressed peasantry or to accrue foreign capital, permitted the exploitation of its citizenry; the Japanese migration companies, which were known for their "usurious and fraudulent practices"; and ambitious Japanese and Hawaiian agents, who personally benefited from Japanese labor migration.[32] Thus, lacking legal rights and equal protection under the law, these migrants wrestled with the dual system of justice that operated in Hawaiʻi. The origins of this system can be traced back to the early contract labor period, beginning with the arrival of the first Japanese laborers in 1868, as these workers were entirely at the mercy of plantation owners. The unequal power differential on the plantations replicated itself in the courtroom, providing the basis for the dual system of justice that emerged in Hawaiʻi. According to scholar Sally Engle Merry, "the law was one of the core institutions of colonial control, serving the needs of commerce and capitalism."[33] The law became a tool by which the plantation owners attempted to establish complete economic and legal control over the lives of the migrants through legal measures and labor contracts. These regulations would echo their experience under martial law when authorities incarcerated Japanese and outlawed labor movements and strikes. As noted by a Japanese newspaper reporter, violence against the Japanese was not uncommon, and anyone who dared to challenge the existing plantation hierarchy faced grave consequences:

> During those days, the general rule was that the manager was as a king who held the power of life and death over the workers. The local courts were controlled by him but there was nothing anyone could do about it. Some managers were said to have regarded their mules as more valuable than the workers. It is said that a Scotch plantation manager on the island of Hawaii used to say outright that the death of one or two Japanese was of no consequence, but that he did not want to see any harm come to his mules because they cost him approximately a thousand dollars each. Actually speaking, it was a fact that the plantations of those days took better care of their mules than they did their contract laborers.[34]

This belief that laborers were inconsequential and valued less than work animals was reflected in the judicial system. Whites were rarely punished for their crimes against Japanese and other ethnicities on the plantations, a precedent that would be echoed in the various incarceration centers across the islands.

Extralegal Control and Violence

From the very beginning of the immigration period, it soon became clear to workers that they would often be at the mercy of whites who could administer physical discipline with impunity. One of the first murders recorded in the Kingdom of Hawai'i was the 1853 case of *King vs. H.N. Greenwell,* which involved a prominent planter on Hawai'i Island who brutally murdered his Chinese cook, Salai, after he attempted to run away.[35] According to witnesses, as Salai tried to escape from a window after being tied up the previous day, "Mr. Greenwell ran after him and caught him, and began striking him with his fists, he knocked him down and then got on to him and struck him with his fists."[36] Later, despite Salai "trembling and shaking like a beast that had been badly used," with "hands and forehead [that] were turned blue," Greenwell called Salai into the house, where witnesses reported hearing "20 cracks" of a whip while the "Chinaman was wailing like a goat." Salai was later bound "so hard" that his "hands and feet were black and swelled up" by a "small rope which was sunk into the flesh it was so tight." Left untreated, without food or water, he died the next day.

Despite this graphic testimony, Chief Justice William Little Lee ruled that, although Greenwell had severely whipped Salai, "he did not die from this or any other inflicted injury, but in due course of nature, from long sickness and his voluntary exposure for several nights, without food or raiment, to the rain, cold and hunger in the forest" while he was fleeing from Greenwell. Lee agreed with defense witnesses who testified that Salai's escape and failure to seek treatment were typical behaviors of Chinese, who "commit suicide on trivial occasions."[37] In light of these mitigating circumstances and because of the unstable personalities of the Chinese, the court acquitted Greenwell of the murder of Salai after half an hour of deliberations.

The case of *King vs. H.N. Greenwell* reflected both the legal and everyday battles on the plantations, which were, according to author Richard Edwards, a "contested terrain" where planters tried to extract as much labor as possible from their workers.[38] At the same time, laborers sought greater control over their work, personal autonomy, and economic freedom. This terrain was visited by violence on the part of planters and workers. On October 28, 1889, Katsu Gotō, who had often volunteered to act as an interpreter for the Japanese in court proceedings, paid the ultimate price for his support of the Japanese community. He was lynched and found hanging from a telephone pole due to his alleged activism for Japanese laborers on the plantations.[39] Gotō belonged among the first group of Japanese to migrate to Hawai'i aboard the *City of Tokio* in 1885, and he lived in Hawai'i during a period of emerging worker discontent and labor struggle on the plantations over low pay and harsh working conditions. As a successful storekeeper, Gotō often served as a translator and advisor to the workers on the plantations. His involvement—or "interference," as the owners often saw it—reportedly served as one of the motives for his murder. Gotō also posed an economic threat to white-owned businesses in the area, as many laborers patronized his store because he sold goods at lower prices. He extended lines of credit to plantation workers and provided lodging for laborers, all of which made his store an informal gathering place for the migrant Japanese community.[40] To some, Gotō's brutal murder ended many of the threats he posed to white authority; the public spectacle of his lynching was designed to weaken Japanese resistance through its highly visualized brutalization of a Japanese male body, a man who had challenged white plantation hegemony. Decades later, following the outbreak of World War II, authorities would arrest other leaders in the Japanese community in a similar effort to control the remaining Japanese population who feared a similar fate.

Some white plantation owners did treat their workers humanely, such as George Wilcox, owner of Grove Farm on Kaua'i, who allowed his workers to rest and smoke when they reached the end of a row of cane. He also "pampered" them by transporting them on trucks or drays to their worksites instead of making them walk. In addition, Wilcox discharged a manager who had been with him for eight years after he knocked down a worker in fury when the worker accidentally set fire to a cane field with a lighted cigarette.[41] Exceptions like Wilcox, who looked after the well-being of his workers, are found throughout Hawai'i's plantation history. Some whites did align themselves with the Japanese in their legal and labor battles against oppressive planter authority. However, violence directed at minorities was not uncommon, and many perpetrators were never arrested or punished. In

1891, at Olowalu, Maui, a Japanese worker was burnt to death after an overseer pushed him into a blazing brush fire after a slight argument. Since that incident, where the overseer escaped punishment for his murder of a worker, Japanese laborers referred to the plantation as "*Oniwaru*" or "Bad Devil" plantation.[42] In January 1892, a Caucasian field boss shot Ihei Higashi in the leg without provocation. When the case was taken to the circuit court, the offender was fined and sentenced to six months in jail. However, the verdict was appealed to a superior court, and the field boss was acquitted of all charges after allegedly bribing the judge and witnesses. When the Japanese community, outraged at this miscarriage of justice, started a fund drive to appeal the case, the Caucasian overseer hurriedly called in and requested the mediation of the Japanese Section of the Immigration Bureau and the Japanese Consulate. The matter was settled when Higashi received $350 in compensation and returned to Japan. This case illuminates the shared interest held by the planters and Japanese government officials, who desired to create a subservient labor force and encourage further migration from Japan at the expense of these laborers' rights. Japanese were considered particularly expendable when they attempted to challenge the plantation system in Hawai'i—the source of white power and hegemony—by supporting or participating in labor strikes. Numerous strikes and work stoppages mark the history of the Japanese in Hawai'i, all designed to address worker grievances over low wages, inadequate housing, and poor, if not dangerous, work conditions.[43]

Workers also resorted to violence as a way of protesting against harsh and unfair treatment. While most daily acts of violence and resistance went unrecorded, evidence reveals that workers did not submissively accept ill-treatment and often resorted to aggression, both on a collective and an individual level, in revolt against intolerable and inhumane living and working conditions. In 1866, a "gang of coolies" on Maui resisted the orders of their overseer and, armed with knives, "rushed forward to seize him," stopping only when the overseer fired his gun and wounded one of them.[44] A group of "heathen Chinese" in 1879 similarly attacked their *luna* (overseer) at the 'Ō'ōkala plantation on Hawai'i Island with cane knives and hatchets and ceased only when one of them was shot "point blank."[45] Authorities later arrested and removed fifty-six of the rioters for punishment. Workers at the Wai'anae plantation attacked "Captain Ross" from behind with a hoe as he bent down to examine a water course; he received two heavy blows to his ribs, and "a third blow aimed at the head was partially warded off, not without injury to the arm raised in defense."[46] Twenty-one "infuriated Japs" similarly "hacked up badly by hoes," the head *luna* at Laupahoehoe in 1900.[47] Three years later, on a Maui plantation, a gang of Chinese laborers attacked an Irish *luna* because he had hit one of them. Immediately, "the whole gang turned on him, and in a few minutes, he was buried under a ten-foot pile of cane stalks."[48] Friends eventually dug him out, but he quit his job after being "nearly paralyzed with fright," fearing that the Chinese would set fire to the pile. In 1915, after being threatened with dismissal for "lagging," a Filipino laborer "seriously and possibly fatally wounded" A. A. Robinson, *luna* on the Pa'auilo plantation in Hilo, by fracturing his skull with a hoe.[49] *Lunas* were particular targets of worker violence as they imposed planter will and wielded total control over their lives and bodies. Many workers sang songs lamenting the brutality and hardship they experienced at the hands of owners and overseers that would later resonate in inmates' experiences within certain incarceration centers.[50]

Worker violence directed toward plantation authority led planters to issue a general rule: "In no case shall any laborer be permitted to raise his hand or any weapon in an aggressive manner or cabal with his associates or incite them to acts of insubordination."[51] Despite planters' penalties—fines, physical violence, verbal reprimands, and arrest—it proved inadequate in deterring violations. Authorities later cited their contentious relationship with Japanese workers on the plantations as cause for increased restrictions against the Japanese that ultimately preceded martial law. As plantations, working conditions, and owners varied widely throughout Hawai'i, it is challenging to characterize workers' experiences even on one island. Yet, it is clear that some Japanese were willing to challenge their exploitation, not due to issues related to race, but rather in their quest for individual autonomy and self-preservation as they labored in often debilitating working environments. Authorities, however, failed to make that important distinction, and the association of Japanese with violence and mayhem would influence later understandings of this ethnic group and impact martial law policies that targeted Japanese.

"The Evil Designs of Some Employee"

Worker Agency and Resistance

In their acts of violence, workers expressed discontent with their treatment and protested against exploitation. After a Chinese laborers' riot on the Lihue Plantation, Wray Taylor of the Bureau of Immigration discovered that labor aggression was the result of widespread discontent: laborers were arrested for "not working quick enough," had their wages docked "without any explanation," and suffered abuse at the hands of *luna* William Zoller who "admitted that he had laid hands on laborers at different times."[52] Frustrated and angered that the planters failed to address their grievances, workers resorted to violence to express their dissatisfaction and gain some satisfaction through retribution that some planters referred to as "The evil designs of some employee."[53]

Arson and Recalcitrance

Laborers occasionally expressed their anger against their bosses by committing acts of arson. In 1865, following the death of a Chinese worker, several Chinese attempted to burn down a building on the Princeville Plantation on Kaua'i. Authorities charged them with murder and sent them to Honolulu for sentencing.[54] After a fire gutted a sugar mill in Kāne'ohe, with losses totaling $30,000, the *Pacific Commercial Advertiser* commented that "it may be well to urge our planters to be more guarded against fires" as the "risking of a building worth from twenty to fifty thousand dollars, wholly unprotected, and liable to be destroyed by accident or through the evil designs of some employee, is too great for any one to incur."[55] But fires continued to occur: in 1867 at Halawa and 1870 at Makawao.[56] Masuda Takashi, president of a Japanese labor recruiting company, recorded in his diary an arson incident involving workers from Kumamoto, Japan: "I told [Robert] Irwin that people from Higo Kumamoto work very hard, but they are quick tempered and unless they are handled with care, they may make some trouble. My prediction unfortunately proved correct later. Immigrants from Higo set fire to a sugar plantation and this became a big issue between the Japanese and Hawaiian governments."[57]

Workers developed other day-to-day methods of resistance that were more subtle and often more vexatious to plantation owners. Although workers did not control the means of production, they could control the pace and quality of their labor and thereby carve some measure of independence and resistance. Many workers were deliberately inefficient and sought to minimize their daily labor through recalcitrance, feigning illness, and work slowdowns. One account published in the *Pacific Commercial Advertiser* detailed how Chinese laborers were notorious for traveling to the cane fields like "snails, but return like racehorses" as they have "not the least desire or intention of faithfully serving any white employer."[58] Employees also sang songs of their disobedience that celebrated their absenteeism from work and preference for wine rather than labor.[59]

Their failure to conform to the regimentation and disciplined pace of plantation work constantly frustrated their bosses, who attempted to monitor their every behavior. Most workers did not overtly flaunt their recalcitrance; instead, they covertly smoked, gossiped, and rested when the watchful eyes of the *luna* were not upon them. They became skilled in deception, appearing to be productive and energetic workers while taking every opportunity to avoid real productivity. G. W. Bates, who visited Hawai'i in 1853, described this continuous game between worker and overseer:

> No beast of prey watches his victim with closer scrutiny than the kanaka [Native Hawaiian] watches his employer. In his presence, he makes every

> effort to appear active and useful; but the very minute he disappears it is a signal for a general cessation of work, and one keeps a "look-out" while the group indulges in every variety of gossip. On the reappearance of their master, the sentinel gives the alarm, and every man is found to be at work as though he meant never again to lay down his tools. The owner may have watched them through a clump of foliage; but they will swear him out of the use of his eyes, and insist on it he was altogether mistaken.[60]

Japanese laborers engaged in similar tactics to avoid work. On one Kohala plantation, *luna* Jack Hall bemoaned his difficulties with supervising Japanese women as "it always seemed impossible to keep them together, especially if the fields were not level."[61] As a result, many of these women were "usually scattered all over the place." As many as possible "were out of sight in the gulches or dips in the field where they could not be seen, where they would calmly sit and smoke their little metal pipes until the luna appeared on the skyline when they would be busy as bees." Even when under the direct supervision of the *lunas,* workers used their numbers to challenge the ability of the overseers to monitor and control the labor of the entire group. Some used fleeting opportunities to take unscheduled breaks, to the chagrin of *lunas* whose control over the labor force was always tenuous.

Malingering and Alcohol/Drug Usage

Workers not only pretended to be busy but also faked illnesses to avoid work altogether. According to scholar Ronald Takaki, laborers "became adept actors, falsely feigning sickness, or pleading a death in the family or some other domestic calamity."[62] To deceive plantation doctors and to secure medical excuses from work, some individuals even drank shoyu (soy sauce) to raise their body temperatures. In 1873, one English traveler said, "it reminds me very much of plantation life in Georgia in the old days of slavery."[63] With some amusement, she wrote: "I never elsewhere heard of so many headaches, sore hands, and other trifling ailments. . . . [I]t is very amusing to see the attempts which the would-be invalids make to lengthen their brief, smiling faces into lugubriousness, and the sudden relaxation into naturalness when they are allowed a holiday." Those workers caught not performing work or feigning illness were subject to fines, punishment, and, in some cases, incarceration for violating their labor contracts. Authorities enacted similar policies during martial law as they prohibited workers from leaving their jobs unless approved and regulated labor contracts due to the acute labor shortage in Hawai'i. In response to the daily drudgery of hard labor, many plantation workers resorted to drugs, including opium, heroin, morphine, and alcohol, to avoid work.[64] Although it is impossible to know the extent of alcohol and drug usage, many workers used these substances after work, on weekends, and during their lunch breaks. Beginning in 1860, the Chinese could legally sell opium in the kingdom following negotiations by U.S. minister William B. Reed, who forced China to legalize incoming opium shipments in the treaties negotiated in 1858 after the Taiping Rebellion.[65] Between 1864 and 1868, the opium trade in Hawaiʻi increased from $15,000 per year to $60,000.[66] In 1874, with fewer than 2,000 Chinese men in the Islands, the Custom House reported the arrival of more than thirty-four pounds of opium and one thousand "pills"; it was asserted that three-fourths of the Chinese at that time were addicts.[67] Opium was a profitable business on the plantations, and workers took advantage of the availability of the drug. Visiting a Hilo plantation in 1874, Isabella Bird noted that while the Chinese were "quiet and industrious," they openly smoked opium.[68] One year later, officials charged fifteen Japanese laborers with assaulting Henry Treadway, their overseer. The assault reportedly stemmed from their "lost time" because of using opium, for which Treadway planned on "docking" them.[69] In her travels through the islands, M. Forsyth Grant also reported the widespread use of opium on the plantations: "Opium is the great curse of the Chinese—they lose their health, are unable to attend to their work or business, but still the drug has such a fascination for them that they cannot give it up."[70] Grant described opium users as having "faces the colour and appearance of parchment, their eyes heavy and dull, their hands trembling." Despite these effects, according to Grant, "the pernicious habit is so strong that they are unable to avoid it."

Alcohol was more pervasive than opium and was more extensively consumed on the plantations. A correspondent for the *Pacific Commercial Advertiser* visiting the Wailuku plantation on Maui in 1872 described an *awa* shop, which sold an alcoholic drink made from a root "pretty well patronized by the natives."[71] On Saturday nights, plantation camps were animated with drinking parties; throughout the night, "an uproar was made with drinking and singing."[72] Because they perceived problems with alcohol usage by the workers, planters passed a new law in 1882 "totally prohibiting the importation and sale of all spirituous or intoxicating liquors, except for medical and mechanical purposes."[73] However, this law was relatively ineffective in prohibiting the production and usage of alcohol. The *Kohala Midget* voiced the frustration of many plantation owners in 1911, declaring: "No employees can drink booze and do six honest days' work in a week. They are not 'up to scratch.' Even if they can keep awake. They are not as 'at,' physically, as men who don't drink. Their brains are muddled by booze."[74] However, most workers knew that drugs and alcohol only offered temporary respite from the backbreaking labor and drudgery of plantation work or melancholy thoughts of home.

Ha'alele Hana

Despite repeated beatings and imprisonment, some workers attempted to escape the plantation to gain their freedom. One worker, Masaji Watanabe, "hated being worked on the plantation like a beast of burden."[75] Despite repeated beatings by the manager, who often left Watanabe's "back covered in blood" from whippings with a thick leather lash, Watanabe finally escaped from the Waianae plantation. Others, such as a Chinese worker from Līhu'e Plantation, feigned sickness and disappeared without a trace after being carried ashore by two native sailors and placed in front of the inter-island wharf. Newspapers speculated that "probably he is safely housed in the dwelling place of some friend" after taking advantage of his sickness to escape plantation work.[76] *Ha'alele Hana,* or desertion from service, was particularly common during the nineteenth century. As early as 1882, W. C. Parke, marshal of the kingdom, complained about the mounting expenses of a police force tasked to arrest plantation troublemakers. Parke blamed rising costs "solely" on "the increase in sugar plantations throughout the Islands, and these arrests have enormously increased the expense of the prisons and lock-ups."[77] Six years later, another marshal, John H. Soper, similarly attributed the rising costs of the police force to "keeping the Oriental, Portuguese, and native Hawaiian labor in their place." In 1892, authorities arrested 5,706 individuals for deserting their contract service on the plantations—of these arrests, 5,387 were convicted. To control the problem of *Ha'alele Hana,* planters formed surveillance networks and an informal system of mutual assistance to capture deserters. Others offered rewards for capturing runaways as "incentives" to identify deserters and report suspicious individuals or "wandering laborers" to the authorities. However, these tactics failed to deter many workers from leaving their contracts to escape from the regimentation, low wages, and harsh conditions of plantation labor.

As soon as the opportunity arose, either at the end of their labor contract or through desertion, many laborers left the plantations for work in the bustling city of Honolulu. In 1859, the editor of the *Polynesian* called attention to the movement of Chinese laborers from the plantations to Honolulu: "In February next the last Coolie contracts expire and we may then expect a still further increase of liberated laborers from the plantations on the other islands, to swell the crowd of Chinamen now already prowling about Honolulu without any apparent means of livelihood."[78] As their experiences on the plantations dissipated their hopes for a new and better life in Hawai'i, thousands of laborers decided not just to leave the sugarcane fields but the Islands. Many migrated to the United States, particularly following Hawai'i's annexation and the prohibition of contract labor in the Territory of Hawai'i: Laborers were no longer bound to the plantations, and thousands boarded ships for the continent in search of a better life.

On plantations everywhere, Japanese laborers read advertisements that enticed them to move to the mainland, where wages were higher and their labor was in demand. "Want to Get Thousands of Japanese" was the headline article of the *Hawaiian Star* that described the "American Fever" sweeping through the Japanese population, "causing a lot of agitation among them" as advertisements for free transportation and wages of $1.45 per day were circulated among the laborers.[79] Recognizing that labor was paid more in California than in Hawai'i, planters considered offering monetary inducements to try to persuade laborers to stay on the plantations. Some frustrated planters even refused to return passports to their workers. Unable to discourage workers from leaving for the mainland, planters turned to the government for assistance. Under pressure from the sugar companies, the Territorial Legislature passed a law in 1905 that required an emigrant agent to pay a $500 annual fee for a license.[80] It also specified that anyone engaged in business as an emigrant agent without a license would be guilty of a misdemeanor and fined $500. The law aimed to harass labor recruiters and restrict their activities. Ultimately, the planters succeeded in limiting Japanese migration through the passage of the 1907 Gentlemen's Agreement, a voluntary accord between the United States and Japanese governments that virtually ended the migration of workers from Japan and prohibited Japanese laborers from leaving Hawai'i to work in the continental United States.[81] Unable to return to their home country or to seek higher wages and improved working conditions elsewhere, Japanese laborers realized they had no choice but to struggle for a better life in Hawai'i.

Conducted on both individual and collective levels, resistance against planter hegemony and dominance characterized the early Japanese history in the Islands. Despite the dual system of justice and federal and local legislation designed to restrict the rights and movement of the Japanese, numerous laborers remained defiant. White plantation owners frequently clashed with Japanese laborers. Conflict on the plantations became a source of anxiety for many whites as the Japanese represented the largest ethnic group in the Islands, almost doubling their population in the two decades following Hawai'i's annexation by the United States in 1898 and averaging about 40 percent of Hawai'i's population from 1900 to 1940.[82] With the outbreak of war, the large number of Japanese laborers posed a unique dilemma to military authorities who needed laborers to rebuild Pearl Harbor and support wartime mobilization, yet questioned their loyalty to the United States.

Strikes

In the early years of Japanese migration, laborers were encouraged by the Organic Act on June 14, 1900, which established Hawai'i as a territory of the United States and subsequently abolished the labor contract system.[83] While many planters had heralded Hawai'i's territorial status as the culmination of their efforts to disenfranchise Native Hawaiians and Asians, annexation had unexpected repercussions. Under the laws of the United States laborers could not be legally sanctioned for protesting against and breaking their labor contracts. Previously, contact laborers could not strike as they were bound by contract to work for a specific number of years. Authorities could arrest and prosecute workers for violating their agreements. Immediately following the passage of the Organic Act, the Japanese went on strike in several places to enforce the law. On June 20, 1900, two hundred Japanese laborers on the Spreckelsville plantation in Maui struck, demanding the termination of all labor contracts. "Armed with clubs and stones," which they "freely used and threw," the strikers resisted nearly sixty policemen and *lunas* who carried black snake whips.[84] Although the strikers were "most thoroughly black snaked back to their camps," their contracts, which had bound their bodies "as property of the sugar planters, to be abused and even whipped," were eventually canceled. During this strike, however, "several hundred Japanese from other camps," similarly armed, had gathered, ready to resist white authorities who bypassed the crowd. Stories about these events, reported by the *Hawaiian Star,* were widely disseminated throughout the plantations.

Consequently, the newspaper editorialized, "The Japanese have the idea that the white forces were afraid of them."[85] Some whites speculated that "perhaps it would have been better had the Government force gone in and dispersed this gang, with a good thrashing thrown in," to dissuade Japanese laborers from this notion. This editorial and its thinly veiled threat of the use of force failed to have the intended effect of deterring future labor movements. Before the year's end, twenty-four strikes occurred at forty-six establishments.[86] Over eight thousand laborers, who incurred $21,445 in lost wages, participated in the strikes, costing employers $10,300.

Despite realizing the financial burden they would have to shoulder, workers went on strike over grievances with overseers and demanded increased wages, reduced work hours, the reinstatement of discharged workers, and mandatory holidays. Others immediately left the plantations for Honolulu, searching for employment opportunities in the city and causing an uproar among the planters who desired a stable labor force. In his report for 1900, Hawai'i's governor Sanford B. Dole observed that "a large number of Japanese contract laborers have taken advantage of this immunity" and have either deserted work or "become irregular and uncertain in their performance."[87] Dole reported that many plantations have become "greatly prejudiced in the operations for want of labor" as workers abandoned their contracts for higher wages elsewhere and exacerbated existing labor problems. Laborers also left the Islands, searching for better opportunities in the United States. A year after the Organic Act took effect, 4,079 Japanese left the Territory. At the same time, only 589 arrived, giving rise to dire predictions by the planters who lamented the drop in plantation stock prices and warned that "if no relief is forthcoming, the most disastrous results will surely follow."[88] The twentieth century would similarly witness a number of strikes involving Japanese laborers. In 1900 alone, thirty-one labor strikes occurred on the various plantations in the Hawaiian Islands.[89] However, these strikes were generally confined to a limited locality, often lasted just a few days, and received little attention in the press.[90] Yet, in 1907, the governments of Japan and America enacted a treaty called the Gentlemen's Agreement Act that prohibited the migration of workers from Hawai'i to the mainland United States. This single piece of legislation dramatically affected the fortunes of laborers who could no longer escape to better working conditions or higher pay. Instead, they were forced to confront plantation managers with their complaints, which soon escalated into major movements such as the 1909 and 1920 strikes, as workers advocated for better pay and improved working and living conditions.[91] These strikes marked a fundamental shift from previous labor movements in their character and their impact as they extended far beyond the plantations to involve the planter elite, high-ranking government authorities, and influential leaders within the Japanese community. Authorities would arrest and imprison strike leaders and support efforts to break strikes by evicting striking workers and fining recalcitrant workers.

While it is difficult to identify the collective impact of these actions on later incarceration and martial law policies, similar policing occurred throughout the various incarceration centers. Authorities would regulate inmate access to matches that they used to light their cigarettes, monitor inmate labor, and prohibit alcohol consumption. Armed guards supervised inmates even when they went to the latrine and segregated Japanese inmates from the larger community and other prisoners. Thus, plantation control strategies would continue reverberating in wartime policies enacted decades later with the heightened danger allegedly posed by the Japanese. While all workers were subject to army regulations that dictated wages, working conditions, and allocations of workers to various industries, "enemy aliens" who were primarily Japanese endured additional restrictions such as gathering and travel restrictions, and authorities required them to turn in cameras, portable radios, flashlights, firearms, and other items that could be used for espionage purposes.

"Japs Must Be Taught a Lesson"

The Growing Threat of Japanese

After 1900, the relationship between plantation managers and Japanese laborers remained tense, often breaking into open, sometimes violent confrontations as planters sought to impose greater control over the migrant population while laborers sought greater autonomy and independence. It would also parallel growing tensions between the United States and Japan over Japan's aggressive expansion throughout the Pacific. Thus, as workers organized themselves and initiated strikes, many faced state-sanctioned violence closely monitored by authorities in Washington. Anxious to control Japanese laborers who were becoming more "aggressive" and "self-assertive" because "the labor force is overwhelmingly Japanese," many planters and police authorities felt that the "Japs must be taught a lesson."[92] Commissioner C. P. Neill of the United States Department of Commerce and Labor explained that it was a "lesson in mind" of the "kind that the militia can best teach." Neill's suggestions were forwarded to President Theodore Roosevelt, who wrote to William H. Taft, then Secretary of War, regarding Neill's memorandum:

> I call your special attention to that phrase of Mr. Neill's letter where he speaks of finding on that part of the officers of the law a very distinct impatience with those forms of law which hamper summary action on the part of police and militia, and of the feeling which he asserts exists that the safeguards of the law for the protection of the individual citizen need not be so carefully observed in dealing with Japanese laborers. This is a very important matter.

Although Hawai'i had become a Territory of the United States with the passage of the Organic Act, Roosevelt did not intend to extend equal rights and protection granted under the law to Japanese laborers. Both Roosevelt and Neill hinted at the possibility of utilizing federal troops to quash future uprisings, a suggestion embraced by the *Honolulu Advertiser*, which later called for a company of troops to be stationed at every large O'ahu plantation during the 1909 strike. As Japanese also began to establish an urban presence on every island, their visibility and expansion into other areas of the economy heightened fears of their growing economic and cultural influence and political loyalties.

The Emergence of Dynamic Prewar Urban Japanese Communities

Although most Japanese started as plantation laborers on O'ahu, many were employed in other industries. In 1940, Honolulu had the largest number of professional workers in the Islands, and out of a labor force of 25,363 Japanese, nearly 33 percent, or 8,439, were Issei.[93] With almost 17,000 Japanese workers in Honolulu, large urban Japanese communities existed by the start of the war. Many Issei openly embraced their Japanese culture in ethnic enclaves like Liliha, Kaka'ako, McCully-Mō'ili'ili, Kalihi, Mānoa, and 'A'ala, where visitors to the Islands would have been amazed at the "old world customs" openly practiced by the Japanese. Unlike the neighbor islands, O'ahu had large urban populations of Japanese who, to the fear and suspicion of civil and military authorities, embraced elements of Japanese culture during a period when Japan was militarizing and expanding. By the 1930s, there were over a dozen vernacular serial publications, and many Issei read the news in two prominent daily Japanese newspapers, the *Nippu Jiji* and *Hawaii Hochi,* each of which had a circulation of about fifteen thousand.[94] Since 1892, 107 Japanese newspapers have been published throughout Hawai'i, with most published on O'ahu.[95] Japanese movie theaters such as Nippon Kan and Honolulu Za showed the latest films from Japan, and both Issei and Nisei sang Japanese songs they learned through Japanese radio programs and from records available locally. Although the Nisei were American citizens due to their birth in an American Territory, a majority of Hawaii Nisei (73,281 out of 119,361) also carried Japanese citizenship as late as 1940. Their dual citizenship was due in part to the restrictions that limited their ability to expatriate between the ages of seventeen and thirty-seven as they were eligible to serve in either the Imperial Army or the Imperial Navy[96] Although most Nisei identified as American, military and civil officials continued to question their loyalties and affiliations.

The Japanese Navy also regularly visited Hawai'i. Between 1876 and 1939, there were forty-one visits by the Imperial Japanese Navy.[97] These courtesy visits allowed American and Japanese naval officers to establish professional contacts, allowed the Japanese to observe Pearl Harbor, and reaffirmed ties between Japan and its citizens abroad in the Islands. Many Japanese in Hawai'i celebrated these visits, which were publicized in Japanese newspapers. Officers and men were greeted with warm hospitality by businesses, civil and religious organizations, and homes of Japanese on O'ahu, Maui, and Kaua'i. While in the Islands, naval officers delivered public lectures on Japan's aims in China. Encouraged by the Consulate Office of Japan and the Japanese Chamber of Commerce, Hawai'i Japanese purchased 3 million yen worth of Imperial war bonds to support Japan's war efforts in China. They also contributed 1.2 million yen to the National Defense and Soldier's Relief Fund, donating more per capita to the National Defense Fund than residents of Japan. These transactions were primarily handled by Honolulu branches of the Yokohama Specie Bank and the Sumitomo Bank or through consular agents active on each island. The *Nippu Jiji* and other Japanese language newspapers also assisted in the war effort by collecting blankets, lead plates from auto batteries, tinsel foil from cigarette packages, and Kodak film wrappers to help the war effort. Local *kumi* (groups) of housewives collected and prepared *imonbukuro* (comfort bags) for troops fighting in China. A few Japanese women also sewed one thousand stitch belts as amulets to protect Japanese soldiers in combat.[98]

Due to the large number of Japanese concentrated in rural and urban areas, many Issei could converse in Japanese and encouraged their children to learn Japanese by enrolling them in Japanese language schools. To develop a more stable labor population and ensure Japanese children could easily transition to schools upon returning to Japan, sugar planters in Hawai'i and their Issei parents encouraged the establishment of Japanese language schools that also provided childcare services for Japanese laborers who worked during the day. These language schools were separate from the established English standard schools that the Territorial government supported as a means of racial segregation. In 1920, the Federal Commission of Education, reporting on the status of public instruction in Hawai'i, noted the existence of 163 Japanese language schools educating nearly twenty thousand students.[99] By 1935, 85 percent of Nisei students attended Japanese language schools after regular school hours. Those who sought more intensive Japanese education became *Kibei,* Nisei educated in Japan, who later returned to the United States.[100] Many of these language schools were associated with the 77 Buddhist temples and shrines on O'ahu, the most significant number in the Hawaiian Islands, home to 75 of the 149 Buddhist and Shintō priests in Hawai'i.[101] Due to the close affiliation between Buddhist temples and language schools and suspicions that both institutions fostered nationalistic sentiment within Hawai'i's Japanese community, some whites alleged that the language schools were "under the control of reactionary Buddhist priests" who undermined the efforts of "genuine Americanization."[102]

The Japanese "Danger" among Nisei

For white elites, the dangers that the Japanese posed even within urban communities seemed confirmed by the dramatic events in Hawai'i in 1928, when Myles Fukunaga, a young Nisei man, kidnapped and murdered the son of a prominent white family.[103] Before the body of his victim was found, Fukunaga had demanded a ransom of $10,000 as part of his revenge against the Hawaiian Trust Company that he blamed for his family's misfortunes.[104] He also hoped to earn enough money to allow his parents to return to Japan and enable them to have a better future.[105] After an extensive search, authorities would later arrest Fukunaga and convict and execute him in O'ahu Prison within weeks. Despite the haste in which Fukunaga was identified and punished for his crime, the island's white oligarchy that dominated pre–World War II Hawai'i was shaken by the brash kidnapping of a white boy whose father was the vice-president of a prominent company. Particularly threatening was the possibility that beneath the innocent visage of a typical Japanese lurked murderous intent toward whites. Thus, Fukunaga's crime became associated with the danger individual Japanese posed even within urban communities where whites and Japanese were in close contact, further strengthening existing suspicions about the large Japanese population in Hawai'i. This concern among whites that Japanese residents might more frequently resort to violence against them had particularly severe consequences over time. This fear had become so pervasive during the Fukunaga case that, for the first time, the possibility of imposing martial law emerged in the Islands to maintain white hegemony and order. A few years later, Honolulu again witnessed a crime that raised suspicions about the local Japanese population. The Massie rape and trial renewed demands for law and order and exacerbated fears of the Japanese in Hawaiʻi, both on the plantations and in urban settings.

The Expansion of the American Military in Hawaiʻi and the Massie Case

While the Fukunaga case seemed to illustrate the dangers the Japanese posed to white elites, the Massie case only three years later sparked similar fears among military leaders in the Islands. The military had long been interested in the Islands well before World War II due to Hawaiʻi's strategic location in the Pacific. Only a decade after the annexation of Hawaiʻi by the United States in 1898, Congress authorized the construction of a naval base at Pearl Harbor. This military base enabled the United States to occupy a strategic bastion in the middle of the Pacific where United States maritime strength would be used to advance and protect American foreign policy interests as the island of Oʻahu was destined to become the central fortress on the Alaska-Hawaiʻi-Panama defensive perimeter.[106] As the military expanded its presence throughout Hawaiʻi, the Japanese became the focus of regulations and surveillance, similar to what had existed on the plantations where white elites created informal and formal control strategies designed to create a stable labor force.[107] Subsequently, as the military increased its presence in Hawaiʻi, officials became increasingly concerned about the growing conflict between military personnel and the various ethnicities in the Islands.

These concerns were magnified during the world-famous Massie case in 1932 when Navy wife Thalia Massie accused a group of local men—including two Japanese Americans—of assault and rape. These events spurred calls as early as the 1930s for the institution of martial law and for establishing a commission form of government meant to subvert traditional legal channels and rights and to counter the rampant Japanese threat that extended now to a dangerous second generation of Japanese in Hawaiʻi.[108] However, at this time, prominent local businesspeople seemed uneasy with this solution as it essentially would break their political and financial control over the Islands. To allay hostilities and to explain what had happened in Honolulu, businessman Walter Dillingham wrote *A Memorandum,* which, despite a statement cautioning that it was "For Private Circulation and Not for Publication," he sent to mainland newspaper editors and members of Congress. While arguing that it was "the greatest importance that this city, which is the playground of the personnel of the Army and Navy, be so operated and controlled as to keep it decent and safe," he held that "Honolulu is better able to cope with its problems through leaders and organizations made up from its citizens than by placing this important function of government under politically appointed officers from Washington."[109] Given recent reforms made in territorial laws, he predicted a future where the "standards of American ideals" would be as high as in any mainland community. Ironically, those ideals would be continually achieved at the expense of minority rights. The military began actively investigating the Japanese in the Islands, who seemed to threaten military personnel and, by extension, national security.

Consequently, many Japanese were of particular concern to both planters and military officials. The Japanese would become the largest ethnic group in Hawai'i, almost doubling their population in the two decades following Hawai'i's annexation by the United States in 1898 and averaging about 40 percent of Hawai'i's population from 1900 to 1940.[110] O'ahu had the largest Japanese population, with 60,593 in Honolulu alone out of 157,905. Most Kibei—American-born Japanese educated in Japan—were also found on O'ahu (565 of the approximately 700 Kibei in Hawai'i) and were of particular concern to military officials as the public education they received in Japan included military training and emperor worship.[111]

Military Investigations of the Prewar Japanese Community

Thus, before the war, military officials conducted extensive studies on the loyalties of the various generations that comprised the Japanese population. In the weeks preceding the attack on Pearl Harbor, at the request of presidential envoy John Franklin Carter, businessman Curtis B. Munson filed an intelligence report that he sent to the president on November 7, 1941. As historian Michi Weglyn concluded, the findings "certified a remarkable, even extraordinary degree of loyalty among this generally suspect ethnic group."[112] In his study, Munson divided Japanese Americans into four groups: Issei, Nisei, Kibei, and Sansei. The report focused on the other three groups by dismissing the Sansei because they were primarily children. Of the Issei, he noted that they were "considerably weakened in their loyalty to Japan by the fact that they have chosen to make this their home and have brought up their children here."[113] He explained, "They expect to die here." He described the Nisei as "universally estimated from 90 to 98 percent loyal to the United States if the Japanese-educated element of the Kibei is excluded. The Nisei are pathetically eager to show this loyalty. They are not Japanese in culture. They are foreigners to Japan." While conceding that the Kibei "are considered the most dangerous element," he also noted "that many of those who visited Japan after their early American education come back with added loyalty to the United States. In fact it is a saying that all a Nisei needs is a trip to Japan to make a loyal American out of him." Following his West Coast investigations, Munson went to Hawai'i to continue his work, where he reported, "we believe that the big majority anyhow would be neutral or even actively loyal."[114]

A second study was completed on November 4, 1942, by Captain Frank O. Blake, who confirmed these findings. He issued a memorandum to the U.S. Army headquarters of the Hawaiian Department regarding what he described as the "Kibei project"—a survey of the records of Kibei in the Islands completed by Lt. Kanemi Kanezawa.[115] Kanezawa was formerly a member of police Captain John A. Burns's Espionage Bureau, established in December 1940 to examine personal loyalties, general Japanese sentiments, and potential racial tensions. Kanezawa thus had considerable experience investigating the Japanese community.[116] Kanezawa identified about 700 Kibei who returned by July 1, 1935, from an extended stay in Japan with information regarding whether they were interviewed, incarcerated and released, or were in Japan, in the U.S. Army, or an unknown location.[117]

Although authorities had not "processed" the approximately 20 Kibei on Kaua'i by the date of the report, of the 726 Kibei identified, 181 had been incarcerated, or about 34 percent of those questioned. Authorities also investigated all Navy and Navy contractors of Japanese ancestry, and of the 2,000 surveyed, 143 were deemed dangerous to naval security—most of them Kibei. The report noted that "the Kibei themselves are facing the greatest dilemma of their lives—the country in which they were born being at war with the nation in which they were raised. . . . Torn between two nations, many of them frankly express that they are at a loss as to what their sentiment should be." However, the report added that "from the viewpoint of Internal Security, the general run of Kibeis are not of immediate danger individually," although "Kibeis are dangerous as a group composed of individuals who might translate some underlying sympathy for Japan into action inimical to the welfare of the United States." The report added that "most of the Kibeis are not loyal to Japan in the true sense of the word, neither are they loyal to the United States," creating a complicated situation for both them and military authorities, who were deeply concerned about the influence of this group. The report concluded that "while the Kibei group is potentially dangerous in this area and situation they may properly be handled as citizen evacuees in a mainland relocation" and that Kibei are "deserving of and will repay if fairly treated, any effort on their behalf." Notwithstanding the findings of these reports, military officials were still deeply troubled by the large Kibei population in Hawai'i and on O'ahu in particular.

Complex Loyalties and Identities within Hawai'i's Japanese Communities

Despite these suspicions and aspects of Japanese culture visible throughout Honolulu, Japanese prewar identity and loyalty were more complex than associating ethnicity with allegiance to Japan, particularly for the Nisei. Although many Nisei attended Japanese language schools, their effectiveness in teaching Japanese to Nisei was somewhat limited. Most Nisei in Hawai'i attended public schools in the morning and Japanese language schools in the afternoon, although many did not take their language studies seriously. O'ahu's Nisei also benefited from the Americanizing influences of McKinley High School, often called "Tokyo High."[118] As O'ahu's only public high school, its principal, Miles E. Cary, introduced Core Studies with a core curriculum emphasizing citizenship, leadership, and critical thinking.[119] During this time, students were influenced by two ideals expressed in the Declaration of Independence: "That all men are created equal in the sight of God and are entitled to an equal opportunity to make the most of their talents; and that when the existing social order is inimical to equal opportunity, the system should be overturned."[120] However, the promise of equality and opportunity would be unfulfilled when Nisei, with excellent academic and employment records, were passed over when the Big Five corporations recruited management personnel. Additionally, many recent arrivals from the mainland—including American military personnel—often distrusted the Japanese due to preconceived racial beliefs. Due to long-standing racial biases, the Nisei were confronted with limited economic opportunities, perpetuating their subordinate economic and social status in prewar Hawai'i.

Patriotism through American Military Service in World War I

Seeking better economic opportunities and the chance to demonstrate their loyalty to America, about 29,000 first- and second-generation Japanese registered with the Selective Service, which totaled 71,280 registrants in the Territory following the passage of the Selective Service Draft Act on June 18, 1917. Previously, the Japanese had been prohibited from joining the National Guard, but that restriction had been modified when Congress lifted the restrictions preventing "friendly aliens" from volunteering. In August 1917, 838 Japanese were accepted into the Japanese Company or "Company D" of the First Regiment of the National Guard of Hawai'i. "D" Company did not get a chance to engage in active combat. Still, the *Pacific Commercial Advertiser* reported their "loyalty to the American flag" and "the enthusiasm displayed by the Japanese."[121]

As the experience of World War I veterans illustrated, some Japanese were initially deemed ineligible due to their Japanese citizenship. Civil and military authorities in the pre–World War II period often cited the large number of Hawai'i Nisei (73,281 out of 119,361) who carried Japanese citizenship as evidence of loyalty to Japan.[122] Many Nisei held dual citizenship and were considered Japanese citizens by blood and American citizens by birth. Expatriation from Japanese citizenship was a long and complicated process frequently handled by consular agents and always had to be accomplished through the Japanese consulate. The ambiguities of dual citizenship were only one of several circumstances complicating the lives of Hawai'i Nisei before World War II. Additionally, with the Supreme Court ruling on O'ahu resident Takao Ozawa's petition for citizenship, Issei would be denied American citizenship due to their national origin of birth until after World War II. Thus, Issei could not renounce their Japanese citizenship without becoming stateless people.[123]

For Hawai'i's Japanese, who often lived near both civil and military officials, the prewar period was fraught with contradictions and the challenge of balancing loyalties to both America and Japan. The prewar period was characterized by numerous incidences on and off the plantations of Japanese resistance to white authority and exploitation that brought together shared interests by civil and military officials to control the perceived Japanese threat. As the Japanese engaged in strikes, committed acts of arson, and protested their exploitation through malingering, drug use, and drinking, white perceptions of the political, economic, and social threat of the Japanese only grew. At the same time, planters and military officials sought to expand their presence and influence in the Islands, increasing conflict between these groups within rural and urban areas throughout Hawai'i. Thus, racial fears and economic interests of the plantations and military grew in the decades before World War II, as did Japanese activism. Ironically, many Japanese highlighted their oppression through the American tradition of protest and resistance. To white elites, however, the visibility and activism of the Japanese community was evidence of their inability to assimilate and their loyalties to Japan rather than a nuanced understanding of the complexities of citizenship and the limits of American equality and liberty granted to them as Japanese. Therefore, as early as 1932, there were calls for the United States to administer commission rule or martial law in Hawai'i, which would become a reality less than ten years later. The presence of so many "undesirables" in Hawai'i, of which the Japanese constituted the majority, directly affected the Territory's status, the decision to impose martial law during World War II, and the incarceration of select members of the Japanese population. Efforts to reshape Hawai'i's legal and political systems also underscored the close alliance of the white oligarchy and the military, which shared similar objectives of protecting white supremacy and white economic and political interests.

The enactment of martial law in Hawai'i and the incarceration of individuals represented a crisis in constitutional rights that reflected long-standing racial fears among the military and select members of the Islands' white elite. These groups were aligned against the very segment of the population martial law was designed to contain: the Japanese. Yet, martial law impacted communities to varying degrees and had very different meanings for those who ultimately benefited from or suffered under martial law regulations. While some Japanese embraced the opportunity to demonstrate their loyalty and patriotism to America through Morale Committees and later military service, others endured community surveillance, censorship, investigations, and incarceration. Experiences on each island also varied, depending on the degree of mobilization and militarism that occurred, highlighting the complexity of this period, particularly for military officials who were intent on identifying threats within Japanese communities across the Islands. Residents also faced personal and official questions about their loyalties and allegiances that became life-changing decisions during this period of unprecedented changes and upheaval with the outbreak of war.

2 Community Mobilization and Surveillance under Martial Law

> *[The Japanese will] achieve absolute domination of the islands within 20 years. . . . If you leave things that way, you've lost Hawaii within a few years. The Japs there are not only a menace now—what's going to happen 10 years from now. . . . This isn't the last war with Japan. Think of the hazard to the United States if the Japanese achieve absolute domination in the Hawaiian islands.*[1]

These statements, made in 1943 by John A. Balch, former president of the Mutual Telephone company in Hawai'i, argued for the "shipment" of twenty thousand Japanese families to the midwestern states and Mississippi valley to protect Hawai'i from the large Japanese population in the Islands.[2] Secretary of the Navy Frank Knox also advocated mass evacuation of the Japanese to a neighboring island, such as Moloka'i, to contain the threat of the Japanese population.[3] However, not all whites shared Balch's opinion of the Japanese; many of those who did occupied essential positions in Hawai'i's government, the business community, and the military. Further incarceration was discouraged not because of an "enlightened" racial policy but because of logistical concerns and the labor shortage in Hawai'i. Gen. Delos Emmons, the army commander who replaced General Short as Hawai'i's military governor, shared these concerns as the Japanese, who constituted one-third or more of the population, were an important part of the labor force during a period in war-mobilized Hawai'i when laborers were in short supply. Additionally, the lack of materials to construct proposed camps to house the entire Japanese population and the scarcity of transportation to transfer Japanese between islands also weighed heavily on Emmons's decision not to incarcerate all Japanese in Hawai'i.[4] As officials concentrated their efforts on protecting the Islands and rebuilding the military after the Pearl Harbor attack, a mass evacuation of Japanese from Hawai'i would have significantly hampered the war effort.

Yet those who remained were not immune to the racial hysteria that resulted in the incarceration of 2,270 Hawai'i residents. The outbreak of war immediately impacted those working in military facilities. It resulted in the mobilization of Hawai'i residents, including Japanese, involved in defense repairs and preparations and Morale Committees to promote interracial unity. Although many of these activities were sincere expressions of patriotism, they were also efforts to deflect the suspicion focused on them due to their Japanese ancestry. Officials seemed to focus community surveillance in urban areas, particularly on O'ahu. In response to continued community investigations by entities such as the Honolulu Police Department, who reported their findings to the Military Governor, members of the Japanese community engaged in self-censorship. Residents immediately removed public displays of Japanese culture, Japanese candidates were discouraged from running for political office, and Americanization efforts were widespread throughout the Islands. Fear of and discrimination against the Japanese suffused popular public sentiment, and many Japanese were aware of the possibility of their incarceration, resulting in the avoidance of the families of inmates as they feared a similar fate. Officials would incarcerate residents from urban neighborhoods on O'ahu and the rural towns on Kaua'i, Maui, Moloka'i, and Hawai'i Island. The availability of facilities and the extent to which military officials could exercise their authority would create diverse experiences for Hawai'i residents. O'ahu inmates experienced more direct military control due to their proximity to the Military Governor and critical bases. In contrast, authorities often relied upon existing mechanisms of control and relationships established on the plantations within these rural communities. Regardless of the motivation for incarceration, however, those who remained free were not immune from the impact of military control as their lives were fundamentally transformed under martial law.

Martial Law in Hawai'i

Through the implementation of martial law, the military was finally able to engage in extralegal actions against the Japanese that they justified by the "exigencies of war." At the outbreak of war, a reluctant governor, Joseph Poindexter, enacted martial law at the insistence of General Short. Poindexter was only convinced to do so by believing that martial law would be lifted "within a reasonable time."[5] Subsequently, a proclamation was issued declaring martial law and relinquishing the entire civilian governmental authority to the Army. Although the territorial governor and some leading members of the Hawaii Bar Association informed Army officials directly that they had gone too far in suspending normal liberties, even in such an emergency, military officials expressed little concern over the implications of martial law in either Hawai'i or official circles in Washington. Many accepted Army control as necessary due to the necessities of war. It was generally thought that the civilian courts would be reopened and criminal jurisdiction returned to the territorial government once the danger of imminent invasion had passed. However, it was not until March 1943, more than fifteen months later, that military officials who had ruled Hawai'i lifted the suspension of constitutional guarantees, including the right to a jury trial in criminal cases and the privilege of the writ of habeas corpus.[6] In essence, the dual system of justice that had operated within Hawai'i's legal system became irrelevant, given the all-out suspension of civil rights under martial law. Authorities only fully lifted martial law on October 24, 1944, more than two years after the Battle of Midway.

What was unique about the institution of martial law in Hawai'i was its lack of precedence in any United States Territory. Its scope, length of time, and lack of necessity highlighted its underlying motive of controlling the Japanese population. In October 1941, the territorial legislature, anticipating a war emergency, enacted the Hawaii Defense Act. This act authorized the civilian governor to exercise sweeping executive powers in any war emergency. However, civilian courts would be responsible for enforcing the laws with full provision of due process for any individual accused of violations. Military officials considered this statute on December 7. Still, they ignored civilian rights and constitutional law in favor of martial law, which had been advocated as early as 1928 during the Jamieson case when Myles Fukunaga, a young Nisei, kidnapped and murdered the son of an influential white family. The Defense Act became important in discussing whether Army rule was necessary. Many civilian leaders in Hawai'i contended that the act gave the governor ample powers over security in the civilian community, with no need for Army courts to enforce the laws. In the early months of 1942, however, the Defense Act was rendered irrelevant by the preemptive effect of martial law.

Behind the Army's readiness to take over every detail of government in Hawai'i only hours after the Pearl Harbor attack was Lt. Col. Thomas H. Green, an Army adjunct who was the chief legal officer for the military command in Hawai'i. He had spent the better part of 1941 planning the details of martial law, and thus, a bevy of "general orders" was in his files and ready for promulgation long before the Pearl Harbor attack.[7] During the military rule in Hawai'i, until late October 1944, officials issued some 181 general orders under the names of the commanding general Delos Emmons and Colonel Green, the latter having been given the title of "Executive, Office of the Military Governor." Under that title—and operating from the Office of the Territorial Attorney General at 'Iolani Palace, which the Army had appropriated for its Military Governor's functions—Green controlled much of civilian life and criminal law enforcement in Hawai'i until mid-1943.[8]

Gen. Delos Emmons, who took command of the Army in Hawai'i in January 1942 and succeeded to the appropriate title of Military Governor, authorized Green to extend Army control even to the full range of federal administrative functions. These eventually included all the wartime powers exercised by the Office of Price Administration, the War Production Board, the War Labor Board, and other "alphabet industries." The Army's general orders in Hawai'i also controlled wartime wages and working conditions. The military regulated labor allocations on the plantations, including "sweetheart deals" with the sugar and pineapple plantation companies. They kept their labor force in place but contracted workers to the Army's military construction projects.

The Army won over powerful employer interests and thus gained political influence within the civilian community by criminalizing job switching and absenteeism from work. Under martial law, employees had to obtain employer permission to leave a job. It was an offense to be absent from a job without permission. Therefore, organized business groups enthusiastically supported Army rule as military officials criminalized job absenteeism, or *Ha'alele Hana*, which had plagued plantation owners for years. Before and during the war, plantations, particularly on O'ahu that were often close to military bases, granted access to the military as part of the HSPA's "outstanding record of cooperation and assistance" to military forces.[9] During the war, the planter's Provisional Police organization formed in 1940 assisted in the "defense of Hawaii and the fulfillment of the mission of the armed forces in Hawaii." Planters made all plantation facilities, machinery, equipment, and staffing available to the military during the war as part of their personal and financial support for the war effort.

December 7 and the Battle of Ni'ihau

Due to the cloud of suspicion and fear surrounding the Japanese community and the need to prove their loyalty due to anti-Japanese sentiment that became part of sanctioned public discourse, thousands of Japanese engaged in super-patriotism in the wake of the shock of the Pearl Harbor attack. Some community members initially thought the planes flying overhead were part of the frequent military maneuvers in the latter months of 1941. Newspaper editor Yasutaro Soga described the Pearl Harbor attack as "a thunderbolt out of the blue" and was so incredulous that the Japanese would attack Hawai'i that he dismissed initial reports as training exercises.[10] Issei Suikei Furuya recalled that he "was overcome with emotion and did not know what to do" upon hearing that the Japanese military had bombed Pearl Harbor and that the United States was at war with Japan.[11] Samuel Sasai, later a 442nd Regimental Combat Team member, was home on Sheridan Street helping his father repair a leaky garage roof. Early that Sunday morning, Sasai noticed black smoke clouds rising over Honolulu's western side. As he and his father had become accustomed to constant military drills and practices, Sasai recalled that "both of us commented how realistic the maneuvers were that morning."[12] His sister was in the kitchen preparing breakfast and listening to the radio when the announcer broke the news that Japan had attacked Pearl Harbor: "This is the real McCoy! Take cover! This is no drill! Take cover!" As the Sasai family gathered in disbelief around the radio, the announcer provided details about attacking aircraft with Japan's "meatball" insignia. Sasai remembered that "both my parents looked at each other and used the same despairing word—"*Masaka* (can it be)?!"

Many Nisei were not only conscious of the burden of loyalty that faced them in the coming days but also questioned the fate of their alien parents. That day, George Akita wrote in his journal: "It's funny how the course of our lives can be changed in such a short space of time. . . . I guess we Japanese are in for it now. Especially Mom and Pop; they're aliens."[13] Akita worried about the fate of his parents, "torn between two nations" and "haunted by [the] fear that they might have to be separated from their children in the event that this government feels it expedient to deport all nationals." Akita realized that their limited English language skills and Japanese citizenship placed his parents and other Issei in danger of arrest and incarceration. He recognized that "they will be looked upon with suspicion" in the tension-filled days following the bombing.

As on O'ahu, rumors ran rampant about alleged incidents of Japanese sabotage, including Japanese parachutists landing on Kaua'i as part of a potential invasion that would be facilitated by Japanese residents, heightening existing fears. Although these rumors remained unsubstantiated, a mysterious incident on the island of Ni'ihau immediately following the Pearl Harbor attack seemed to confirm the disloyalty of the local Japanese population. On December 7, Japanese naval airman 1st Class Shigenori Nishikachi, returning from O'ahu, crash-landed on the island of Ni'ihau, owned by the Robinson family and inhabited primarily by Hawaiians. Howard Kaleohano, a local worker who had witnessed the crash, ran to pull out the unconscious pilot, confiscating his pistol and papers. Due to difficulties communicating with the pilot, neighbors of Kaleohano's summoned two Japanese: Ishimatsu Shintani, born in Hiroshima, Japan, and Yoshio Harada, a local Japanese American. While waiting for the boat to take Nishikachi to O'ahu and the authorities, Nishikachi asked Shintani and Harada for help retrieving his gun and papers. While Shintani refused, the pilot convinced Harada to help, and together, the two men terrorized the inhabitants of Ni'ihau for several days.

During a botched kidnapping attempt, where Nishikachi and Harada held Ben Kanahele and his wife captive while they searched for the missing documents, "the pilot fired three times, wounding Ben in the left chest, left hip, and penis."[14] Kanahele was infuriated by these injuries, and, despite being seriously wounded, "using the same grip he used in handling sheep, Ben picked up the pilot by the neck and leg and dashed him against the stone wall" of the building. Kanahele then drew his hunting knife and cut Nishikachi's throat. After witnessing the pilot's death, Harada killed himself with the gun. Authorities later awarded Kanahele and Kaleohano medals and honors for their courageous and heroic actions. However, officials censored news of this event immediately following the Pearl Harbor attack.[15] Although historians debate the motivations behind Harada's actions in the "Battle of Ni'ihau," this singular event cast doubt on the loyalty of the nearly 160,000 Japanese in the Islands.[16] While some may have identified more closely with their country of birth, any pro-Japanese sentiments they did feel did not translate into any acts of sabotage. It also did not justify the civil and human rights violations that hereafter took place. However, this reasoning was lost in the tumultuous days that followed as the Battle of Ni'ihau provided further impetus to incarcerate suspicious individuals.

Experiences of Japanese Labor

Suspicion of the Japanese also extended to workers required to report for work on the military bases to repair the damage inflicted by the December 7 attack. Officials had to weigh labor needs against Japanese fears. Although military and territorial officials believed that the Japanese community harbored dangerous elements, Japanese laborers still needed to conduct repairs on the military bases as they comprised a large portion of the skilled labor force. Joe Tanaka, who went to work on December 8, noted: "It was ironic that here in Hawaii, the Japanese were working in high security places and in California they were relocated."[17] Tanaka pointed out that "all the skilled labor in Hawaii was Japanese so everything would have come to a screeching halt if they interned the Japanese here." However, the expertise of the Japanese laborers did not shield them from blatant hostility and threats of violence. Masato Inouye, whom a private defense contractor employed, spent December 8 filling sandbags at Pearl Harbor. "When we finished our work," Inouye recalled, "the soldiers on guard told us to get the hell out of there or they'll let us have it and chased us all the way from Pearl Harbor to Dillingham Boulevard near Gaspro. I'll never forget that day."[18]

A similar fate befell Richard Nishioka, who also reported to work at Pearl Harbor on December 7, as military personnel made little distinction between enemy combatants and longtime employees. When Nishioka finished work at 1:00 a.m., military personnel detained him, and "a soldier put a .45 to my head and dared me to run."[19] Authorities held Nishioka for five days. FBI personnel repeatedly questioned him about his citizenship and his responses to scenarios such as "what I would do if Hirohito came down the street?" In response to such an outrageous and impossible scenario, Nishioka asked: "What I going to do? I don't even know what he look like." Although Nishioka did not recall the interrogator's reaction to his straightforward and honest response, later, soldiers "made me sleep on the concrete floor, and made me march a mile to the mess hall." Nishioka remembered a particularly humiliating experience: Soldiers "stripped me naked and even checked my buttocks to see if anything was hidden in there." Eventually, authorities released Nishioka, but officials barred him and other Japanese workers from their original jobs because of the danger they presumably posed. According to Nishioka, only private contractors could employ Japanese, but these workers "had to wear black badges that clearly spelled out 'Restricted.'" George Tanna, one of these laborers, recalled that besides wearing these badges, he worked under the supervision of armed guards who were visibly "trigger happy."[20] Although the military brought in Caucasian workers from the mainland to complete skilled jobs, the use of Japanese workers continued to the consternation of officials. Tanna explained, "we were more efficient than they were because we worked with our bare hands while they used gloves that got in the way."[21]

In addition to needing workers to repair damaged facilities, military officials required soldiers to guard critical sites and installations, even though military officials often made little distinction between the Japanese enemy and Japanese Americans. On December 7, 1941, authorities ordered all Reserve Officers' Training Corps (ROTC) members to report to the University of Hawai'i campus. At the time of the Pearl Harbor attack, enrollment in ROTC was mandatory for all male students except those with "exceptional reasons." Consequently, many Nisei belonged to ROTC. Yoshiaki Fujitani recalled his experience on the day of the attack: "We were handed the old Springfield '03 rifles we used in our drills and parades and told to install the firing pins that had been taken out to prevent accidents. Armed with this five-round, bolt-action rifle with chrome-plated bayonets for parade use, we were mustered into the Hawaii Territorial Guard (HTG), which gained distinction as the only ROTC unit in the country to see any military action."[22] For nearly two months, ROTC members guarded "water tanks in the hills, gas tanks at Iwilei, and the piers of Honolulu Harbor," even though members of the Japanese community were being arrested, incarcerated, and harassed as dangerous elements in the population. Nearly "80 percent" of the members of ROTC were young men of eighteen or nineteen years of age and of Japanese ancestry. Eventually, authorities raised concerns about arming Nisei at key governmental and military sites. In January 1942, officials disbanded the Hawai'i Territorial Guard. In response to this "rebuff and rejection," community leaders such as Hung Wai Ching, Shigeo Yoshida, and Mitsuyuki Kido began recruiting volunteers to form a labor battalion. It was officially known as the 34th Construction Engineer Regiment but was commonly referred to as the Varsity Victory Volunteers, or the "Triple V" or "VVV."[23] For nine months, the men of the VVV built barracks and roads, fixed fences, broke rocks in the quarry, and performed other construction work essential to the defense of

Hawai'i. Community volunteers met different needs and efforts spearheaded by Morale Committees that were eventually established on most islands.

Morale Committees and Wartime Patriotism

On December 18, 1941, military officials established a Morale Section that created various subcommittees within different ethnic communities to promote racial unity and address anti-Japanese sentiment in the Islands. The Emergency Service Committee, for example, was organized to work with the Japanese community. The formation of Morale Committees during the war indicated the underlying racial tensions in Hawai'i, as extensive efforts were made to mobilize the Japanese community and other ethnic groups to contribute to the overall war effort.

Before World War II, some Nisei and non-Japanese had formed the Committee for Interracial Unity in Hawai'i. This multiethnic group of civic and military leaders included YMCA leader Charles Loomis, Chinese American YMCA Secretary Hung Wai Ching, and Japanese American school principal Shigeo Yoshida. These highly articulate, educated individuals who would later comprise the Morale Section represented three major ethnic groups in Hawai'i—white, Japanese, and Chinese—but were not beholden to their ethnic group. Loomis was a respected outsider from the mainland who was not part of the exclusive circles of the Islands' *kama'aina* (native-born) elite. Ching, the son of Chinese immigrants, was a YMCA administrator with strong ties to influential individuals like the University of Hawai'i Board of Regents Chair Charles Hemenway, who was one of the founders of the University of Hawai'i, president of the Hawai'i Trust Company, and a former attorney general of the Territory. Born to Japanese immigrant parents, Yoshida excelled as a debater at the University of Hawai'i under the tutelage of individuals like Hemenway and became one of the few Nisei administrators in the Territory's Department of Public Instruction. As scholar Franklin Odo noted, "Unlike men who were executives of Big Five firms or ethnic organizations, these were leaders by virtue of their association beyond their own ethnic boundaries."[24] These men were uniquely qualified to direct their energies to the overall Morale Section effort rather than one individual group.

During the Pearl Harbor attack, individuals connected with various community groups, including the Committee of Interracial Unity, reported to Robert L. Shivers, chief of the Honolulu office of the Federal Bureau of Investigation (FBI). They gathered to implement the plans they helped to set up before the war as part of advanced preparations to address the potential Japanese threat. They also discussed their plans with the head of the local Office of Civilian Defense. As a result of these meetings, a Morale Section was created in the Office of Civilian Defense on December 18, 1941, as part of the Office of Military Governor on January 26, 1942. According to Shivers, the Morale Section "was appointed by the Army and worked under the immediate supervision of the Assistant Chief of Staff for Military Intelligence [and] maintained a close liaison with the FBI and the Military Governor's Office."[25] The purpose of the Morale Section was to serve as an intermediary between the Army and civilian community on matters related to public morale and to work toward the maintenance of a "unified and cooperative community."[26]

Under the Morale Section were several ethnic or national subcommittees that worked among their respective groups to disseminate military orders and alleviate any problems. The Japanese subcommittee of the Morale Section was organized as the Emergency Service Committee (ESC) in February 1942 on O'ahu.[27] Similar groups were organized on the other islands—the Kaua'i Morale Committee in May, the Maui Emergency Service Committee in August, the Lāna'i Emergency Service Committee in January 1943, and the Hawai'i AJA Morale Committee in April 1944.[28] In addition to thirteen Nisei men, Loomis and Ching of the Morale Section served as ex-officio members of the ESC. In the ESC alone, there was an advisory committee of about eighty men of Japanese ancestry who were leaders of their respective districts.[29]

Besides the ESC, the Honolulu Police Contact Group and the Citizens' Council were organized to promote racial unity in Hawai'i. The Honolulu Police Contact Group was sponsored by the Honolulu Police Department and led by Captain John Anthony Burns, who had headed its Espionage Division and worked under the direction of the FBI. Besides encouraging the active participation of Japanese Americans in the war effort, it "helped to allay the fears of the other racial groups where the Japanese were concerned, thus contributing to the overall unity of this community."[30] Leading professional and business leaders comprised the Citizens' Council to keep Hawai'i's citizens "united in purpose and action." These groups emerged throughout the Territory and helped to avert racial tensions in various racial communities.

Actions of the Morale Committees

During the war, authorities confiscated $2.4 million in frozen bank assets from three leading Japanese banks in the Territory to limit local efforts to support the Japanese military. This money was converted into war bond purchases.[31] Through letters and personal phone calls, the ESC collected $147,408.75 to be invested in war bonds. In June 1943, ESC members raised over $10,000 for the "Bombs on Tokyo Campaign."[32] The money was presented to Lt. Gen. Robert C. Richardson Jr., who succeeded Gen. Delos Emmons.

In addition to collecting money, many Japanese also responded through individual demonstrations of loyalty. Often holding down more than one job, many Japanese served as block wardens, Red Cross workers, firefighters, medical workers, and laborers. They responded to urgent pleas for blood by hosting numerous blood drives and encouraged the purchase of war bonds. Block wardens patrolled their areas, investigated fire hazards, and enforced the 6 p.m. curfew and blackout regulations established under martial law. Volunteers also crewed first-aid stations and the blood bank and provided emergency ambulance services. The eight hundred volunteers who had received emergency medical training under the United Japanese Society in Honolulu went directly from their certification ceremonies on December 7, 1941, to the aid of the wounded at Pearl Harbor. As members of the Kiawe Corps on O'ahu and Kaua'i and of the Menehune Minutemen on Hawai'i Island, Japanese volunteers cleared kiawe thickets for evacuation and military camps, built trails, and strung barbed wire along the coastline.[33] On Sundays, Japanese women devoted their free time to Red Cross activities, such as folding bandages and knitting woolen socks. Others joined the Women's Division of the Office of Civilian Defense (OCD), studied safety measures, disseminated necessary information, and worked on particular projects such as Christmas gifts for service members.

Although many of these activities were sincere expressions of patriotism, they were also efforts to deflect the suspicion focused on them due to their Japanese ancestry. Fear of and discrimination against the Japanese suffused popular public sentiment, and the military officials who now ruled Hawai'i closely monitored the actions of the Japanese community. The activities of the members of the Morale Committees revealed the extreme insecurity and racial tensions that existed in World War II Hawai'i. As the military conducted its roundup of suspicious individuals, it effectively silenced any voices of dissent in the Japanese community. Local military personnel defended this program as the surest way to "neutralize" the subversive element they feared existed among the Japanese community, stressing their superior understanding of the local Japanese.[34]

Under martial law, Japanese newspapers in Hawai'i were ordered to stop their presses. Although no similar orders were issued to other Japanese businesses and institutions, the doors to Japanese schools, Buddhist temples, and Shintō shrines closed as most teachers and priests had been incarcerated. Almost overnight, the Japanese community was deprived of its social, educational, and religious leaders, which created a void in leadership and aroused ambivalence and anxiety among the Japanese about their future in Hawai'i. This tactic so successfully suppressed the leaders in the Japanese community that in 1943 and 1945, with only one exception, no individuals of Japanese ancestry were elected to office in the Territory despite Japanese constituting nearly 29 percent of the total voter pool.[35] Only a few years earlier, in 1941, six representatives and one senator of Japanese ancestry were in the territorial legislature, and six Japanese on the county boards of supervisors. Many Japanese candidates who had previously been politically active decided not to run for public office during the war due to the volatile situation. Possibly, some had heard of the incarceration of World War I veteran Sanji Abe, the first territorial senator of Japanese ancestry in Hawai'i, whom authorities had arrested and detained after finding a Japanese flag in his movie theater in Hilo.[36] Abe's experience reflected the challenges and suspicions surrounding the Japanese community in Hawai'i, as even honorably discharged U.S. veterans could be incarcerated.[37] In addition, Japanese voters hesitated to support Japanese candidates for fear that the Japanese community would be seen as trying to take over the government. The Japanese community did not want to exacerbate already strained race relations, as the war allowed other ethnicities to express long-standing racial antagonism toward the Japanese. The planters had pitted various groups against one another on the plantations as part of their "divide and rule" strategy, and hostility toward the Japanese remained.

Community Mobilization of the Japanese on Kaua'i

The first Morale Committee on the neighbor islands was established on Kaua'i on May 26, 1942, as part of extending war mobilization efforts to all islands of Hawai'i. However, the local population had already been mobilized along racial lines in the Kauai Volunteers under the direction of military and plantation personnel. Paul Townsley, a Līhu'e Plantation official, was the commanding officer of the Kauai Volunteers. Within three weeks after enlistments were opened on March 8, 1942, three battalions were formed: the first from Kekaha to Hanapēpē, the second from Kalāheo to Līhu'e, and the third from Kapa'a to Kīlauea. Initially, only persons of "non-oriental ancestry" could enlist, but in September 1942, Koreans and Chinese were allowed to join. The regiments comprised 90 percent Filipino and eventually numbered more than 2,200. Members of the Volunteers did their usual work during the week and trained on Sundays. The regiment organized its military police and a mounted detachment to patrol *mauka* (inland) ranch country and was available for scouting expeditions in case of an attempted enemy invasion. Included in official Volunteers' equipment were *bolos*, "overgrown cane knives whittled down to a razorblade sharpness . . . the favorite weapon of the Filipinos."

Denied the opportunity to participate in the military defense of Kaua'i due to residents' fears, the Japanese comprised most of the Kiawe Corps. Work crews turned out each Sunday for over two years. They contributed thousands of hours clearing brush, burning rubbish, stringing barbed wire, building trails, and clearing areas for military camps and evacuation grounds. As a project of the Kauai Morale Committee, participants were predominantly Japanese and included many Issei. Each Sunday, more than one thousand assembled at locations around the island where a convoy of trucks met them.

At the outbreak of war, members of the Kauai Morale Committee also helped to organize a family survey, and over five hundred individuals made "house to house visit[s]" to Japanese homes. In response, "they were severely criticized by a few for using the FBI as the authority or high pressure methods." However, the morale report noted that the "Committee in no way gave such instructions to arouse criticism."[38] Yet the parallels between the house-to-house interviews and the FBI investigations and questioning that resulted in the incarceration of individuals were unmistakable. Possibly, the imprisonment of hundreds of Japanese on Kaua'i inspired a proactive approach as the efforts, programs, and outreach of the Kauai Morale Committee revealed their intent to serve as the primary organization for the internal surveillance of the Japanese community on the Garden Island to a degree unprecedented among the neighbor islands.

In addition to contributing to the island's defense by fortifying the military infrastructure, members of the Kauai Morale Committee promoted the internal security of the island as they took an active role in dissolving thirty-six language schools, associations, and Buddhist temples on Kaua'i whose leaders authorities had incarcerated. Celebrating this undertaking as a "complete success," members then promoted an educational campaign to "give intelligent, moral, and social guidance toward American victory and the acceptance of the American way of life in the Japanese community."[39] By the end of 1944, the Central Committee reported 200 meetings and workers' conferences with a total attendance of 8,858 people who listened to lectures given by the officers in charge of military intelligence and by the members of the Central Staff. Authorities approved the subject matter for speeches delivered in English and Japanese. They also distributed over 7,500 posters in seven months and 1,500 flags as part of service flag rallies with over 2,400 in attendance. The American Legion and the U.S. Army jointly sponsored them.[40] Members organized Mothers' and Girls' forums to discuss "social and sex problems," English classes for Japanese aliens, fundraisers, bond purchases, and blood donations. They also promoted enlistment into the armed services. Members served as the liaison office for those who had been incarcerated and their families, condoning if not promoting the actions that had taken place thus far by the military authorities against the Japanese on Kaua'i. They, along with other members of Kaua'i's population, including affluent whites, were also keenly aware of the outside public opinion of the Japanese on the Garden

Island, which could shape the military response to the island. Concerns about anti-Japanese sentiment would be particularly keen with the announcement of the results of the 1942 primary that revealed the likely election of four Japanese candidates.

Even before the primary election, many candidates understood their tenuous position. They consulted with political advisors and even the Military Intelligence Department, which issued the following statement: "The Military authorities have no official pronouncements. Politics is a matter of civilian concern and we are not making any decisions for them."[41] However, following the primary election in which Japanese ancestry candidates were nominated—including Yutaka Hamamoto, Noboru Miyake, George K. Watase, and Wallace Otsuka—an inflammatory editorial in the *New York Daily News* gained wide mainland publicity and was reprinted in the Honolulu newspapers:

> The Territory of Hawaii held its primary election Sunday and the sour part of the news is that five out of the seven Japanese candidates who ran for various nominations won out. . . . It seems inescapable that we have got to exercise some old style imperialism in Hawaii for the duration of the war to be on the safe side. We cannot afford the risk of having any apple-carts upset in those islands by the present or former subjects of the Mikado and if the Japanese in Hawaii don't like that attitude they had better go back where they or their ancestors came from.[42]

However, on October 10, 1942, while the Central Staff of the Kauai Morale Committee was in session, Maj. Charles A. Selby appeared and stated, "The editorial which follows up the New York Times comment on the Japanese candidates is going to appear on Tuesday, October 13, 1942. The situation is more serious than I anticipated. Gentlemen, it is in your laps." He left the room without further explanation, and the Central Staff scheduled meetings with the four candidates to discuss the situation. With the publication of Clarice Taylor's *Garden Island* editorial, "Kauai Out on a Limb," the Japanese candidates knew its contents, which ran with the approval of military authorities. Taylor noted that although "it is undemocratic and an invasion of the rights of free men to place pressure on our three candidates at a time when we are fighting a war to preserve freedom," she added that "the answer to this is that it is better to relinquish our rights for the time being rather than lose them forever."[43] Thus, even on the neighbor islands, some public figures highlighted the increased scrutiny and pressure facing Japanese residents within and outside their communities.

This conciliatory response to mainland pressure to remove Japanese candidates was echoed in the reaction of the Kauai Morale Committee, whose members actively intervened in this situation to encourage the withdrawal of the candidates. Initially, some resisted these pressure tactics. When Masaru Shinseki, vice-chairman of the Kauai Morale Committee, went to speak with Yutaka Hamamoto, Hamamoto flatly stated, "I have 'guts,' I will run." However, after days of negotiation and deliberation with members of the Kauai Morale Committee, eventually, the four candidates withdrew their candidacy, but not without considerable hesitation from some members. As Noboru Miyake explained, "The candidacy of American citizens of Japanese ancestry for political office in Hawaii has become the occasion for adverse, even uninformed comment and criticism . . . but I do not wish, by any act of attitude of mine, to create any situation which may react unfavorably against the territory of my birth, this territory of the United States."[44] The Territorial Governor Ingram Stainback widely praised the four candidates in the papers for demonstrating "the spirit of cooperation here in Hawaii by giving up their political careers for the good of the territory" as the rights of these individuals, like their incarcerated counterparts across Kaua'i were sacrificed for the alleged good of the majority.[45]

Community Mobilization of the Japanese on Maui

In August 1942, the Maui Emergency Service Committee was formed, and the Lanai Emergency Service Committee was established nearly six months later, in January 1943. These committees promoted racial unity by spearheading the "Speak-American" campaign, organizing blood drives, purchasing war bonds, and collecting funds for the Red Cross and the Army and Navy Emergency Relief Societies. Over one thousand individuals joined the Maui Volunteers to help safeguard the island after enemy submarines shelled Maui on December 15 and 30, 1942, inflicting damage on Kahului harbor and other areas around town.[46] Following the December 15 attack, the *Maui News* reported that shrapnel ironically hit a large "Bonds for Bombers" poster of the American Can Company. Still, this incident "only served to stimulate Maui Pine's spirit in the Defense Bomb Drive."[47] War also arrived on the shores of Maui when a torpedo sank the United States Army Transport *General Royal T. Frank* on January 28, 1942.[48] A rescue ship brought the thirty-six survivors to the Hāna wharf, where first-aid units and ambulances were waiting. Twenty-four other crew members were considered lost as eyewitnesses reported that the ship went down in thirty seconds after the torpedo struck the boiler room and the ship exploded.

As Maui mobilized for war, Maui resident Kazukiyo "Jiggs" Kuboyama especially recalls the rationing and limited supplies of daily necessities that civilians faced: "Everything was rationed. Rice and everything, you have to have a coupon to go and get. Those days, everything was rationed, gas, food, all was rationed. You had to have a ticket even for cigarettes, liquor." Amy Kiyota recalled the requirement for civilians, including children, to carry gas masks, and drills would be practiced at schools where trenches were dug due to the belief that another attack was possible:

> Everybody carried gas mask. No matter how big or how small you were, you carried the gas masks. And the school yard was all dug with trenches, trenches here, trenches there. And we'd always have drills so that when the air raid siren would go off, the class would have to get out of the rooms and you have to know exactly which trench to go in. . . . I don't know how many years we carried that gas mask, but it was something you just had to do and we never grumbled. You know, you had your school bag, your gas mask, and as small as we were, we knew just how to put the gas mask on, you know, we practiced so often.[49]

Daily lives were transformed so that even children became aware of the change in community dynamics. Kishi Mukaisu recalled the racial slurs other groups leveled at the Japanese: "'Jap, Jap.' We were referred to as 'Jap.' They would look at us and call us 'Jap.' Even in the conversation they would say, 'Jap, Jap.'"[50] With war exacerbating preexisting racial tensions, many Japanese became aware of the possibility of being incarcerated even though publications censored news of the incarceration of Japanese residents.

According to author Gail Bartholomew, who examined the *Maui News*' World War II coverage, "very little statistical or descriptive information was offered in the pages of the *Maui News* regarding the program of relocating local Japanese into internment camps."[51] In contrast to the newspaper's enthusiastic support for other war policies, such as encouraging Americanization efforts, there was "editorial silence" on Japanese incarceration. Nevertheless, news of the imprisonment of prominent individuals became widely known in the Japanese community. Myrtle Hashimoto recalled, "We heard that all the teachers and priests were being interrogated. And my mother being a teacher, she was a nervous wreck. She didn't know what was going on. My dad said, 'They're looking for traitors.'"[52] Hashimoto recalled that another woman who was a teacher had a nervous breakdown after authorities interrogated her. Due to this experience, the teacher had to seek psychological treatment at the Hawai'i State Hospital in Kāne'ohe. Fearful of being arrested by authorities, Hashimoto's mother lived in fear as "she didn't know what would happen to her, and the other teachers were taken to concentration camps. The priest, too. The whole school they were just taken. The menfolks especially were taken."

On the other islands, the police actively arrested Buddhist priests, Japanese language teachers, consular agents, and prominent businessmen soon after the outbreak of war. Even before the war, preparations began as early as October 1940 to organize and train police reserves, and by 1941, there were more than one thousand Provisional Police officers in Maui County.[53] On the evening of December 7, military intelligence in Honolulu sent orders to arrest and detain "numbers of enemy aliens." According to the police annual report, "the speed and thoroughness displayed in completing this assignment spoke well for the officers assigned." Officers sent these individuals to Maui County Jail, and "custody of these men was assigned to the regular jail staff, with a special army detail for added security." Word soon spread in Maui's Japanese community about the arrest of specific individuals. With no crime but their ethnicity, many other Japanese, such as Kazukiyo "Jiggs" Kuboyama, wondered if they would be next and pondered the reasons for their incarceration:

> You kind of felt sorry, wonder why they were taken. We couldn't understand because they were like anybody else, but it just happened that maybe the position they held and because they were leaders of the community, they were the ones most likely [to be interned]. Or they just so happened to go back to Japan and come back. So now, all these people who came back [to Hawai'i right before the war started] were the ones who were interned at a concentration camp. We were really surprised at some of the people they selected.[54]

On Maui, each arrested individual was given a questionnaire with a notice that it was necessary for government officials to take "reasonable precautions" with the outbreak of war:

> National interests and your personal safety require this. We appreciate that you are inconvenienced. . . . We know that you being detained leaves some of your property, particularly real property, unguarded. It is our desire to protect each and every bit of your property pending your detention. This being the case, we ask that you fill in the blanks below. Some of you will immediately believe that this is a ruse to make you divulge your holdings in order that the government might take possession of the same. While the government might do that, it could do the same without the aid of any information that you might give it. THIS QUESTIONNAIRE HAS BEEN PUT UP IN ORDER THAT WE MAY BETTER ABLE [*sic*] TO PROTECT YOUR PROPERTY. You need not fill it out if you do not desire so to do so.[55]

As many Issei were incarcerated, it is difficult to determine if they understood the questionnaire or trusted its stated intent as authorities began to arrest prominent individuals throughout Maui while simultaneously promoting efforts to mobilize the local population to support the war effort.

Community Mobilization of the Japanese on Hawai'i Island

At Kīlauea National Park, Superintendent Edward G. Wingate recalled hearing about the Pearl Harbor attack around 8:15 in the morning. After immediately realizing that "it is the real McCoy," he began calling the Hilo Police Department. He then went to the Army Recreational Camp to confer with Col. C. W. Bonham, who was in charge.[56] Authorities mobilized the National Guard, who assumed duty stations and issued arm and identification bands. Although Wingate reported "tension and some excitement" with the park's closure, the primary concern of park officials was to distribute passes to allow visitors to return home that night. Many of the activities of park officials after that concerned "the numerous reports of strange lights, behaviors and noises . . . as well as several reports of failures to black-out properly."[57] As park officials enforced martial law regulations, military and police personnel across the Islands began arresting Japanese suspects.

Despite an established military presence on Hawai'i Island, there appears to have been less pressure to develop a Morale Committee as the Hawai'i AJA Morale Committee was formed in April 1944, over a year after Kīlauea Military Camp had closed in 1942 and nearly two years after the first Morale Committee was established on Kaua'i.[58] It also lacked the same record of achievements as the morale groups on the other islands. One account from Kona in 1944 was highly critical of the group:

> It seems that this committee is another one of those which the [Niseis] welcome to get on the "band wagon" either to show their super-patriotic spirit or to conceal their pre-war pro-Japanese activities. According to a reliable source, two members of this Kona Morale Committee were formerly staunch pro-Japanese leaders. Some wonder why the naval [intelligence] or the F.B.I. have never questioned their loyalty. One doctor expressed that they should be the first ones to be picked up, but they have not been approached as yet. Probably, because of poor leadership, the community as a whole has very little respect for this Morale Committee.[59]

While this is only one person's opinion of the Hawai'i AJA Morale Committee, not all Japanese embraced the mission and actions of the Morale Committees, and some were suspicious of the motivations for participation. However, the Hawai'i AJA Morale Committee only existed for three months before all the morale groups united. It formed a Territorial Emergency Service Committee in June 1944 that was active until September 1945, when it disbanded. While initiatives to promote

Americanization and demonstrations of loyalty continued throughout the Islands, ironically, so did surveillance efforts of the Japanese by military and civilian officials as they remained under a cloud of suspicion.

Community Surveillance and the Search for "Enemy Espionage and Sabotage" in O'ahu's Japanese Community

The Police Espionage Bureau

As early as 1935, the Army established the Army Service Command, which created a partnership between "civil control forces" and the military to prevent sabotage and local uprisings.[60] The Army's plan for civilian warfare in Hawai'i also led to the creation of a paramilitary organization called the Provisional Police in July 1940. Led by plantation manager T.G.S. Walker, its mission was to prevent and suppress any emergency, such as "sudden and unpredicted overt acts by disloyal inhabitants."[61] Through the efforts of the Army, the Honolulu mayor, the chief of police, and plantation managers on O'ahu, the Provisional Police was established to allow civilians to defend Hawai'i against possible attack. Throughout the fall and winter, plantation employees, members of the American Legion, and utility workers were trained in guard duty around the island. By April 1941, some 1,500 guards were ready for action; by May, more than one-third had participated in Army maneuvers.[62] The idea was to free the regular militia from guard duty by utilizing plantation laborers who were familiar with local faces and terrain and could be efficiently managed and mobilized through Hawai'i's existing plantation hierarchy.

In addition to the Army, the Federal Bureau of Investigation (FBI) also became interested in looking for subversives within Hawai'i's Japanese community. In August 1939, just before war broke out in Europe, the FBI reopened its Honolulu office, which it had closed years earlier. FBI agents joined the efforts of Army and Navy intelligence staffs, which had been compiling lists of anti-American suspects, mainly those of Japanese ancestry. Together, they developed more detailed information regarding the Japanese population in the Islands, focusing surveillance on the older group of 35,000 aliens and the younger 120,000 Japanese Americans, many of whom held dual citizenship.

The FBI also gained the assistance of the Honolulu Police Department (HPD), which formed an Espionage Bureau at the FBI's request.[63] This entity was established in December 1940, following the approval of Police Chief Gabrielson, the mayor, and the Board of Supervisors. The police bureau employed a Japanese, Korean, Hawaiian, and "Hapa-Haole" (Japanese-White), all of whom spoke Japanese, to investigate matters for the FBI, Army, and Naval Intelligence to engage in undercover activities within Hawai'i's Japanese community. Police Captain John A. Burns served as the head of the Espionage Bureau from January 1, 1941. He liaised with certain Japanese who advised the United States military and civilian intelligence bureaus on Japanese activities.[64] Throughout 1941, a total of 550 investigations were carried out by the Bureau, with the majority of cases (86%) referred through the FBI.[65] Burns recalled that much of what the Espionage Bureau did was respond to questions raised by the FBI about people's backgrounds, general reputation, and activities to determine personal loyalties. Espionage Bureau personnel also examined general Japanese sentiments and potential racial tensions.[66]

Kanemi Kanezawa, a member of Burns's staff at the Espionage Bureau, recalled that their work differed from regular police work. "The investigations," Kanazawa pointed out, "were done discretely and indirectly. . . . Our investigations were based upon second- or third-hand hearsay evidence. It would never have stood up in a court of law."[67] However, these investigations were critical in the "Preparedness" of the HPD to counter a potential wartime emergency.[68] Thus, Gabrielson advocated that police departments should "have a record and also a cross index of all aliens so they could be apprehended on very short notice" during times of war.[69] Although how the FBI utilized the evidence gathered by the Espionage Bureau is unknown, as relations between the United States and Japan deteriorated in 1941, demand for intelligence on the Japanese community increased. Fortuitously for Burns, six months before the attack on Pearl Harbor, Japanese community leaders of the O'ahu Citizen's Committee for Home Defense called a public meeting at McKinley High School, where they proposed an organization of Japanese Americans to police the Japanese community in the event of war.[70] The FBI and Chief Gabrielson agreed that such an organization was not acceptable. However, they did consent to an alternative proposal to create an organization called the Police Contact Group, a network of loyal Japanese Americans who would regularly report to the HPD through Burns.[71] Gabrielson asked Burns to coordinate efforts and to submit names to the FBI for clearance. The first meeting was scheduled for Monday, December 8, and was canceled after the December 7 bombing of Pearl Harbor.

However, one week before the attack, investigations into the Japanese community had already begun. Burns recalled that Robert Shivers of the FBI called him into his office and, with "tears in his eyes," confided that "we're going to be attacked before the week is out."[72] Burns reported that Shivers asked him to "try to see if you can get your men without letting anybody know it, see if there is any kind of signs in the community" of any "abnormal feeling" that would indicate prior knowledge of the attack.[73] According to Burns, he sent out four men under his command; despite "meeting ten or fifteen guys and observing their conversations" every day, "we found nothing that gave us any [hint]" of local collaboration.[74] While Shivers never revealed the source of his information before the week was out, his prediction came true. By noon, December 7, mere hours after the Pearl Harbor attack, Burns was closeted in meetings with Shivers and Col. George W. Bicknell, head of counterintelligence for the U.S. Army in Hawai'i. Together, they went over lists of possible security risks, and each of the three men had a vote. "If two of us voted yes," Burns recalled, "he was a risk." Burns noted that these individuals had been "completely investigated" partly through the efforts of the Espionage Bureau.[75] Thus, as arrests began that day of suspected individuals in the community, HPD officers provided critical staffing. "I had asked the chief for one hundred cars and one hundred men when we went to start this pickup business," Burns recalled. "So we generally had one policeman driving the car, or reserve policeman, one federal government guy . . . sometimes there were three" as suspects were arrested.[76] Although some could argue that a selective infringement on the civil rights of specific individuals that was the basis of these arrests was a more reasonable response than the incarceration of the entire Japanese community in Hawai'i, Burns's findings that "there would be no sabotage by the Japanese" contradicts the necessity of these actions.[77]

Within a week of the Pearl Harbor attack, federal authorities stopped consulting Burns and his Espionage Bureau about who should be incarcerated; instead, they continued to use this unit to track down rumors of evidence of Japanese disloyalty.[78] None, however, led to any evidence of espionage. Yet, the Police Contact Group, which constituted "over fifty guys, scattered throughout the islands," was active throughout 1942.[79] Burns noted that while the Group was "never organized," it became a "helluva good idea" because it became a suitable method of "getting information out where the paper didn't get it, or didn't put it rightly."[80] Burns added that it served a critical purpose of "quieting rumors down, because the boys who in one district would pick up that their people in that community got a big rumor they could call me, get the straight information, and take it back and cut the rumor." Besides promoting blood bank donations and war bond sales, Burns noted that it "furnished a very valuable asset on what's going on in the community," giving him evidence of Japanese loyalty. At the same time, he simultaneously pushed for allowing Japanese Americans entry into the armed services. However, in both his biography and oral history, Burns fails to note the police surveillance of the Japanese community that continued at least throughout 1942, based on the information obtained by his Police Contact Group.[81] Additionally, from the Contact Group's more diligent workers came the leaders of the Emergency Service Committee, which served as the Morale Section of the Japanese community to spearhead various efforts to prove the loyalty of its members.

HPD Special Detail: A "Crime Prevention Agency" Operating in Japanese Communities

The military continued to monitor local sentiment in the days and weeks following the Pearl Harbor attack. Within two hours after the attack, military censors were installed at all communication agencies. The Army and Navy censors handled civilian correspondence until February 1942; after that, mail censorship was done under the auspices of the Federal Office of Censorship, though it remained closely allied with the military and the Military Governor's office. One responsibility of the censorship office was to monitor morale in the Islands and compile bimonthly reports, which were furnished to Navy Intelligence and focused on topics such as "Racial Problems," "War Worker Morale," "Japanese Morale," and "Interracial Friendships and Marriage," and quoted a selection of "typical comments." They also compiled statistical reports on the frequency with which issues were mentioned and on changes in the general tone of comments.[82]

Although the censorship reports provided thousands of anonymous individuals' voices and private opinions, FBI officials desired more specific knowledge of local Japanese attitudes and sentiments. On January 8, 1942, the FBI inaugurated a course of instruction in "civilian defense" for members of the HPD at Central Intermediate School. At the opening ceremonies, Shivers explained to police executives the need for officers to receive FBI training. According to Shivers, "In this war, the civilian populace is going to be guided by the man on the beat and by executives of the police department," as HPD officers were encouraged to "guide" the civilian population through the tumultuous war period.[83] In fulfillment of this prediction, a few months later, a select group of police officers was charged with conducting "Special Detail" in neighborhoods in urban Honolulu and visiting island residents. One of seven designated police officers—James Akana, Marcus Colburn, Neil Donahue, James Dulaney, Ansley N. Neptune, Ernest Nowell, and William G. Ross—joined bilingual officer Eichi Hongo in daily patrols. In addition to enforcing blackout restrictions as part of martial law, they handled traffic and curfew violations, arrested juvenile delinquents, raided gambling dens, and visited community bomb shelters. Reports were sent to Chief Gabrielson and Captain Dewey O. Mookini of the Patrol Division. Meetings were held in Burns's office as officers recorded their daily activities and candid observations of life in Hawai'i under martial law.

However, as part of Special Detail, the officers' responsibilities extended beyond regular patrols throughout O'ahu neighborhoods. Describing themselves as a "Crime Prevention Agency" rather than an "Enforcement Agency," Special Detail officers explained that "our main purpose for patrolling . . . was because of the numerous Japanese residents" residing in neighborhoods like Liliha, Kaka'ako,

McCully-Mōʻiliʻili, Kalihi, and Mānoa.[84] According to the officers, the intent of these patrols was not to "pick on them or try to find fault with the people" but to "help them out in their misunderstandings and by our assistance, it would help to a great extent, in keeping them out of trouble."[85] Despite the innocuous description of their activities, most police visits specifically targeted members of the Japanese population living in ethnic communities who were previously the focus of military and FBI surveillance that had resulted in arrests and incarceration. Reports provided authorities with detailed information from these visits about the occupants' age, profession, wartime volunteer activities, attitude, and other household members and extended family members.

In response to "numerous" queries about whether officers could enter a person's home without authorization, on March 2, 1942, provost Judge Lt. Col. Neal D. Franklin issued the following statement publicized in the *Honolulu Advertiser:* "Justice cannot wait now, under martial law, for the formality of a search warrant. We don't have time."[86] The urgency of Franklin's statement was reflected in the actions undertaken by HPD Special Detail officers, who used martial law regulations as a pretext for visiting Japanese homes and investigating the inhabitants. According to Officers Neptune and Hongo, "As usual, we entered the houses with the pretense of checking the radios, and after 'breaking the ice,' we made them feel at ease and proceeded to explain our undertakings in that area."[87] In a report filed by Nowell and Hongo, they explained how their "Good Will tour" served a benign purpose to help people "become better Americanized."[88]

While officers often conducted regular patrols, interviewing residents door-to-door, they also resorted to subversive means of identifying residences to visit. During their patrol of King Street in August 1942, Nowell and Hongo described how they "soft footed it over fences and through back yards stopping from time to time" as they listened to personal conversations or for the illegal usage of radios.[89] When left alone to patrol the McCully area, Hongo mentioned how he "began my work by 'snooping' inbetween houses listening in to the conversation going on in houses" and later talked to residents "explaining my purpose in the area."[90]

Although officers often traveled in pairs, Hongo explicitly explained wartime regulations to Issei, who did not speak English, while his partner talked to their Nisei children. While trying to "weed out" potential nationalistic sentiment within the Japanese community, the officers suggested to residents that "the First Aid Unit could always stand a few more volunteer workers, and also encouraged blood donation" to show their loyalty to America.[91] In many instances, officers explained their activities in the context of preventing potential criminal activity from occurring or stopping the illegal activity that Japanese residents were unknowingly committing during wartime.[92] The "help" that the officers provided extended to personal visits to ensure compliance with martial law regulations and personal exhortations of demonstrations of loyalty and support for Americanization efforts in their neighborhoods. During their visits, they also encouraged residents to ensure others adhered to regulations. While visiting Keisuke Nishimura, officers Dulaney and Hongo "suggested to him that he should talk to his friends and neighbors in regards to our conversation, and should have them to cooperate in everyway with this Government, and to live and think like good Americans" by donating blood, purchasing defense bonds, and volunteering.[93]

Personal Investigations and Intimidation: Fear of the Police

This transformation of the physical environment of Hawai'i's Japanese communities and homes and the upending of traditional generational roles facilitated by police visits sparked further mistrust of officials by many Japanese. However, according to special duty officers, many residents appreciated the efforts of the police and their "goodwill" visits. For example, Taro Tasaka of Kapi'olani Boulevard initially "held back the fear she had inside of her."[94] But, "after talking to her in Japanese and making her feel at ease," she was so relieved that she "broke down, expressed her previous emotions, and showed her gratitude by thanking us with tears in her eyes." To the officers, "such an [incident] as this really shows what good results we can obtain by treating people with Kindness—applying the 'GOLDEN RULE'—regardless of Citizen or Alien." Thus, officers understood their actions as benevolent outreach to the Japanese community to smooth racial differences and encourage Americanization.

Despite the positive perspective HPD officers presented about their actions, many instances indicated residents' fear of police visits. When investigating shortwave reception noises at Wiliwili Street, Dulaney and Hongo took the opportunity to question the occupants, Shinichi and Muichi Shimamura. According to the police report that day, "We first asked the former whether they had ever listened to Japan. He immediately replied 'No!'"[95] Dulaney and Hongo noted that "he was rather afraid of policemen so we told him that he did not have to fear us." Despite these reassurances, Shimamura continued to be cautious in his responses to the police.

As officers encouraged residents to speak to others about their visits and be "Good Samaritans" by complying and adhering to the law, some apprehensively awaited an unannounced visit by the police.[96] For example, Kamado Uyehara of Fern Street mentioned to officers that "after receiving information that the Police were checking that district, he wondered why we had not checked his home earlier. He stated he had been expecting our call everyday in the past."[97] Others seemed overly anxious about the officers' visit and likely prepared well in advance. Nowell and Hongo noted that Torahichi Suzuki of Date Street "wanted so much to be with the Law, that he insisted, to a point of irritation, that we check his house thoroughly" to ensure compliance with blackout measures.[98] A group of Issei also noted that they all retired into their homes after 8:00 p.m. because they were afraid of being arrested.[99]

While officers reported that many residents were grateful for their visits, others were less than receptive to their efforts. When visiting Rinji Takakawa, officers noted that "he held back and didn't express his thoughts freely. We had to do most of the talking."[100] Besides recalcitrance, others were more open in their displeasure of police intrusion in their homes. When Dulaney and Hongo questioned Takakawa about a large radio reportedly brought to the house, they noted that his daughter, Joan, "did not like our intrusion and resented, very much, our checking the place. She later left the room, crying, due to being scared, we presume."[101] Despite the sensitivity the officers tried to demonstrate in these visits, the officers became upset at her reaction, stating, "We let her know, definitely, that we did not visit them just for the fun of it, but rather because it was a necessity, and if [we] were going to be sarcastic, we could make a very bad report about her." Although the officers explained that "since we did not locate anything in violation of the law, it was for their good," thereby appeasing her worries, "we let her know that she shouldn't take the attitude she had at that time."

Although officers dismissed the younger Takakawa's response to their visit, many Japanese residents were aware that visits by the police motivated by accusations of disloyalty could serve as the basis for arrest and incarceration. On August 5, 1942, officers responded to a complaint by William Pattison of Lime Street, who claimed that his neighbor, Harry K. Teruya, "had always been listening to short-wave" on numerous occasions.[102] Although no violations were found, officers cautioned the residents in the surrounding area about the volume and the "Propagandic nature of the Enemy broadcasts" and continued to patrol the area.[103] Officers also encouraged the owner of the Okumura store on East Mānoa Road to inform them to relay to any "Pro-Japanese" they might know that "those were the type of people we were anxious to meet, to convince them [to become] good Americans." If they still harbored anti-American sentiment, the police would deal with them "severely."[104]

The most revealing example of fear of the police occurred when police visited Teruko Sokabe of Kaaloa Street. Early in 1942, police officers asked Sokabe, whose husband Miyuki had been incarcerated, to make a written statement to the police "in regard to her feelings as to this present situation—her opinion of Japan, where she was born, and the U.S. where she was reared."[105] According to officers, this statement was "for the purpose of letting others know the true feelings of the Japanese Aliens residing here, that is their loyalty for this Government." Although officers mentioned that writing this statement was "not compulsory, but voluntary," and for the benefit of other Issei, Sokabe felt otherwise. Sokabe went to the Swedish consulate the following day as she "felt that we were trying to incriminate her." She stated, "he didn't know what it was all about." According to Dulaney and Hongo, Sokabe had taken the "wrong attitude," and although they felt they were "trying, in every way, to help her, she did not trust us and led us to have no faith in her." Burns was alerted to this case, and the officers were once more sent to her home on December 15, 1942, to resolve this situation, but Sokabe remained undecided about the situation.

Although police officers regarded Sokabe as a "foolish woman," the activities of the police did not inspire confidence or trust in some members of the population. Sokabe and others had husbands who were incarcerated, and visits by the police often followed earlier visits by FBI and military officials who had taken their husbands away.[106] On other occasions, officers were more sensitive to the plight of wives and family members of inmates. While officers were suspicious of the "very large safe and an abundance of Japanese books" at the residence of Iwako Koike, at the time of their visit, Koike was entertaining guests, and "we did not want to embarrass her any further by questioning her in the presence of her visitors."[107] They planned to visit her later, as "we believed that we had to handle her in a very delicate manner because any harsh undertakings on our part would certainly result in her having a bad feeling for [this] Government." The officers' comments revealed their awareness of the plight of the families of inmates whom officials had earlier visited; they justifiably feared future police visits as their loved ones had been taken away without any explanation.

Collaboration and Internal Community Surveillance: Contact Men and the Emergency Service Committee

While police likely relied upon Army and Navy intelligence to identify possible subversive elements in the Japanese community, explaining in part why both federal and local officials visited certain families, officers regularly met with Burns to discuss the progress of their work. Additionally, Burns's contact men encouraged officers to see specific individuals. Although no official sanction was secured, starting on January 14, 1942, a group of district leaders who had been chosen in November 1941 came into Burns's office "four or five Contact men at a time" to discuss "setting at peace the minds of the people and the educational feature" of the visits.[108] Police reports mention several contact men who were identified explicitly with providing support and intelligence to Burns and the police department to ensure the loyalty of the Japanese community under martial law: "Mr. [Kiyotsuchi] Suehiro" (Mōʻiliʻili), Harry K. Masuda (Kalihi), "Mr. Fujikawa" (Kakaʻako), the Reverend Ernest S. Fujinaga (Upper East Mānoa); Kazuo Watanabe (Lower Mānoa Section), "Mr. Kosasa" (Kaimukī), Nelson Kawakami (Pālama), and James K.

Fujioka (Kaheka Lane). These men comprised a small number of the forty-three Contact Group members responsible for neighborhoods in Honolulu alone; twenty-seven others were responsible for other districts around O'ahu, including 'Aiea, Waipahu, Hale'iwa, and Kailua.[109]

Police particularly praised the efforts of Fujinaga, who had assumed a leadership role in the Japanese community and assisted Americanization efforts. According to Dulaney and Hongo, many in the community had "a great deal of confidence" in Fujinaga due to his efforts to install streetlights and implement a correct house numbering system.[110] Following the outbreak of war, Fujinaga encouraged women to volunteer for Red Cross work, gathered men to volunteer for Army Engineer work and other projects, obtained gasoline coupons for gardeners, and took care of the tire requisitions. Police noted his efforts to promote blood donations and sell $9,000 worth of bonds and encouraged Issei residents to attend Fujinaga's English language classes. Additionally, Fujinaga provided names of people the police should visit, people he "felt needed a good talking to due to their being more Pro-Japanese, rather than American." On one occasion, he specifically encouraged officers to visit Mr. Okubo, Mr. Ueno, and Mr. and Mrs. Sumida of Upper Mānoa Road.[111] Other contact men like Kazuo Watanabe engaged in efforts to speak to businesspeople around town to promote Americanism, obtained passes from the Military Governor for Issei going to early Kiawe Corps work, and similarly encouraged blood donations, the purchase of war bonds, and Red Cross volunteer work.

Given the interests of the Police Contact Group, unsurprisingly, it was part of the Emergency Service Committee (ESC), composed primarily of Nisei. They sought to prove the loyalty of the Japanese community in Hawai'i during World War II. Thus, police were also directed to certain homes by Shigeo Yoshida, a leading organizer of the ESC who had been a visitor when police arrived at the home of Iwako Koike.[112] Yoshida asked officers to clarify policies related to Issei visits but encouraged officers to telephone twenty-two-year-old Thomas Toyofuku of Lot 2 lower Oili Road, whose father had been incarcerated. Toyofuku had tried to volunteer for the armed forces but had been rejected because of his dual citizenship. Yoshida requested that officers "go to see whether we could straighten him out," as he was discouraged.[113] Nowell and Hongo told Toyofuku to "keep his chin up and make the best of everything, for himself and for his family" and encouraged him to seek them out if he or his family needed assistance. While Yoshida's suggestion was likely driven by personal concern for Toyofuku, his actions show the close collaboration between Nisei leaders and civil and military authorities to ensure the loyalty of the Japanese community.

While some may have appreciated the efforts of the Police Contact Group and the ESC members, others in the Japanese community were not receptive to these efforts.[114] Some members of the Japanese community referred to ESC and Police

Contact Group members and Burns himself as *inu* (dogs) and accused them of trying to win favoritism by cooperating with the government as they were regarded as "patriotic zealots" and "self-appointed stool pigeons" for the military authorities.[115] In the mainland incarceration camps, allegations of "informer" and "collaborator" used to identify alleged *inu* sparked beatings and riots at Poston and Manzanar; one incident resulted in two deaths and nine wounded.[116] In Hawai'i, similar events did not occur whereby members of the Emergency Service Group or Police Contact Group were targets of violence by disgruntled inmates or community members. While resentment did exist, martial law and the threat of military punishment seem to have deterred actions against these individuals who enjoyed the support of the military government. The selective nature of incarceration in the Islands also ensured that those who remained free complied with the actions of military and civilian officials. Still, the use of the word *inu* suggests that some did not fully embrace the Americanization efforts to prove the loyalty of the Japanese community. These efforts possibly prevented the Japanese population's mass incarceration and became the basis for the postwar activism of Hawai'i's Democratic Party and Nisei politicians. They had ties with the ESC and Burns.

Japanese House Cleaning

Besides investigating bond purchases, addressing rumors, and promoting English-speaking efforts, officers carefully observed the interiors of residences during their visits. They encouraged individuals to remove Japanese objects and heirlooms to prevent potential accusations of disloyalty. Some, such as Helen Shizano Tokuda of South King Street, voluntarily removed or destroyed Japanese cultural artifacts before the arrival of the police. When police officers visited her home, she shared a photo album of a trip to Japan a younger sister had taken in 1939 that contained only sightseeing photos. Tokuda also revealed to officers that "about two months after the war, they found a Japanese flag that their mother had. They immediately burned [it]."[117] When police visited the McCully home of Keisuke Nishimura, they noted the presence of "several articles in their living room that were from Japan, such as bird [miniature] statues, [miniature] houses, etc." After talking to Nishimura about the importance of abiding by existing laws and supporting the war effort, "We suggested to them that anything they had use for they should keep, but if such things as books, etc., were not going to be used, they should do away with them."[118] While Tokuda voluntarily engaged in these actions before the arrival of the police as a demonstration of her loyalty to America, she possibly might have engaged in these actions to prevent the scrutiny to which police subjected the Nishimura home.

As two Japanese authors observed during this period, "The Japanese people at present are subjected to criticism from all sides; every move made by them is observed keenly by the community, and any false move is severely criticized."[119] While the origins of this criticism have been identified broadly in the context of addressing the entire Japanese community, the actions of the police reveal a specific targeting of people in their neighborhoods and homes to ensure community compliance.

Thus, upon visiting the home of Takeo Muraoka of Upper Mānoa Road, Dulaney and Hongo noted "the bad condition of the home and the 2 Japanese Shrines they had. In this regard, we *suggested* to her that she put same away if she really did not need it." According to the officers, "It only tended to create an impression of Japanese Ideals on their part."[120] Although the impact of the officers' advice is unknown, the officers felt it was their responsibility to encourage eradicating Japanese items from households. As such, residents in the Sheridan district reported that "they had been turning the house inside out trying to look for and get rid of unlawful things. All pictures, books, they disposed of by burning."[121]

Additionally, officers noted that reversing generational roles, "even the sons and daughters of the Aliens came over to instruct the parents in the law and in getting rid of anything unlawful." These investigations partly contributed to the fear and anxiety that infused many Japanese communities and residences during the war, even among those who had not been arrested or incarcerated. Consequently, many Japanese voluntarily engaged in individual and community-wide actions of self-censorship to deflect suspicion away from them and avoid community animosity.

Community Self-Censorship: Transformed Communities

This home transformation was also carried out in the larger Japanese community as the physical landscape of Hawai'i was dramatically altered following the Pearl Harbor attack. Previously, the Issei had openly embraced their Japanese culture in ethnic enclaves like Mō'ili'ili and 'A'ala, where visitors to the Islands would have been amazed at the "old world customs" openly practiced by the Japanese: Issei read the news in two prominent daily Japanese newspapers, the *Nippu Jiji* and *Hawaii Hochi,* and sent their children to Japanese language schools.[122] Japanese theaters such as Nippon Kan and Honolulu Za showed the latest films from Japan, and both Issei and Nisei sang Japanese songs they learned through Japanese radio programs and from records available locally.

After December 7, however, the familiar physical landscape of the Japanese community was radically transformed with the closure of Buddhist temples, Japanese language schools, Japanese newspapers, and radio stations, and the incarceration of priests, teachers, and businesspeople. Naval Commander John Ford noted, "They have all taken down their signs and substituted English lettering. For example, 'Banzai Café' . . . is now the 'Keep 'Em Flying Café.'"[123] Numerous businesses removed Japanese signage, began selling more Western products, and offered American forms of entertainment. Two Japanese writers observed this transformation during the war: "Today, no one dreams of going to a Japanese movie. Instead, they have turned to American movies. Aged Issei couples are frequently seen toddling into a jammed theater where Hedy Lamar and Spencer Tracy are being flashed on the screen."[124] While the transformations were voluntary, these changes in the Japanese community reflected the deep anxieties of the Issei, who feared incarceration.

The response of many Issei to this dramatic change was one of "retiring"– withdrawing from public life. The loss of organized community activities, traditional leaders, and social continuity meant "the loss of the guidance on which they had depended in defining the situation of everyday life."[125] As one Issei explained, "We are afraid. We don't know what to do. Even our own children don't let us go out. If we go out, we will be the focus of hate and revenge. So we stay in the house." Even in their own homes, the Issei were not immune to the changes sweeping through Hawai'i as the private or family sphere was transformed in part through the efforts of the police.

"To Promote Friendship, Goodwill, and Americanizm": The Encouragement of Americanization

During their visits, officers often prefaced their comments with questions to determine the loyalty of Japanese residents, such as "What would you do if the Enemy attacked this Island?" or "Would you, as an Enemy Alien, take part for them, or would you fight them?"[126] These questions echoed earlier interrogation questions FBI and military officials asked of Japanese inmates as officers took a particular interest in promoting "Speak American" efforts. When Dulaney and Hongo visited Shigeko Yoshida and her neighbor Yukiko Tamaye in Mānoa following a suggestion from the Reverend Ernest S. Fujinaga, who felt "they needed a good talk from us," the officers clearly expressed their condemnation of any pro-Japanese sentiment to these two housewives: "We flatly told them that any UnAmericanized thinkings would absolutely not be tolerated. We told them that if they thought Japan was better we wanted them to get out; we didn't want them here. They would only cause trouble for the loyal Japanese here."[127] However, if they "showed their utmost cooperation and did their bit," they would be treated fairly. Thus, officers often encouraged Issei to attend English language classes, support volunteer activities, and engage in activities to promote Americanization.[128]

During their visits, officers also inquired about the number of war bonds purchased to indicate loyalty. When officers visited the house of Shimeki Masunari, they pointedly explained to Masunari that loyalty entailed action, not just words: "to be a good american did not necessarily mean to be born in America but, rather the attitude taken in the purchase of war bonds and stamps, the working on vital war projects, and spirit in volunteer work, cooperating with the blackout and the General Orders."[129] Besides Masunari, other Japanese residents were recipients of appeals by the police, who actively monitored and promoted war bond purchases among Japanese families. In one particular instance, Dulaney and Hongo wrote an extensive report about a visit to the home of Shizuo Kimoto of Haoli Street, where they had a "friendly conversation" with his wife, Beatrice Yuki Kimoto.[130] Dulaney and Hongo noted that although Kimoto "felt that it was their duty as good Americans to cooperate in every way with this Government to help win this War," upon questioning her about her specific activities, officers observed that "she could show no proof that they were actually doing something to cooperate." Dulaney and Hongo noted that although her husband was a defense worker making $1.25 an hour and the family had $2,460.86 in the bank, they had not purchased defense bonds. According to the officers, "This all led us to believe that they took no interest in the welfare of this Government." Thus "we definitely let her know that they should be ashamed of themselves for being so selfish, and suggested that she start doing her bit," attempting to possibly appeal to the Japanese value of *haji* or shame to encourage her compliance. After giving her a "good sales talk" about the benefits of investing in war bonds, the officers left after obtaining a promise from Kimoto to discuss purchasing war bonds with her husband. A month later, Dulaney and Hongo returned to the Kimoto residence to determine the progress in complying with their suggestions. To their disappointment, they learned the family had purchased one $25 bond and planned to purchase only one monthly. Despite the family's explanation that they preferred to keep money in the bank in case of an emergency, the officers convinced the family that they could at least invest half the amount in bonds out of the $2,000 they had in the bank. After giving them a "good talking to in regard to the necessity of their cooperation," officers also suggested that they purchase defense bonds for their children.[131]

In contrast to the Kimoto family, Nowell and Hongo congratulated Toshiko Mori of Pumehana Street for purchasing $5,000 worth of defense bonds for her and her Nisei children. Officers also commended the actions of Keisuke Nishimura of Algaroba Street, who had led a group of about 400 in collecting funds for the Victory Kit, visiting 800 homes, and raising $1,200 in donations. They noted that two of his sons were block wardens, that everyone in his family had purchased defense bonds, and that Nishimura "participated in the collection of all Japanese literature that was turned in at the [outbreak] of the War and headed the group in the McCully

District."[132] While Kimoto and Nishimura's actions reveal their commitment to the American government, their activities could also reflect efforts to deflect criticism from the police, who promoted the purchase of war bonds to a degree that has not been acknowledged before.

The Suppression of Rumors

Besides promoting Americanization efforts within the Issei population, police officers actively sought to suppress rampant rumors. Immediately after the attack on Pearl Harbor, the Espionage Bureau investigated rumors that proliferated in the Islands, such as the rumor that Japanese plantation workers had cut arrows in the cane fields to direct Japanese flyers to Pearl Harbor or had set cane fires as signals. Others had heard that Japanese pilots who had been shot down were found with McKinley High School and University of Hawai'i rings, implying they were former residents of Hawai'i.[133] Newspapers reported that Japanese parachutists had landed on O'ahu and that the city water supply had been contaminated, along with other general acts of sabotage.[134] In addition to rumors surrounding the Japanese community, internally, the Japanese community faced great anxiety about their future as literally overnight, 1,444 Japanese—of whom 979 had Japanese citizenship, and 525 were American citizens, though mostly Kibei, or those educated in Japan—were incarcerated.[135] Rumors became particularly rampant as Issei, many of whom had only a limited grasp of English, were cut off from traditional means of information following radio restrictions that prohibited Japanese news programs and the closing of Japanese language newspapers. On October 24, 1942, after a meeting in Burns's office, Dulaney and Hongo went to Kaheka Lane to investigate a rumor regarding the Japanese people having to evacuate as they were allegedly being sent to the mainland. Although the officers reported that people there had not heard of the rumor, they made a special effort to suppress it through individual conversations. They also contacted Kazuo Watanabe, Burns's contact man for lower Mānoa, to relay to others that the rumor was untrue.[136]

A few weeks later, on December 10, officers were dispatched to the Kalihi district to respond to rumors of the dangers of blood donations after "Mr. Matsumura" had died four hours after donating blood.[137] Following Matsumura's death, members of the Kalihi football team refused to donate blood. Officers spent days talking with people, assuring the safety of donating blood. According to an explanation Dulaney and Hongo provided to Noka Shimabukuro, we "informed him that [Matsumura's] death was not because he had donated blood, but was due to the reaction of the blood vessels after the queer feeling, or shock, that took place after he donated his blood."[138] Although they assured Shimabukuro and others that "there were hundreds of others who had donated their blood and had never died," they also added, "Even if he had died from donating his blood, he was dying for his Country, and they, as well as everyone else, should make up their minds to die for this Country, anyways. It would be a worthwhile death, we explained." Though likely exaggerated, this type of extreme patriotism expected of Japanese residents was actively promoted by HPD officers who also sought to eliminate the "Pro-Japanese" threat by eradicating elements of Japanese culture.[139]

Martial law was thus the culmination of extensive studies by military and civilian officials who had examined the Japanese "threat" for years. It is essential to highlight that not all government officials supported the mass incarceration of Japanese residents of Hawai'i, partly due to reports by John Franklin Carter and Curtis Munson, who believed that the overwhelming majority of local Japanese in Hawai'i were loyal. Others, like General Emmons, were concerned about the logistics and the lack of necessary resources that would be diverted to incarcerate the large Japanese population in the Islands. Scholars like Greg Robinson correctly highlighted the limits of President Roosevelt's efforts to control policies like incarceration in places like Hawai'i, noting "the importance of the particular circumstances in shaping actions."[140] Thus, the wartime experience of Hawai'i's Japanese is particularly unique as officials faced the impossibility of mass incarceration in the Islands. Instead, they engaged in other actions that still reflected racist understandings and suspicions directed at the Japanese. Consequently, these investigations' continuation and invasiveness suggest continued questions about the effectiveness of Americanization efforts and selective incarceration in controlling the remaining population in Hawai'i. Authorities believed a threat still existed that necessitated police visits to Japanese communities. Those investigated were from many different social strata than the educational, religious, political, and economic leaders incarcerated, indicating that all Japanese were suspect by their race.

It is essential to note the close collaboration between the HPD and FBI and between ESC members to promote Americanization efforts and the loyalty of the Japanese. This period also ushered in a new leadership role for the Nisei, who were granted new status with the arrest and incarceration of traditional leaders. Their English language skills and ability to communicate effectively with authorities gave them a critical advantage over the remaining Issei, who became a silent generation with admonitions to "Speak American." This generational transformation would also occur in incarceration centers on the mainland, where authorities would grant Nisei leadership roles while their Issei parents relinquished their authority. One of the most prominent and controversial examples remains the actions of the leadership of the Japanese American Citizens League (JACL), which cooperated with federal authorities in the mass exclusion and incarceration of Japanese Americans during World War II. JACL leaders also criticized draft resisters and opposed court cases challenging the legality of imprisonment. While these actions of the JACL have been denounced, in Hawai'i, the Americanization efforts of the Japanese community that were supported by organizations like HPD, the Police Contact Group, and ESC have often been understood positively. To many, these actions created a new future for the Japanese community through their demonstrations of loyalty at home and on the battlefields of World War II. However, it is clear it also created an atmosphere of anxiety and fear in Japanese communities among those who had not been arrested or incarcerated. Possibly, these widespread demonstrations of loyalty like bond purchasing, blood donations, and extensive volunteer work were not simply spontaneous gestures that emerged organically from felt beliefs of allegiance to America; they were actions that the police and a select group of self-appointed individuals within the Japanese community closely monitored and promoted. The wartime demonstrations of American patriotism that became a critical part of the postwar identity of Japanese Americans in Hawai'i were thus a response to the suspension of civil liberties and freedoms by the military as well as heightened surveillance and extralegal actions against remaining community members who were not immune to the anti-Japanese sentiments of military and civil officials.

Subsequently, while some established their reputation during World War II through their efforts to mobilize the Japanese community by cooperating with authorities, others became targets of police visits to ensure compliance with military and civilian orders, revealing the collusion of internal and external interests. Ultimately, the incarceration of individuals from Japanese communities across the Islands would highlight the selective targeting of the Japanese due to underlying and long-standing racist fears by military and civilian officials despite ongoing efforts by the Japanese in Hawai'i to prove otherwise.

3 "They Even Checked Our Assholes"

The Invasiveness of Martial Law and Japanese Incarceration

I must mention that we were forbidden to carry any [cutlery] in the camp. But some of us picked up the metal from the boxes which were sent to the mess hall and made a knife. On December 14th, some of us were assigned to work outside the camp. On their way back to the camp, their bodies were searched, and the inspector found a handmade knife from Rev. Ryoshin Okano. Upon an alarm, 67 guards surrounded Okano and stripped him naked with their pistols pointing at him. . . . At night we were gathered in the open space and we took off our clothes. We had to remain standing for a long time until they finished searching our clothes. Other guards searched our tents and took away our fountain pens and pencils. We were frozen to death in the cold, windy, and barren field.[1]

Yasutaro Soga, a prominent journalist and political leader, told this story in his memoirs about his experience in Hawai'i incarceration centers; it reflected the treatment he and other inmates received throughout the war. The use of extreme force to subdue one man indicates the pervading fear of and paranoia about the Japanese that had built up years before World War II and culminated in incarceration. The attack on Pearl Harbor on December 7, 1941, not only launched America's entry into World War II but also began America's war against a specific ethnic group within its shores: Japanese and Japanese Americans. Although scholars have extensively researched the story of Japanese incarceration on the mainland, a closer examination of the unique experiences of inmates across Hawai'i is still needed, where martial law gave military officials unprecedented power and authority. Isolated from the larger Japanese community and subjected to arbitrary punishments, including interrogations and strip searches, these inmates became victims of racist fears and suspicions.

Further, the military used those incarcerated as "examples" to control the rest of the Japanese population in Hawai'i, who feared sharing a similar fate. A study on the effects of incarceration on Hawai'i's Japanese community during the war confirmed that "an extreme degree of fear was present" due to the loss of traditional leaders and religious institutions.[2] Although incarceration could merely be seen as a product of wartime hysteria, its long history of planning and carefully conceived intent of weakening and controlling the Japanese community undermines this argument. It might be argued that the limited incarceration of residents in response to the Pearl Harbor attack was a more reasonable response than the large-scale incarceration of Japanese on the mainland. However, the problematic logistics of relocating a large number of Japanese in the Islands during a wartime labor and materials shortage made mass incarceration nearly impossible. Additionally, it is important to note that while all residents were subject to martial law policies, authorities overwhelmingly targeted Japanese for surveillance and selective incarceration based on their race, further undermining claims of an enlightened racial policy.

For many of Hawaiʻi's inmates, their experience in incarceration centers echoed their past treatment on the plantations. While the planters governed their workers paternalistically, they also required strict obedience. In exercising the strong hand of "authority," plantation owners devised an intricate system of rules and regulations for their laborers. They also developed a wide range of strategies, including promoting competition between different groups of laborers, establishing a docking system for virtually every kind of misconduct, utilizing police power to support plantation discipline and authority, and resorting to physical violence. Yet the Japanese did not passively accept this treatment and, throughout the early years of the twentieth century, engaged in strikes, various forms of protest, and even criminal activity and violence against planters and their collaborators. As they did so, tensions slowly escalated between whites and Japanese, who engaged in legal battles in the courtroom, verbal debates in the newspapers, and physical confrontations on and off the plantations. This growing resistance against white paternalism and white authority, and by extension, the dual system of justice in Hawaiʻi, led to growing fears of the Japanese population. It also resulted in demands for extralegal restrictions and regulations designed to control and suppress the unruly Japanese.

With lessons learned from over fifty years of experience dealing with the Japanese, territorial authorities and military officials sought complete control of the Japanese community through extralegal means under the exigencies of war. While the Japanese responded with widespread community efforts to counter accusations of disloyalty and suspicion, virulent anti-Japanese sentiment by military and civil officials resulted in martial law that culminated with the arrest and detainment of leaders within the Japanese communities across the Hawaiian Islands. It is essential to note the diverse experiences inmates endured on each island. Although authorities had planned for the possibility of incarceration, the actual logistics of arresting and detaining residents varied. Even authorities on Oʻahu seemed ill-prepared to house the number of suspects they had identified in prewar pickup lists despite engaging in surveillance efforts for years. Until Honouliuli was finally completed in 1943, authorities utilized the existing U.S. Immigration Station and Yokohama Specie Bank and the hastily constructed Sand Island Detention Camp, initially a series of tents surrounded by barbed wire and armed guard towers.

In contrast to the neighbor islands, the arrest and detainment of O'ahu residents would primarily occur in the urban communities of Honolulu as the military would process all inmates at the U.S. Immigration Center before sending them to Sand Island Detention Camp and later to mainland incarceration centers or Honouliuli Internment Camp when it opened on March 1, 1943. The majority of Honouliuli civilian inmates were American citizens of Japanese ancestry. The remaining prisoners were primarily German Americans who were joined by citizens and aliens of Italian, Irish, Russian, and Scandinavian descent. Honouliuli became the largest prisoner of war (POW) camp in wartime Hawai'i, detaining enemy soldiers and non-combatant labor conscripts from Japan, Korea, Okinawa, Taiwan, and Italy.

O'ahu inmates would endure some of the harshest treatment by military officials, likely due to their proximity to the Military Governor and critical military installations, including Pearl Harbor. Despite surveillance efforts, the high concentration of Japanese residents in nearby neighborhoods also likely contributed to military concerns. Thus, the treatment endured by O'ahu inmates highlights the extreme fears held by military officials of the Japanese, whom they treated in the same manner as enemy combatants. Their experiences would challenge any claims of an enlightened racial policy within wartime Hawai'i.

The Arrest of Japanese Suspects and the "Bloodthirsty" Nature of Incarceration

On December 7, while Japanese planes flew over Pearl Harbor, the FBI and Army began their roundup of suspicious individuals such as priests, Japanese language teachers, and even fishermen throughout Hawai'i. Officials were particularly concerned about the influence of Shintō and Buddhist priests as Buddhism as early as 1889 had been closely associated with Japanese immigrants who were followers of the Hongwanji, Jōdo, Higashi Hongwanji, Nichiren, Sōtō, and Shingon sects. By 1941, there were a total of 114 Buddhist temples and shrines in Hawai'i, and according to Bishop Mitsumyo Tottori, whom authorities interrogated following the Pearl Harbor attack, there were roughly one thousand families on O'ahu who belonged to the Shingon sect alone, with eight hundred families on Hawai'i Island, four hundred on Kaua'i, and five hundred on Maui.[3] A 1941 report by the Office of Naval Intelligence depicted the Japanese in the United States as an "inherently religious race" who "depended upon the authority, the ritual, and the doctrines of

Shintoism or Buddhism, or both religions to act as moral factors to guide their personal conduct to aid their spiritual well being, both in life and hereafter."[4] The report further explained that priests of both religions were held in "high regard" and "looked upon" as "leaders in the communities"; the "anti American and possibly subversive elements" it discovered in the Japanese community were traced "almost invariably" to these priests. Their existence within the Japanese community was a source of alarm, and this fear by military officials contributed to their decision to close most shrines and temples and incarcerate most Buddhist and Shintō priests during World War II, with notable exceptions.[5]

Similar suspicions surrounded language school teachers due to long-standing fears about the influence of Japanese language schools on the plantations. Thus, military officials identified Japanese language school teachers as suspects and interrogated and incarcerated them in the days, weeks, and months following the attack. Eventually, authorities arrested 2,270 Japanese and Japanese Americans and imprisoned them at an estimated 17 sites across the Islands as well as on the mainland. Local police, including Japanese, assisted in the apprehension of these individuals, partly due to their knowledge of the whereabouts of individuals they regularly interacted with in the community. Consequently, these individuals' social status and prominence within the community made them easy targets for arresting officers.

The night when authorities apprehended prominent journalist and political leader Yasutaro Soga, he recalled Honolulu "look[ing] like a dead town."[6] Officials enacted a curfew and a blackout. The only traffic on the road was military vehicles picking up suspects to take to the Immigration Building in Honolulu to await questioning. On other islands, police would apprehend suspects and confine them in local jails, prison camps, language schools, and gymnasiums. Authorities would not inform individuals about the nature of their crime, their destination, or even how long they would be away from their families. One prisoner was Torao Taketa, father of Doris Taketa Kimura, who was home when officials came to apprehend her father. She recalled what occurred that day: "They came while we were all sleeping. I don't know who they were—FBIs or whoever. So many of them came and they said, 'Mr. Taketa, you come as you are.' So he had to get dressed and they searched him that he didn't have any weapon or whatever—knife or anything like that. They searched his pocket. They didn't say where he was going to go and they just took him. We didn't know until much later."[7] The family later learned that officials had "put him in a prison" in Wailuku, Maui, where they visited him. However, due to jail restrictions, the family could not bring him anything, and her mother was in shock, asking, "what did he do that they have to take him away?" In the meantime, other community members began to avoid the family, fearing a similar fate. Kimura remembered that "they kind of stayed away I think. . . . They thought that something my dad did wrong, that he was taken away. It was not easy for us."[8]

Upon arriving at their destination, military personnel subjected suspects to a body search and collected their possessions. At the Immigration Center in Honolulu, several rows of three-decked beds and mats were spread over the floor, but by the time Soga arrived, other inmates had taken the beds, and three or four people lay on each mat. Overcrowding became a common problem as authorities picked up more individuals than the facilities could accommodate. Even Col. William F. Steer, former provost marshal for the Territory of Hawai'i, recalled that "it was quite crowded. Man, they were packed in there like sardines. Hot sweaty and pretty bad."[9] Yoshitami "Jack" Tasaka also recalled being "kept all day in a dark room with no light bulb, until called one by one to the final judgment."[10] Tasaka said, "we were forced to languish in this room from one week for a short stay to several weeks for a long examination" as prisoners waited to learn about their fate. "No one slept much that first night," remembered Soga, and the close quarters mainly affected the many elderly inmates.

In the morning, familiar faces emerged from the crowded confines of the rooms. The men shared the stories of their arrests as they nervously awaited the interrogation process. This initial questioning occurred before the establishment of formal hearing boards on December 14, but inmates were similarly questioned by military officials and had few legal rights or protections.[11] Minosuke Hanabusa (figure 1), a retired Wai'anae fisherman who was part of the first group of detainees, recalled his tense wait and his questioning: "I didn't know what they were going to ask. They had a pistol placed in front of the questioning man. They had 2 of them with guns asking me all kinds of questions. I didn't know. . . . I neve[r] did anything like that [espionage] . . . those 2–3 hours, I really suffered from the questioning. Especially when I had no information or knowledge in what they were asking. They had me facing that overnight."[12]

Arrest and interrogation experiences varied for each individual as the treatment's harshness depended on the responsible individual from the Military Police (MP) or Federal Bureau of Investigation (FBI). However, officials conducted many interviews under the veiled threat of force. According to Soga, the attitude of the officials was "bloodthirsty," as they already considered the Japanese guilty.[13] Even after lengthy interrogations, inmates were not allowed to leave the premises or to contact their families about their status and well-being. The Immigration Center became their temporary home until authorities could make further arrangements. Newspaper editor Yasutaro Soga offers some of the most detailed descriptions of life at the Immigration Station:

> At mealtimes, we lined up single file and were led to a backyard under the strict surveillance of military police. Anyone who stepped out of line came face to face with the point of a bayonet. At the entrance to the yard, each of us got a mess kit and food. Then we sat down on the ground and ate.

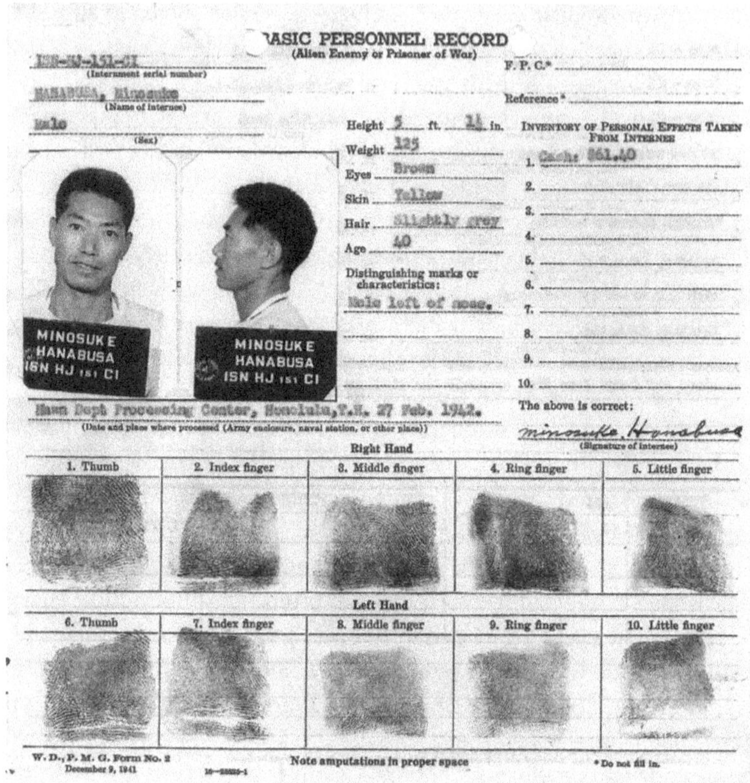

BASIC PERSONNEL RECORD
(Alien Enemy or Prisoner of War)

ISN-HJ-151-CI
(Internment serial number)

HANABUSA, Minosuke
(Name of internee)

Male
(Sex)

F. P. C.*

Reference*

Height 5 ft. 11 in.
Weight 125
Eyes Brown
Skin Yellow
Hair Slightly grey
Age 40
Distinguishing marks or characteristics:
Mole left of nose.

INVENTORY OF PERSONAL EFFECTS TAKEN FROM INTERNEE
1. Cash: $61.40
2.
3.
4.
5.
6.
7.
8.
9.
10.

MINOSUKE HANABUSA ISN HJ 151 CI

Hawn Dept Processing Center, Honolulu, T.H. 27 Feb. 1942.
(Date and place where processed (Army enclosure, naval station, or other place))

The above is correct:
Minosuke Hanabusa
(Signature of internee)

Right Hand

1. Thumb	2. Index finger	3. Middle finger	4. Ring finger	5. Little finger

Left Hand

6. Thumb	7. Index finger	8. Middle finger	9. Ring finger	10. Little finger

W. D., P. M. G. Form No. 2
December 9, 1941

Note amputations in proper space

*Do not fill in.

Figure 1. Incarceration File of Minosuke Hanabusa. National Archives at College Park, Maryland. RG 494. Record of U.S. Army Forces in the Middle Pacific, 1942–46. Record of the Military Government of the Territory of Hawaii. Alien Processing Center. Internee Case Files. Box 217, Stack Area 290, Row 44, Compartment 6, Shelf 3.

> Although there was a covered rest area nearby, we were forbidden to use it. Even if the ground was wet or it had begun to rain, we were forced to eat sitting on the ground. After ten or twenty minutes, we were taken back to the room. We were not allowed an occasional breath of fresh air or exercise at all. Of course we had to wash our own utensils. After we returned to our room, a few of us were called in turn and ordered to clean our area and the toilets.[14]

The harsh treatment endured by individuals like Soga highlights their perceived threat as military officials considered Japanese language newspapers and their editors dangerous influences within the community due to their long history of activism in plantation labor strikes, high-profile crimes like the Myles Fukunaga case, and the Massie trial and efforts to outlaw foreign language schools as part of Americanization campaigns in the 1920s.[15] Many Japanese inmates were middle- and upper-class professionals who had advanced economically beyond most plantation workers. According to inmate Hisashi Fukuhara (figure 2), "Ordinary farmers didn't go. Everyone was either a store manager or banker o[r] newspaperman."[16] As leaders, they had been well insulated within the Japanese community from other ethnic groups or social classes. They were publicly humiliated and degraded before these other prisoners, damaging their sense of self-worth and identity. Consequently,

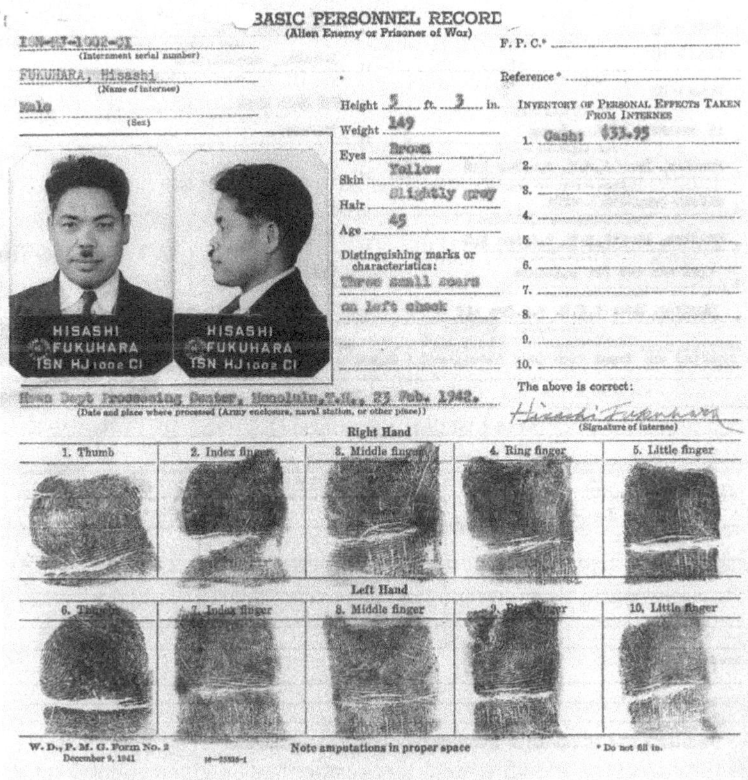

BASIC PERSONNEL RECORD
(Alien Enemy or Prisoner of War)

[illegible]-1002-CI
(Internment serial number)

FUKUHARA, Hisashi
(Name of internee)

Male
(Sex)

F. P. C.*

Reference*

Height 5 ft. 3 in.
Weight 149
Eyes Brown
Skin Yellow
Hair Slightly grey
Age 45
Distinguishing marks or characteristics:
Three small scars
on left cheek

HISASHI FUKUHARA ISN HJ 1002 CI

HISASHI FUKUHARA ISN HJ 1002 CI

INVENTORY OF PERSONAL EFFECTS TAKEN FROM INTERNEES
1. Cash: $33.95
2.
3.
4.
5.
6.
7.
8.
9.
10.

The above is correct:

(Signature of internee)

[illegible] Processing Center, Honolulu, T.H., 23 Feb. 1942.
(Date and place where processed (Army enclosure, naval station, or other place))

Right Hand

1. Thumb	2. Index finger	3. Middle finger	4. Ring finger	5. Little finger

Left Hand

6. Thumb	7. Index finger	8. Middle finger	9. Ring finger	10. Little finger

W. D., P. M. G. Form No. 2
December 9, 1941

Note amputations in proper space

* Do not fill in.

Figure 2. Incarceration File of Hisashi Fukuhara. National Archives at College Park, Maryland. RG 494. Record of U.S. Army Forces in the Middle Pacific, 1942–46. Record of the Military Government of the Territory of Hawaii. Alien Processing Center. Internee Case Files. Box 217, Stack Area 290, Row 44, Compartment 6, Shelf 3.

with the incarceration of newspaper editors and reporters, most Japanese presses were forced to close, and many never reopened even after the war's conclusion.

Sand Island

After a few days, soldiers carrying bayonets and machine guns transferred the detainees to Sand Island, where authorities had constructed incarceration facilities on December 8, 1941, using the existing facilities of the Quarantine Station. Despite protests from the acting surgeon general in Washington, who had argued on behalf of the Public Health Service that had occupied the facilities, the Army took over the Quarantine Station.[17] The Army had planned to use Sand Island since April 1941 due to its strategic location. Although it was adjacent to Honolulu, it was separated by water; as an island, prisoners could not escape easily. In addition, it was near the Office of the Military Governor in ʻIolani Palace but in an isolated location away from strategic targets. Further, the facilities at the Quarantine Station were in excellent condition, and authorities could quickly convert it into a camp. Once martial law was declared, the Army took over the facility.

Before inmates entered the camp, officials confiscated all personal belongings, strip-searched them, and checked for weapons. According to Hanabusa, "in the process they stripped us down and even checked the anus. We were completely naked. Not even under shorts. They even checked our assholes."[18] This systematic humiliation of the inmates was part of a concerted effort by military officials to degrade and weaken the leadership of the Japanese community in Hawaiʻi. As Myoshu Sasai recalled, "They were just playing games with us . . . that was also a part of war."[19] While these inmates directly experienced military brutality on a day-to-day basis, incarceration immediately impacted the entire Japanese community as it demonstrated the power of the Army authorities. Incarceration succeeded in its purpose as it instilled timidity in the rest of the community by allowing the military to assume control over literally every aspect of the bodies and the lives of these once-powerful Japanese individuals.

Living Conditions

By the end of the war's first week, authorities had detained about 300 inmates at Sand Island. The physical plant was divided into four compounds: two housed up to 250 Japanese; one compound was designated to hold women of various races; and the final compound was set aside for 25 Germans and Italians. Each compound constituted a distinct unit with a spokesperson to deal directly with the authorities. However, the military did not feel compelled to address inmate complaints, and the military could replace any leaders who caused too much trouble. In his memoirs, Soga detailed an incident on December 30, 1941, when "Admiral" Ohtani upset "Captain E" by insulting one of the soldiers. According to Soga, "Captain E told all of us in a threatening look that Ohtani should have been primarily shot to death."[20] As punishment, Ohtani, surrounded by several guards, was sent to a remote warehouse on the property and confined for a week with water and hard crackers.

The living conditions of his fellow inmates were not much better. For the first six months, authorities housed inmates in tents that the first group of inmates had constructed under guards' direction at night in the pouring rain. "Most of us never did this type of work," remembered Soga, as many inmates were elderly professionals who were unused to manual labor. "We were soaking wet from rain and perspiration, and finally we finished building tents about 9 o'clock at night."[21] When the inmates finally erected the tents, the exhausted men lay on makeshift beds and slept in wet clothes. Officials did not improve their housing in the morning or for months afterward. Throughout the winter and spring, inmates lived in this manner. During the day, the tents became unbearably humid inside, and when it rained, water dripped through the porous canvas and flooded the ground. The tents also provided little protection against the night chill or the wind that swept through Sand Island. Many inmates wore the same clothes in which they were apprehended and were not allowed additional clothing until restrictions were relaxed. Authorities housed inmates in these conditions until the barracks were completed in May 1942, providing a vast improvement in accommodations.

Daily Life

Life at Sand Island was characterized by military regimentation and alternating bouts with feelings of fear and boredom. Officials held morning and evening roll calls daily, with each company rotating the camp's kitchen duty, latrine cleaning, and general maintenance work. At first, Suikei Furuya noted that kitchen patrol (KP) was used as "light punishment" by authorities, but as authorities began lifting restrictions, it became part of the routine work.[22] Often, officials would call roll for trivial matters and require inmates to get into formation throughout the day. At other times, upon hearing whistling, inmates gathered and lined up for inspections as many as seven to eight times a day, demonstrating the complete authority of the military.

Aside from routine chores, inmates picked weeds, cleaned the yard, and swatted flies to keep busy. Hawai'i Island inmate Otokichi Ozaki recalled that authorities treated Honolulu inmates harshly, especially compared to later arrivals. "Our hearts went out to them," Ozaki remembered, "when one man said, 'My friends, our hands have been picks, hoes, and shovels.'"[23] Ozaki explained, "although there was nothing to do, we were expected to do something—even pull the grass around our tents where there was none." He highlighted that although authorities were particular "to the point of being ridiculous, about censorship, sanitation, and cleanliness," they seemed "unconcerned" about their health.[24] No one was excused from "fatigue duty," as these meaningless activities were called, except those who were ill. Under the terms of the Geneva Convention, inmates could not be compelled to work other than to assist in maintaining the camps. However, on more than one occasion, elderly inmates were used as strikebreakers and put to work constructing the double wire fences around the camp after construction workers hired for the task walked off the job. "What I didn't understand," remembered Furuya, "was that the old men were put to work despite available young inmates like me."[25] Although military officials denied this incident occurred, the Japanese government filed a formal complaint soon after.[26] As aliens, many of the inmates filed grievances through the Japanese government. They understood from their incarceration experience that they were considered guilty until proven innocent within the American justice system. While the validity of this claim cannot be determined beyond this oral testimony and the formal complaint filed by the Japanese government, the use of Japanese inmates for labor ended, and no other reports were filed after that.

Although authorities prohibited alcohol in camp, smoking was permitted, and inmates each received a ration of rolled and unrolled cigarettes. It was not uncommon to see a gathering of seven or eight people taking turns puffing on a single cigarette to make the best use of their meager supply. When cigarette wrappers ran out, which they often did, inmates used toilet paper to roll the tobacco. Matches were similarly limited, and only the company commander could obtain them. As a result, many resourceful individuals split matches in two to make them last longer. Inmates referred to Saichiro Kubota of Kaua'i as "*hidane otoko*" as he appeared early each morning, lit a piece of string from the battalion chief's tent, and went from tent to tent, battling the Nu'uanu wind to offer a light for their cigarettes. Otokichi Ozaki recalled that inmates affectionately called him "*kimoiri don*" for his service to the inmates as he did "menial tasks for our benefit" while working in silence.[27]

Despite overt hostility from most of the guards, who were Reserve Officers Training Corps (ROTC) cadets from the University of Hawai'i, there were small acts of kindness that mitigated the harshness of the incarceration experience. As Furuya recalled, "the son of a senator Heen [deliberately] used to drop his unsmoked cigarettes for us. He probably did it because he knew Mr. Ohtani who was a spokesperson representing us in the camps."[28] However, these acts of kindness were few and far between as racial and class differences and language barriers separated guards from the prisoners. For the most part, inmates' lives were defined by regimentation and degradation.

Authorities did not permit detainees to have paper, pencils, or matches to light their cigarettes at night. When night fell, darkness enveloped the camp as lights were forbidden. Officials restricted all activities, and inmates could not leave their tents after 6:00 p.m. except to use the bathroom. When they left the tent for that purpose, guards often challenged them and they had to answer "prisoner"; otherwise, guards would shoot them. Even their most private functions were monitored and controlled by the military. The inmates had to suffer daily injustices under the threat of death, reaffirming their status as prisoners.

Although inmates rotated their duties, there was a hierarchy of positions in the camp that generally privileged whites at the expense of Japanese inmates. These rankings paralleled their earlier experiences on the plantations, where occupations were stratified according to race since racial discrimination was a "formal policy."[29] While a German cook prepared the food, the Japanese were restricted to KP and assigned miscellaneous duties and menial tasks. Meals were often western dishes with few fruits or vegetables and "smothered in butter," making them nearly inedible for the Japanese. The meals at Sand Island resulted in so many protests that the Office of Internal Security had to address a complaint filed by the Japanese government on behalf of the inmates.[30] In addition, no private time was allowed, even during meals, with at least one guard in the mess hall. Hisashi Fukuhara discussed the mess experience: "At the beginning in camp, over there at the mess hall where we went to eat, the guards had bayonets attached to their rifles, and they lined up on both sides of the mess hall, and we had to walk down the middle. They thought we would try to escape. Yea, we had to walk down the middle."[31] Guards often cautioned inmates about leaving too much food as scrap; some even forced inmates to eat what they had left uneaten.

Military Restrictions

Barbed wire fence surrounded the camp, with a white line drawn ten feet from the enclosure. Anyone found in that zone was considered an escapee and shot. In one instance, a Buddhist priest, a Shintō priest, and a principal of a Japanese language school were found wandering beyond the white line. Fortunately, guards did not shoot them. When authorities sounded the alarm the prisoners returned to the designated area.[32] Still, inmates widely circulated this story as a reminder of the constant military presence and a warning about the strict surveillance of their actions.

There were also limits to fraternizing with other prisoners. In his memoirs, Yasutaro Soga recounted an incident where the Reverend Kuchiba of Hongwanji Betusin, Matsuda, the Branch Manager of Shokin Ginkō, and another man were caught violating the rule of three people conversing at one time. Although this law was intended to prevent planning escapes or prisoner uprisings, it was inherently designed to weaken the internal bonds of the community and the leadership organization. In this specific case, as punishment, each had to carry a large shovel and dig outside the compound for unexploded shells from the Pearl Harbor attack. This job was dangerous and usually left to the Japanese inmates, whom authorities considered expendable.[33]

Communication with friends and family on the outside was similarly restricted. Everything addressed to the inmates was thoroughly inspected and, in some cases, confiscated. Letters were only sent out once at a particular hour of the week and were subject to military censorship. According to the wife of Jukichi Inouye, a Sand Island inmate, there were "a lot of windows" in the letters as the military censors cut out certain portions, "especially the date and what you did that day."[34] In addition, the letters' contents were limited as each detainee was only allowed one sheet of stationery and one envelope, all kept under lock and key. Since letters had to be written in English, the few who understood English were kept very busy with correspondence since these letters were the only means of communicating with the outside. The difficulties in correspondence were illustrative of a series of laws and regulations within the camp designed to isolate individuals from one another, their families, and the wider community.

Intimidation and suspicion infused the atmosphere of the camps. When two people were mistakenly declared missing from the roll call, authorities alerted the camp until they were "found." Similarly, when a soap container was misplaced, officials searched everyone until they could locate the missing article. Although authorities later recovered the container, they discovered a piece of a nail and some money on one individual during the search. As a result of these infractions, this particular individual was forced to forfeit his cigarette ration for several weeks.[35] No one was safe from these inspections, and unless individuals reported various violations, they could also be found guilty of the crime. In addition, inmates often participated in designating punishment for fellow inmates, making justice even more arbitrary and spreading tension, division, and mistrust in the camp.

The arbitrary nature of justice and the pervasive threat of punishment in the camps profoundly affected many inmates who distrusted authority. They understood that their actions were monitored and examined by the military guards who could shoot them at the slightest provocation. Authorities would merely regard them as another casualty of the war. In one incident, "old man Tachibana" refused to leave the incarceration center—despite having been pardoned—because he feared reprisals by the authorities. On the morning of the Pearl Harbor attack, several Japanese fishermen were killed by Army machine gun fire. Among the casualties were two friends of Tachibana's, a former fisherman. When authorities paroled him, Tachibana refused to leave Sand Island and requested a written document proving his innocence. Otherwise, he said, he could be picked up again. Tachibana again resisted when a guard attempted to put him into a car. Instead, he opted to walk home. He believed he would not know where they might take him if put into the car.[36]

Despite proof of his innocence, Tachibana's paranoia about the military had some basis, as several people in the camp did not meet any criteria to justify incarceration. Their cases were seen as particularly arbitrary extensions of "justice." Authorities incarcerated the wife of Shigemaru Miyaoh because they mistakenly believed her to be her mother-in-law, as both of them signed their names "Y. Miyaoh."[37] Officials detained both women while the rest of the family was left to raise Miyaoh's three young children, the oldest of whom was only five. Although Miyaoh testified at military hearings that she was merely a housewife and was not involved in any church activities, authorities did not allow her to return home. In another instance, when authorities came to pick up Mr. Yamane because he had visited Japan immediately before the war, his English-speaking wife protested to officers against her husband's arrest. Many Japanese, particularly the Issei, had maintained close ties to friends and family members who lived in Japan. Understandably, many had traveled to and corresponded with relatives in their home country before the war. Yet, this reasoning failed to dissuade authorities, and officials incarcerated them until the war's end.[38]

Psychological Impacts of Incarceration

Daily camp life affected individuals in various ways, as their unknown fates and the ever-looming threat of violence disturbed inmates in different fashions. Some became dissolute and hardened, and at least one had a nervous breakdown. For example, the priest of the Inari Shrine thought he was pregnant, and authorities had to release him for psychiatric treatment. Although he eventually recovered, stories such as this were typical and indicative of the daily stresses of the camp.[39] Hanabusa explained some of the challenges that the inmates faced that contributed to the physical and mental stress of camp life: "It was just spiritual despair. We didn't know how long we were going to be there or when the war was going to end, it wouldn't have been too bad if we knew how long we were going to be there. If they told me I would be there so many months, it would have been bearable. That's how we were all suffering."[40] Many became withdrawn due to the inactivity in the camps and their inability to challenge their imprisonment. Some mainly felt the social stigma of incarceration, according to Soga, "especially those inmates who used to boast in the Japanese communities." As he noted, they "looked . . . depressed" and were "but the shadow of their former selves."[41] In essence, the military accomplished its goal of breaking the leadership of the Japanese community through incarceration. While some resisted, many became despairing and depressed. "We ended up where we were," remembered Furuya. "We couldn't do anything about it. It couldn't be helped."[42] An attitude of *shikataganai*, or "it can't be helped," permeated the camps.

One of the first deaths in the camp was Hisahiko Kokubo from Kaua'i, who died suddenly. Although three doctors—fellow detainees from Honolulu, Maui, and Hawai'i Island—had done what they could without medical equipment, Kokubo passed away in his tent. When authorities removed Kokubo's body, fellow inmates put their hands together in prayers as a final gesture to him. As the vehicle taillights faded into the distance, Ozaki recalled "an indescribable emptiness" that filled many inmates.[43] Many reflected that "for a pioneer, who devoted his life to the advancement of his fellow countrymen, to be rewarded at sixty-four with a lonely death behind barbed wire is too tragic a fate."

Officials used race to justify the arrest and dehumanization of Japanese and other suspicious Europeans living in Hawai'i. In addition to detaining Japanese residents, authorities investigated 114 Germans, 2 Frenchmen, and 17 Italians for possible covert activity.[44] On O'ahu, officials housed them separately from most Japanese men and segregated them from the women. However, the separation of nationalities was not always successful. In Soga's memoirs, he recounts numerous occasions when Japanese inmates were mistakenly incarcerated with Germans and Italians. In January 1942, the Reverend Deme of Waipoa was suddenly paroled from the Japanese camp but with no official explanation accompanying his release. Later, new arrivals told inmates that Deme was being held at the Immigration Center and kept with the Germans. This case of mistaken identity was because Deme is also a German name. His first name, "Josen," was misspelled as "Joseph," and officials treated him like a German. Other occurrences of mistaken ethnicity included the name Maeda being mistaken for the German name Meida and Ipponsugi for the Russian name Iponsky.[45] The Sand Island Detention Camp was in operation for fifteen months, and during that period, about $500,000 was spent on various additions and improvements. On September 9, 1942, Red Cross representative John Sulzer visited Sand Island and noted that of the 358 total prisoners, which included Germans, Italians, and Prisoners of War (POWs), 300 were Japanese men, and 19 were Japanese women. He noted the existence of several one-story wooden barracks that were "well ventilated, well lighted and having shuttered windows."[46] Showers provided hot and cold water, and prisoners could purchase items from the canteen. Sulzer only criticized the fact that "It appears to us that many foreign civilian internees are held here a little too long before being transferred to a permanent internment camp, but on the other hand one must consider the great difficulties of transportation." Overall, Sulzer was effusive in his praise of Sand Island, but six months later, officials moved inmates to Honouliuli.

In March 1943, authorities moved all remaining inmates to the new Honouliuli Internment Camp in 'Ewa, and Sand Island became part of the expanded Honolulu Port of Embarkation. The Immigration Center continued to operate as the temporary custody of aliens pending interrogation and incarceration hearings on Hawai'i, Maui, O'ahu, and Kaua'i.[47] According to the U.S. Army, "hearing boards were established to [ensure] fairness" in evaluating each case.[48] Investigators made an important distinction between "Citizen Japanese" and "Alien Japanese," acknowledging the fact that "by law they have been specifically denied the privilege of becoming United States citizens."[49] According to officials, agents investigating Japanese employed on naval projects and the loyalties of suspect individuals should keep in mind fourteen different factors, including family ties in Japan, education, religion, membership in Japanese organizations, and even previous donations to the Japanese army and navy relief efforts in the prewar period. Authorities brought individuals first before the Preliminary Hearing Board, which was comprised of a Counter Intelligence Corps (CIC) officer or agent and one representative from the Federal Bureau of Investigation (FBI) and Office of Naval Intelligence (ONI). If the members decided to incarcerate the person, the CIC presented their case to the Civilian Hearing Board, consisting of two Army officers and three civilians. Suspects were allowed to bring in witnesses and have an attorney present, although many could not afford the cost of legal representation. Following the Board's recommendation, the case went before the Intelligence Reviewing Board, composed of the heads of the three counterintelligence agencies—the CIC, FBI, and ONI. They could either concur or make an opposite recommendation. Then, the case would be sent to the Military Governor's Review Board, where the final recommendation was made and signed by the Military Governor, and a subject would either be released or incarcerated. According to inmate Myoshu Sasai, they were allowed to call their lawyers. Still, authorities told them it "would be probably a waste," as officials would only question them and they were not allowed to challenge their incarceration.[50] For many, hearing boards were a mere formality before they were sent to incarceration centers on the mainland or Honouliuli on the 'Ewa plain on O'ahu.

Honouliuli

Jigokudani (Hell Valley)

Honouliuli was a U.S. Army Internment Camp that opened on March 2, 1943, in Honouliuli Gulch, west of Waipahu (figures 3, 4, 5). It was the largest and last utilized civilian confinement site in Hawai'i and was used to house POWs until 1946. Various sources cite different reasons why authorities moved inmates from Sand Island to Honouliuli. According to Lt. Louis Springer, commander of the Sand Island camp from March 19, 1942, until May 9, 1943, Sand Island was unsuitable

Figure 3. Inmate Barracks at Honouliuli Internment and POW Camp. Japanese Cultural Center of Hawai'i, R.H. Lodge photographer, #910. "Honouliuli Internment & POW Camp—barracks and tents." AR 19 Archival Collection.

as a prisoner of war or alien internment camp. It violated international law as it was subject to a direct attack by enemy landings. Another report states that Sand Island facilities were needed to expand the Honolulu Port of Embarkation. While the War Department approved the construction of the POW camps, the Provost Marshal General of the Office of Military Governor supervised the operation and internal administration of the inmates. A double fence with watchtowers equipped with machine guns and floodlights surrounded the camp with separate accommodations for officer POWs whom authorities held in buildings or cantonments with different accommodations for general and field officers.

During World War II, Honouliuli was referred to by various names in army documents and consular reports, including "Honouliuli Camp." It was called "Camp Honouliuli," "Internees Compound #6," "Honouliuli Internment Camp," and "Alien Internment Camp." According to Col. S. H. Spillner, the camp was selected as it was "an area that was remote from active Military unit activity and a safe place for Internees (From possible Govt. of Japan Bombings)."[51] Built by the Hawaiian Civil Engineering Department, Honouliuli is in a gulch about five hundred to seven hundred feet wide at the camp location, with steep slopes rising on both sides. The Army cleared

Figure 4. Honouliuli Internee Barracks. Japanese Cultural Center of Hawai'i, R.H. Lodge photographer, #2446. "Honouliuli internee barracks." Hawai'i's Plantation Village Collection.

trees and grass in the densely vegetated valley to provide clear views from guard towers and thus enhance security. Authorities divided the camp into seven compounds: a compound for administration and guards, one for civilian inmates, and eventually five compounds for POWs. The first and smaller section of the camp housed the inmates. The POWs lived in the larger section toward the back of the gulch.[52] Authorities further partitioned the camp into barbed wire enclosures for occupants based on their military status—officers, enlisted, and non-combatants. Okinawan POWs referred to the upper valley as the "Italian quarters" as it housed Italian war prisoners, named the middle section "Hirara" [or Hira/Hirayoshi] corps and described the bottom section as "Fukuchi" [or Fukuji] corps.[53] Authorities separated Japanese Americans from German Americans, and women lived in different accommodations from men. Approximately 320 inmates were kept at Honouliuli, constructed to house citizens, resident aliens, and POWs.[54] A report at the time described the camp:

> The kitchen and mess hall for Japanese internees is equipped to feed up to one thousand internees. The internees live in prefabricated "sixteen-man" demountable barracks. All latrines have modern plumbing with

Figure 5. Honouliuli Internment & POW Camp—Barracks and Tents. Japanese Cultural Center of Hawai'i, R.H. Lodge photographer, #2137. "Honouliuli Internment & POW Camp—barracks and tents." Hawai'i's Plantation Village Collection.

> hot and cold showers. A post exchange is available for the purchase of cigarettes, tobacco, and miscellaneous items for sale. There is also a tailor shop, an equipped dental office, and a dispensary for necessary medical treatment. A recreation field has been cleared and fenced in for the use of the internees.[55]

Upon arriving in Honouliuli, authorities gave inmates two pairs of green khaki pants and replaced them when they became worn. As inmate Jack Tasaka recalled, "It did not rain much, and ill ventilated. We were afflicted with a scorching, intense heat throughout the year. Under this boiling heat, internees were naked all the time, wearing only short pants."[56] Inmates cut the long-legged khaki pants that authorities had distributed to them, and instead of shoes, they made *geta* (Japanese wooden clogs) from scrap pieces of lumber, making a loud clatter wherever they went. If inmates worked around the camp, authorities would pay them 80 cents, and with coupons, they could buy "candy and things" from the store in the camp.[57] However, authorities were still constructing the facility when the first prisoners arrived.

Dan Toru Nishikawa was among the first group to arrive at Honouliuli. He recalled that "koa trees grew out of floor cracks reaching to the ceiling," and as inmates labored to clear the camp, Nishikawa remembered that "tons of mosquitoes hovered even during the daytime, and we could hardly sleep for some time."[58] In recognition of their miserable living conditions, Nishikawa renamed Honouliuli "*Jigokudani*" (Hell Valley) for the camp location and wrote the word on a kitchen apron in a bold-faced letter with a paintbrush.[59] From then on, many inmates described Honouliuli as *Jigokudani* due to its isolated location, the heat, and pests. Despite these challenges, inmates became determined to improve their situation.

Daily Life in Honouliuli

In contrast to Sand Island, authorities seemed to relax prisoner restrictions and treat inmates more humanely in Honouliuli. Nearly two years had passed since the Pearl Harbor attack, and fears of a Japanese invasion and concerns about the loyalty of the Japanese population had diminished. Thus, although inmates were under armed guard, and the camp was surrounded by barbed wire, inmate Toso Haseyama remarked that he felt "nothing in particular" with the MPs watching them.[60] Haseyama explains, "Since this was America, and everything was so easygoing." Inmates were housed in various barracks and experienced a predictable regularity that characterized their days.

Inmates would wake around 6 a.m., and at about 7, they would line up at the mess hall for breakfast. Authorities allowed inmates to hold various jobs to assist in camp operations, and individuals who worked in the kitchen would leave earlier to prepare breakfast. To help prepare lunch, inmates would arrive by 11 for the noon meal and return at 5 for dinner preparations. A bell would announce mealtimes, and everyone would line up for food. In contrast to Sand Island, many inmates reported that officials served Japanese food to accommodate the prisoners' tastes. There was a Japanese cook; others also learned to cook while helping in the kitchen. Haseyama recalled, "There was a worker who made kamaboko [fishcake]," and there was rice for inmates to eat.[61]

When inmates arrived in Honouliuli, the Red Cross could deliver care packages from their families and even from the Empress of Japan. She sent *Ohta Isan* (a digestive), *Goto-san* (a cold medicine), fresh *gyokuro* (quality green tea), and other products through the International Red Cross. She also sent the inmates *haccho miso* (a type of bean paste) in a *shitodaru* (72-liter cask) from the Imperial Household Agency. Although authorities initially wanted to discard the miso as it was covered in blue mold, Haseyama recalled learning that the mold was evidence of its high quality and required a long fermentation period. After assuring authorities he would take responsibility for any inmates becoming sick from the miso, he and others used the miso to make soup. They grilled the miso after adding chopped green onions and sugar cane syrup in abundance from their stock room.[62]

Haseyama recalled he gained weight during his imprisonment because life was so regimented with regular meals. Before the war, he worked until eleven or midnight and weighed less than a hundred pounds. Haseyama reported that "after I went in there, I gradually gained weight and my waist went from twenty-eight to thirty, then thirty-two, and then thirty-four. I got that fat. However, because they couldn't move around very much and lacked exercise, some of the kibei nisei had numerous complaints like bad stomachs and indigestion."[63] If prisoners became ill, they would report their ailment to officials who would provide an MP escort to accompany prisoners to see their physicians outside Honouliuli.

To pass the time, inmates sought approval from authorities for activities they had previously banned. For many inmates, their incarceration afforded them the free time they did not have outside. Inmate Harry Urata took a very pragmatic approach to understanding his situation, noting, "I thought it's better to do something worthwhile you know?"[64] Urata, a Kibei, went to the warden's office seeking approval for English lessons. According to Urata, there was a graduate from a mainland college from whom ten to fifteen people began taking English lessons. Urata explained the permissiveness of authorities, stating, "what I heard is we not prisoner of war, so you know, kind of lenient you know. They said, for your health, if you think you like to do little work and it's up to you."[65] Inmates organized themselves into various units, cultivated vegetable gardens, and grew string beans, corn, tomatoes, lettuce, carrots, beets, cabbage, radishes, eggplant, and watermelon. According to Toso Haseyama, "Later, I went to grow vegetables. I would go after eight [a.m.] and come home by ten [a.m.]. That would be one day's work. (I received eighty cents a day in pay.)"[66] Many inmates enjoyed gardening, and while MPs stood guard to monitor the prisoners and ensure they did not escape, "they didn't scold us or really check on our work," and inmates could socialize with one another. Other prisoners like Haseyama cleaned bathrooms as authorities inspected the toilets weekly. Inmates were also responsible for the general maintenance of their living area as six people were housed in a cottage and slept on bunk beds. They cleaned and mopped the floors daily to ensure their communal living space remained clean.

Inmates and Mental Illness

Despite improving living conditions and more humane treatment by authorities, inmates still experienced the effects of incarceration. Some inmates called themselves "Tokkuri Miso," or bean paste in a sake bottle. As inmate Jack Tasaka explained, "you could stuff miso all the way into a large Tokkuri, similar to a gallon size bottle of Takara Masamune fine sake, and shake the bottle upside down. Although a trace of miso may drop, most of the miso will stay firmly inside the bottle."[67] Inmates used this expression to describe their self-pity, enclosed by barbed wire and unable to escape. As Tasaka pragmatically explained, incarceration would have been a "paradise" if only "we could ignore our mental anguish, we could eat without working, live sluggishly in idleness." He also felt great sympathy for individuals who remained free as authorities considered them "enemy aliens" or called them "Jap." They were under constant threat of being incarcerated at any moment.

With little to occupy their time during much of the day, inmates conversed about various topics, including specific individuals' physical attributes. According to Tasaka, there was a "Ranking List of Peckers" because there were no partitions in the bathrooms and restrooms, and inmates could compare each other. Prisoners began making "idle observations" and exchanged comments such as "A's was long" and "B's was thick" with a "referee" to determine the final ranking among inmates.[68] Despite this bawdy talk among prisoners, many reported that they had no sexual urges in camp, and inmates would say to one another, "my pecker is strangely quiet," or "I have no erection these days." In considering the cause for this condition among the men, Tasaka believed inmates were "enervated" by the stress of their incarceration as "I had thought our peckers stopped listening because of our extensive mental anxiety," although inmates were not physically exhausted. Some believed tranquilizers that authorities allegedly put in the water and food the inmates consumed caused this condition, and some prisoners refused to drink the coffee or soup. Tasaka reported that certain inmates had nervous breakdowns upon hearing this rumor. Still, he pragmatically remembered that authorities extensively restricted their behavior and would not have allowed any sexual activity.

Tasaka's comments reflect some of the psychological pressures inmates faced. While some tried to cope with their incarceration as best they could, others began suffering from mental illness due to imprisonment. Still today, Sand Island and Honouliuli are the only sites where prisoners started to manifest symptoms of mental illness. Nishikawa once encountered an inmate sleeping in a tin latrine filled with water. When Nishikawa questioned the inmate, he explained that he could turn the water into any juice by his body temperature. Thus, when he wanted papaya juice, the water would turn into papaya juice; when he desired orange juice, the water would turn into orange juice. Later, Nishikawa found him sleeping in a tree, and this inmate also pretended to be a samurai. After Nishikawa reported him to authorities, officials took him to the hospital for treatment. But Nishikawa still "felt like crying" about the effects of incarceration on fellow prisoners.[69]

Tasaka also recalled that "everyone experienced mental anguish, worrying about this and that," even though authorities had taken care of their essential needs.[70] In explaining the stress that many inmates felt, Tasaka recalled that when he was a child, and his mother was cutting the nails on his hands and feet, she used to say to him, "*kugami rakuzume,*" which meant, "our hair grows quick in hard life, while our nails grow quick in easy life."[71] Thus, inmates often worried about their families and circumstances while languishing in the camp, feeling helpless to do anything about the situation.

The Creativity of the Inmates

To maintain their sanity, inmates devised ingenious ways to pass the time. When supplies came into the camp packed in boxes, inmates would disassemble them and use the wood to make toys. As Toso Haseyama explains, "we'd make them and, in order to paint them, we would order the paint via the outside visitors who came to see us on Sundays."[72] Inmates also made a guitar out of an old Armour brand canned ham container to which they attached a rod and strung wires. As a hybrid ukulele, guitar, and three-string Okinawan Jabisen (guitar), the "ham-can guitar" became very popular among the inmates who wrote music and sang songs accompanied by the instrument. Tasaka recalled that the "music really consoled my fellows and me during those prosaic days" as inmates passed the time playing music.[73]

Inmates also requested nails and hammers from their families and even supplies for flower arranging. As Haseyama explains, those "things were allowed in freely and easily," not "things which would kill someone such as a pistol or a knife."[74] Inmates requested board games like *Go* and *Shogi* and held friendly competitions with one another.

Under the pretense of desiring flowers to make camp life less depressing and to prevent uprisings within a discontented population, inmates requested permission from authorities to allow their family members to bring flowers. However, inmates were more interested in the large glass jars containing the flowers as they used them to make alcohol in their rooms. Inmates would purchase grape and orange juice at the PX once a week and save sugar in handkerchiefs from the mess hall. Tasaka explains the ingenious way inmates obtained yeast from their family members who would hide it on their bodies: "At our visitor day once a month, family members brought yeast concealed in a bra" or attached it to their panties.[75] Upon arriving at camp, they would visit the restrooms to remove them from their undergarments and pass the yeast packets to the prisoners. Women were essential accomplices in obtaining illegal contraband, unheard of at other camps.

After mixing the ingredients, inmates would mix them once a night and filter the contents to prevent heartburn using two jars and a handkerchief. Tasaka and his bunkmates would bury their bottles as, according to Tasaka, "informers in the camps secretly told the office about our wine" as they desired early release.[76] As in other camps in Hawaiʻi and on the mainland, inmates were aware of *inu,* or informers, who willingly collaborated with authorities to secure their own release. At Honouliuli, Tasaka recalled a "ranking of informers"—those who would "ensnare others in order to save themselves"—and he believed that his arrest was due to the collaboration of "N-dog" due to the topics that authorities raised when they questioned him.[77] Officers who learned about the bootlegging from these *inu* called inmates to the mess hall. Twenty to thirty MPs searched the camp and confiscated twenty to thirty gallon jars.

Although some drank their homemade alcohol regularly and even before it had correctly fermented, Tasaka and his bunkmates would save up their alcohol and host farewell parties for the departing inmates who were leaving for the mainland, particularly the Issei. As part of these celebrations, Tasaka and the men would hire two skilled shamisen players called "male geisha" and pay them coupons that the authorities gave them to purchase goods at the PX.[78] Tasaka recalled that the rates for the geisha were 10 cents an hour for one person, 80 cents an hour for eight geisha, and $1.60 for two hours. The geishas were so famous for farewell parties that inmates requested them early to ensure availability. Authorities sent a number of Oʻahu inmates to Jerome, Arkansas, followed by Crystal City, Texas, where they joined other prisoners from Hawaiʻi who had arrived in three groups between November 1942 and February 1943. Subsequently, many of their families joined them for the duration of the war.[79]

POW Relations

While authorities transferred some inmates to mainland incarceration centers, Honouliuli remained one of the largest POW sites in the Pacific. According to the Provost Marshal Section, authorities detained approximately 17,124 POWs and inmates in the Hawaiian Islands from December 7, 1941, to September 2, 1945. Still, the maximum number confined at any one time was 11,351 individuals.[80] During the war, officials brought in approximately 5,000 Italian, 4,766 Japanese, and 3,723 Okinawan POWs to alleviate the acute wartime labor shortage in the Islands.[81] On December 7, 1941, military officials arrested Lt. Kazuo Sakamaki while authorities apprehended priests, language school teachers, newspaper editors, and other prominent individuals within the local Japanese community. He had participated in the Pearl Harbor attack at Waimānalo, Oʻahu, in a Japanese midget submarine. Sakamaki became the first POW in Hawaiʻi, and Italians and Okinawan POWs later joined him following Allied victories in 1943 in the Atlantic and Pacific Theaters. At the height of operation, there were over four hundred tents, including single pyramidal and double tents at Honouliuli. Camp officials disinfected newly arrived POWs and gave them standard clothing and supplies. Most lived in small six- to eight-man tents, used pit latrines, and took cold-water showers. Under the Geneva Convention, POWs were prohibited from military-related work, and officers were exempt from mandatory work detail. Enlisted men were required to do some essential jobs within the camps and could volunteer for other work assignments, including outside the camp, where they could work twelve hours a day. Thus, authorities allowed POWs outside the camp to work on various projects while local inmates at Honouliuli remained incarcerated. Over time, their military surveillance decreased, with fewer guards assigned to the prisoners. After the war, POWs were under an honor system at Schofield Barracks, behind barbed wire but without guards.

In an unusual twist of fate, inmates whom authorities had arrested for perceived danger due to their ties with Japan helped to improve relations between military officials and POWs. These connections, particularly their language skills and cultural knowledge, helped prevent potential deaths. Nishikawa recalled that sometimes POWs stopped eating, and some were on the verge of suicide. While working as a translator, he found many issues were "the result of miscommunication."[82] Nishikawa recalled one instance where a group of POWs refused to eat because Sergeant Loveless had given them hoes to do hard work. When Nishikawa questioned the officer, he explained that International Law required keeping a clean living environment for prisoners. As their living area was overgrown with weeds that invited mosquitoes, he provided them with hoes to assist them in cleaning their living quarters.[83] Following Nishikawa's explanation to the POWs, they began eating again.

In another instance, many newly arrived POWs believed that American soldiers would kill them and refused to take any food from their enemy country. Nishikawa explained that the Nisei in camp would be preparing their food to alleviate any concerns about the food preparation and that the Empress of Japan provided the tea and miso soup through the International Red Cross. Pragmatically, Nishikawa told them that "it was your fate that you survived, and the exchange boat would probably take you back to Japan in the near future. In the meantime, you can build your body by eating good here, and when you return to Japan, you can again service your country."[84] The group's leader agreed in response to this explanation, and everyone ate again. Other times, Japanese POWs feared that their food was poisoned, and it took assurances from the inmates and promises that they could eventually return to Japan by exchange boat to encourage them to eat.

Negotiating with Authorities: *Jigoku de Hotoke* (A Friend in Hell)

Possibly due to the relaxing of regulations and the passage of time, guards began recognizing the inherent humanity of the prisoners. Many of the guards at Honouliuli came from the University of Hawai'i ROTC, and according to Nishikawa, "they had a fairly good feelings about Japanese in Hawaii."[85] In explaining his wartime experiences, Tasaka lamented, "I happened to be assigned to Honouliuli Detachment," referring to the fact that some Japanese in the Islands became guards. In contrast, others became detainees in the war environment, though they all were Hawai'i residents.[86] Many inmates spoke positively about Sergeant Loveless, who, according to Tasaka, "was benevolent and humane."[87] When his supervisors demoted him for unknown reasons, the "internees, having appreciated his kindness, felt great sympathy for him, and expressed our love and respect to him even more." Even after authorities released the inmates, some wanted to invite him back to Hawai'i for a party in honor of him, but they never located his whereabouts after the war.

Due to the relationships between guards and inmates, prisoners began voicing their concerns about improving their living conditions. When Nishikawa requested food to prepare a special diet for a patient who had just returned from Tripler Hospital, a Major General Army Surgeon who inspected the camp replied that those supplies—fresh eggs, vegetables, and fruits—should be delivered each day. However, Nishikawa showed him they had only received chili con carne, egg powder, beans, and cane syrup. After the officer questioned the MPs, they returned with fresh eggs, vegetables, oranges, and choice meat. According to Nishikawa, "at that time, we realized that we had been treated outrageously for more than a year starting at the Sand Island."[88] From then on, inmates actively voiced their concerns and requested better food.

Later, Nishikawa mentioned to another inspector that "most of our internees grew up in Japan and preferred to eat fish better than meat." He said the Army had jurisdiction over their camp, and canned sardines were the only fish available. Nishikawa immediately told him, "We are good American citizens and has committed no crimes; yet we have been imprisoned. It has nothing to do with who is in charge of us . . . Army, Navy, or civilian. Although I apologize it is a difficult demand, we would appreciate if you could help us." The inspector mentioned that he would try to contact the Navy to offer to exchange items for some fish but could not guarantee anything. About one week after he left, inmates received a six-foot box with a 150-pound sea bass that the cooks prepared a portion of as sashimi while boiling and sautéing the rest. Nishikawa was so grateful that it became "one of the unforgettable events in my life." That experience taught Nishikawa to "speak my mind on whatever the issue" to advocate for himself and other inmates.

Inmates also benefited from their familiarity with some of the soldiers who guarded them, including local Japanese. Nishikawa recalled an MP mess sergeant named Kyochi who brought tofu to inmates as he previously was a drinking companion of a mutual acquaintance. "Based on those past associations with him," Nishimura explained, "I was able to ask him to buy special food items such as miso, shoyu [soy sauce], ginger, and pepper—which were not in our rations—using our coupons."[89] Although inmates had limited power and authority in the camps, they could still capitalize on their prior relationships and connections within the Japanese community to mitigate some of their hardships. They also could improve the conditions of camp life that were not possible in other incarceration centers.

For some, incarceration was a challenging experience due to their sacrifice as U.S. Army veterans of World War I. Others were fathers and relatives of young men who had enlisted to prove their loyalty to America during World War II. In petitioning for his release from Honouliuli, former senator and World War I veteran Sanji Abe highlighted the fact that his son George, a United States citizen, had volunteered in the armed services: "I hate to take advantage of my son's voluntary action and use it for my benefit, but I am compelled to call your attention of one instant as proof of the spirit of patriotism of my home, environment, and influence as an American citizen of the past that prompted son George to volunteer to join the combat division of the United States army, a supreme sacrifice a citizen could offer to the country."[90] Abe further noted that he had sworn allegiance only to the United States during his government tenure, and the Army honorably discharged him.

Sanji Abe's son George was not the only Nisei to volunteer in the United States armed forces to prove his loyalty after authorities had incarcerated his family. Tasaka recalled that Bolo Shirakata, who worried about his incarcerated sick father's health, similarly volunteered to support his father's release. The meeting between father and son before Bolo was sent to the mainland to receive basic training moved many who were aware of their situation to "tears of indignity and sympathy."[91] Although Bolo returned to Hawai'i after fighting in Italy and France, his father died. According to Tasaka, "the built-up anxiety and illness shortened his life; otherwise, he would have lived longer." In other instances, however, incarcerated fathers received messages of the deaths of their sons in combat. Harry Urata recalled the reaction of one inmate who pointedly asked: "Why my son is in Italy killed in action. Why I got to stay over here!" highlighting the cost of incarceration.[92] Although authorities later released that inmate, he returned home only to grieve the loss of his son.

The Experience of Families

As many inmates were the breadwinners of their families, the remaining family members often faced significant hardship and financial difficulties with the closure of Japanese banks and freezing of assets. While some families received aid from the Red Cross, many more struggled to make ends meet. For example, Dan Toru Nishikawa's wife was a Nisei who owned a dressmaking school; authorities ordered the closure of her shop following her husband's arrest. With a seven-year-old son to support, Nishikawa recalled that "she could not see any light and was totally lost."[93] To raise money to support herself and her child, she sold all of their possessions "for a song." She also moved in with her sister, who lived in a rural area. In the meantime, their son worked as a yard boy at a church and delivered English newspapers to supplement the family income. Many would depend upon the wages that inmates earned while in camp. Tasaka reported that in Honouliuli, carpenters, barbers, tailors, doctors, and chefs earned 10 cents per hour for a maximum of 16 dollars per month.[94] Often, inmates worked in the camps and sent those earnings home to their struggling families. Nishikawa reported that "families of internees suffered from larger mental anguish than those of us internees" as they struggled to make a living. According to Nishikawa, the lifetime "damage" of incarceration for those families was "beyond description."[95]

Although inmates were permitted to meet their families weekly, it was often a bittersweet meeting for both parties. Tasaka witnessed the loneliness new brides experienced with the arrest of their husbands and the struggle that young wives faced while caring for their children alone. Tasaka wrote a poem capturing the difficult moments when the visiting time ended and the children left their fathers:

> A long awaited visiting day,
> A million things to talk about, time flies,
> "Father, let's go home together," child begging,
> Patting child on head, with tearful eyes.[96]

According to Tasaka, "It was a very sad sight that brought tears to our eyes for those of us watching," and many were sympathetic to the plight of these families. Tasaka himself "burned with righteous indignation about such unjust treatment," experienced by those whose only crime was their ethnicity. To Tasaka, the phrase, "*Nasake wa hito no tame narazu*" (kindness is never lost, it brings its reward, or we must reap what we have sown) captured his sentiment at that time as he hoped there would be some retribution for the suffering prisoners were forced to endure at the hands of military officials.

Although they constituted a small percentage of the inmates, the Germans were among the first to complain about their incarceration and martial law. On October 13, 1942, Alfred J. Snyder, Esq., representing Mrs. Albert Mehl, whose husband, an American citizen, had been incarcerated at Sand Island following December 7, sent a letter to the attorney general in Washington, DC. In this letter, Snyder not only demanded to know the present status of Albert Mehl but also the nature of the charges filed against him and an indication of when officials would make a prompt determination of his case. Although the outcome of this petition is unknown, less than a year later, two other German inmates, Walter Glockner and Erwin R. Seifert, challenged martial law by petitioning for writs of habeas corpus, a right suspended under martial law. This petition represented a particular challenge to the activities of the CIC and its right to search and make arrests. Although this attack on martial law was ultimately unsuccessful, Glockner and Seifert were evacuated to the mainland and released, thus achieving their goal. However, this incident opened the door for other attacks on martial law, and mounting political and legal pressure resulted in its demise. On February 25, 1946, the Supreme Court asserted that the Organic Act of Hawai'i did not authorize the convening of military tribunals under martial law, challenging the Army's right to try civilians. Although military officials argued that Hawai'i remained in danger of a Japanese invasion, necessitating military rule, this ruling would effectively challenge military authority in the Islands.[97]

Many have argued that a tolerant racial attitude in Hawai'i and a spirit of "aloha" mitigated discrimination and prejudice and prevented the sort of large-scale incarceration that occurred on the mainland. However, the felt need of many Nisei to prove their loyalty through participating in acts of patriotism or enlisting in the United States military during World War II challenges this view. While the value of *on* or obligation to America did exist within a migrant population grateful for the opportunities in Hawai'i and the United States, fear of a similar fate of incarceration also pervaded the ethnic Japanese community that already had a long, contentious history with elite whites and military personnel. Many Japanese understood that martial law had replaced the dual system of justice in Hawai'i and that they were officially a community under suspicion—which justified their leaders' arrest and indefinite incarceration. While the labor needs of Hawai'i and the difficulties of transporting a large population to a secure area were factors in preventing the mass incarceration of the entire Japanese population, the treatment received by the inmates and the fear prevalent among Japanese complicates accepted explanations for the lack of mass incarceration in the Islands. A combination of these factors and the long history of contentious relations between white elites and the Japanese prove more helpful in explaining the distinctiveness and meaningful intent of incarceration in Hawai'i, culminating in racist fears by white elites.

Consequently, inmates on O'ahu experienced some of the harshest treatment under military rule, partly because of the large number of Japanese who lived near Pearl Harbor. However, residents on the neighboring islands were not immune to incarceration policies, and officials similarly embarked upon the arrest and confinement of Japanese beginning on December 7. Due to the dominance of the plantations on the neighbor islands, the military appropriated plantation and other community buildings and utilized and expanded existing military facilities. Many neighbor island inmates thus had various incarceration experiences as they were moved from one location to the next, contributing to their upheaval and dislocation. Understanding their experience is critical in expanding knowledge of Hawai'i incarceration beyond an urban, O'ahu-centric account, as it highlights the evolution of confinement policies partly shaped by the plantations and the relationships formed within rural plantation communities.

4 The Extension of Military Control on the Neighbor Islands and the Arrest, Criminalization, and Incarceration of Japanese Residents

When we had to use the toilet, five or six guards would accompany five or six of us to the bathroom. One on one. When we seated ourselves, the guards would stand on a side. They were there on orders and not trying to harass us. That was the first experience like that in my life . . . armed soldiers with fixed bayonets at that.[1]

Myoshu Sasai, a Jōdo-sect Buddhist minister from Hilo, Hawai'i, told this story in his memoirs about his experience in Hawai'i incarceration centers; it captures the humiliation Japanese inmates endured after authorities arrested them following the attack on December 7, 1941. While authorities systematically rounded up and incarcerated O'ahu residents, arrests were also occurring on the neighbor islands, where military officials utilized a variety of sites within close-knit plantation communities. These locations included language schools, jails, and even gymnasiums, as well as a variety of military facilities that highlighted the collective efforts of military and plantation officials to control the Japanese population. Not only were neighbor island residents more likely to be incarcerated than their O'ahu counterparts, but incarceration on the neighbor islands also had clear precedents on the plantations. Wartime necessity formally sanctioned these extralegal forms of control that had been an intrinsic part of the plantations.[2] These communities bore witness to these arrests, and this firsthand understanding of incarceration highlighted the personal impact of these events. The confinement of residents illustrated how relationships forged on the plantations on neighboring islands could influence the decision to imprison individuals, underscoring the arbitrariness of incarceration.

Understanding the story of neighbor island residents is critical to expanding Hawai'i's incarceration story beyond an O'ahu, urban-centric account as individuals had a broad range of experiences on the other islands. Unlike O'ahu and mainland incarceration centers, neighbor island incarceration primarily occurred in rural communities. The experiences of these inmates highlight that while officials had extensively studied the potential danger of the Japanese, little planning had gone into the actual logistics of detaining individuals for an extended period, particularly on the neighbor islands. Thus, incarceration was more varied on the neighboring islands due to the limited facilities in these plantation communities. Consequently, neighbor island sites did not adhere to the traditional categories that characterized incarceration centers on both O'ahu and the mainland, which different U.S. government agencies operated.[3] As most neighbor islands did not have a strong federal presence before the war, military officials relied upon local authorities and utilized existing facilities within these rural communities. Authorities incarcerated residents in places loosely grouped into three categories—community structures, jails and prisons, and military facilities—highlighting incarceration's localized nature. These inmates became symbols of the unprecedented extension of martial law and the sanctioned infringement on personal liberties. Consequently, the very visibility of these inmates, as they were often incarcerated in community buildings, effectively controlled the remaining population who feared a similar fate. Incarceration on Maui, Lāna'i, Moloka'i, Kaua'i, and Hawai'i Island thus demonstrated the successful extension of military control over rural communities connected through the existing plantation system that preceded the outbreak of war to control the Japanese threat.

The Military Appropriation of Community and Plantation Facilities and the Embedding of Incarceration within Rural Communities

While the military embarked upon the incarceration of O'ahu residents in urban areas concentrated within or nearby downtown Honolulu, authorities focused on arresting Japanese residents on the neighbor islands, many of whom lived in distant rural plantation towns. Many plantations across the Territory created self-contained communities for their workers and employees as part of plantation paternalism to cultivate the loyalty and discipline of the workers. While the paternalism of the plantation managers sometimes emerged from a sincere concern for their workers, with owners building hospitals and other recreational facilities, including gymnasiums, planters realized it played an essential role in production and profit making.[4] Thus, lacking the facilities available in Honolulu, military officials appropriated community structures such as on Kaua'i, where one individual, Paul Muraoka, was imprisoned in solitary confinement at the Līhu'e Plantation Gym's shower room for one month.

Although Muraoka did not know the specifics of the crime that resulted in his arrest, he believed it was likely due to his visits to Japan from 1932 to 1934 and his work for the Japanese consulate in Honolulu for six months. In isolation for a month, Muraoka only saw people when they brought his breakfast, lunch, and dinner. To keep himself mentally alert, he kept leftovers to feed ants and "would check to see from what hole they emerged, how many, how they divided the food to carry out, who gave the first notice. Individual responsibilities, etc."[5] Although the specifics of his accommodations are unknown, Muraoka remembered a window he could look out of, and he started monitoring daily activities to keep himself occupied. When the siren rang the first time, Muraoka noticed that he "saw a large car belonging to a plantation manager speed home." The next time the siren rang, Muraoka ran to the window to see what would occur, and again, he saw the manager departing. By engaging in such activities, he kept from going "emotionally bankrupt" with nothing else to do but wait for authorities to determine his fate. Muraoka likely witnessed the workings of the plantation as sugar production continued despite labor shortages and land and facilities being diverted for military usage. Līhu'e Plantation was part of extensive plans to protect Kaua'i in the event of an invasion, including "sabotage and terrorism on the part of resident sympathizers" that will "probably accompany and may precede the attack," a possibility made very real by the shelling of Nāwiliwili Harbor.[6] On the moonlit night of December 30, 1941, an enemy Japanese submarine about four miles offshore fired on Nāwiliwili Harbor with at least fifteen three-inch shells, most duds, as part of Japanese naval harassment of American territories and coastal regions.[7] One month after this event, authorities sent Muraoka to Kalāheo Stockade. Still, his wife was unaware of his whereabouts as no one had seen Muraoka, and she "didn't expect him to be there."[8]

Besides gymnasiums to promote community bonds and worker loyalty, planters also supported the construction of language schools to encourage the creation of families and a more stable labor force. During the war, however, military officials identified Japanese language school teachers as suspects and interrogated and incarcerated them in the days, weeks, and months following the attack. Officials closed all language schools for the duration of the war and, in some instances, appropriated school property such as the Hilo Dokuritsu Nippon Go Gakkō (Hilo Independent Japanese Language School) on Hawai'i Island for their military use. According to Shiho Nunes, whose father served as the school's principal, December 7 coincided with the school's *tenrankai* (a periodic exhibit of student work) and bazaar. Nunes remembers, "Hardly had it opened when military police arrived to disperse the crowd and shut down the activities." Authorities evicted the family and transformed the school campus into the military police headquarters. They converted the kindergarten building into a jail, and the principal's residence became a holding cell for the temporary detention of aliens. In April 1942, authorities arrested Nunes's father at his former home before sending him to Kīlauea Military Camp and then to Sand Island on O'ahu.

The Criminalization of Japanese Residents and Incarceration in Local Jails and Prisons

Military officials often incarcerated neighbor island residents in local jails and prisons in the continuation of plantation authority and punitive legal control. On Hawai'i Island, authorities incarcerated individuals at Waiākea Prison Camp, Kaunakakai Jail on Moloka'i (figures 6, 7), Lāna'i City Jail on Lāna'i (figure 8), and Waimea and Wailua County Jail (figures 9, 10) on Kaua'i.[9] Conditions in the jails varied widely depending upon the existing facilities, most of which were within communities. On the plantations, the police were a prominent presence

Figure 6. Kaunakakai Jail at Malama Park on Moloka'i. During World War II, authorities incarcerated at least five Moloka'i residents—Yoshihisa Maeda, Masaichi Marumoto, Shigeto Takashima, Shigeki Tani, and Masutaro Teraoka—presumably first at Kaunakakai Jail before sending them to Maui or other incarceration sites on O'ahu and the mainland. Photograph by Kelli Y. Nakamura.

Figure 7. Kaunakakai Jail at Malama Park. Photograph by Kelli Y. Nakamura.

as they often suppressed plantation disturbances and arrested deserting workers. As early as 1882, W. C. Parke, marshal of the kingdom, complained about the mounting expenses of a police force tasked to arrest plantation troublemakers. Parke blamed rising costs "solely" on "the increase in sugar plantations throughout the Islands, and these arrests have enormously increased the expense of the prisons and lock-ups."[10] Six years later, another marshal, John H. Soper, similarly attributed the rising costs of the police force to "keeping the Oriental, Portuguese, and native Hawaiian labor in their place." In 1892 alone, authorities arrested 5,706 individuals for deserting their contract service on the plantations—of these arrests, 5,387 were convicted. Asian workers were particularly outraged as they could not vote and influence police policies, yet they were still taxed and essentially financed the law enforcement needs of the plantations.[11] Military authorities would replace civilian control and remove any pretense of due process, as these inmates were never formally charged with any crime and held under armed guard.

The Wailua County Jail, for example, was the first place on Kaua'i where authorities assembled inmates. The white two-story concrete building with a small one-story barracks was designed by Honolulu architect Fred Fujioka. It

Figure 8. Front View of Historic Lāna'i Jail. Photograph by Kelli Y. Nakamura.

replaced a sixty-year-old jail in Līhu'e. Residents often called it the "Montgomery Hotel, Sheriff Rice's Hotel, the Wailua Hilton, the Haunted Jail, and sometimes, the Alamo" due to the jail's square tower facing Wailua Golf Course.[12] It was built in 1936 during the end of the Depression construction on Kaua'i, including the construction of Wailua Golf Club House, the Kīlauea Plantation Gym, the Waimea Community Hall, Wilcox Hospital, the Ham Young Stores, Kawakami's, and many small shops. Honolulu contractor W. S. Ching built it for $27,500. When it was completed on April 2, 1936, it was considered "simple and modern" and included a kitchen, refrigerated storeroom and pantry, and steel cells with barred windows. The cells often remained unlocked, and the jailer and sheriff built a taro patch, garden, and volleyball and baseball facilities for the inmates. According to one account, the only "prison-like ambiance" in the jail's history occurred during World War II when authorities built a fence and imprisoned residents of Japanese ancestry.

Before authorities brought them to Wailua Jail, at least ten inmates were housed at the Waimea Jail, now the county police and fire station in Waimea on the southwest side of Kaua'i. Mrs. Harada, the wife of Yoshio Harada, and Ishimatsu Shintani from Ni'ihau were some of the prominent inmates housed in these facilities.[13]

Figure 9. Waimea Courthouse and Jail (behind and to the right of the courthouse). Authorities incarcerated at least ten inmates in jail with the outbreak of war. It is the current location of the county police and fire station in Waimea, Kaua'i. Kaua'i Historical Society, "Photo 03–300.JPG." From the Hofgarrd photo album in possession of Kekaha Plantation.

According to a military report, within days after the Pearl Harbor attack, FBI officials gathered Japanese suspects and brought them to the local jail. However, at Wailua, the head jailer was unprepared for the arrival of the men and "not knowing how dangerous these men might be, kept them very closely confined," causing "over-crowding and discomfort," particularly for the elderly who had been receiving medical care.[14] Furuya states, "The prison had iron bars and the bed was an iron slab (*teppan*)."[15] A prisoner later described an 8 × 10 × 12-foot cell with two solid concrete walls, one solid steel wall, and "the entire front of steel and bars."[16] The only light came from a large exposed bulb in the corridor that was the light source for the entire cell block. Showers were located in the bathroom at the end of the hall.[17] Authorities gave the inmates two blankets—one that they used as makeshift bedding on the metal surface and the other as an insufficient covering to protect from the December cold.[18] As the jail lacked toilets, the men used a one-gallon can, and there was no privacy from other inmates.

Compounding the unpleasantness of the jail was the surrounding environment. The prison was situated next to a swamp that was a breeding ground for "Texas-sized" cockroaches, ants, flies, and mice.[19] Furuya reported, "we all got

Figure 10. Wailua Jail. Wailua Jail was the first place authorities incarcerated residents on Kaua'i. It was destroyed by a hurricane and replaced by the Kaua'i Community Correctional Center. Kaua'i Historical Society, "Wailua Jail 2001055134."

swollen faces from mosquito bites" as insects harassed inmates day and night. Janet Chieko Uehara recalled that her father, Kameo Takara, often complained about the "*nankin mushi*" (bedbugs) that were "eating them up."[20] Curtis Wong, who authorities later imprisoned in the camp in 1974, noted, "Kauai's jail provides the optimum physiological conditions for all the rodentia, insectia, and other pestia to carry on their 'swinging parties' and orgies" as the lack of screens in the jail resulted in mosquitoes "feast[ing] on the prisoners" throughout the day and evening.[21]

According to Furuya, authorities arrested him the same day they brought people from west and east Kaua'i to Wailua Jail. When they saw each other in the morning, they said, "Don't ask me how it is! (*Iya dōka to iu na!*)." Furuya was among the first eighteen to twenty people whom authorities initially arrested. He reported over thirty people housed at the jail, twenty-seven of whom would be eventually sent to the mainland.[22] In the morning, the prisoners were given a cracker for breakfast that was so hard, "it wouldn't break even if you bit it, and coffee. That's all," as they waited in their cells with the other prisoners.[23] Authorities treated all inmates as convicted criminals despite many inmates not knowing the cause of their arrests beyond the crime of their ethnicity.

On Tuesday, December 9, a group of Christians visited the jail and reported that five men were in cells meant for at most three individuals. An inspection by the Commanding Officer of the District and Dr. Samuel Wallis that same evening resulted in a report criticizing the health and sanitary conditions with suggestions for improvement. Authorities engaged in an unprecedented partnership with civilian personnel to improve the jail for the inmates' welfare. Mrs. Hale Cheatham, a dietician at the Mahelona Hospital, was responsible for planning meals. At the same time, Mrs. Arthur Achor, a public health nurse, tried to improve the living conditions of the inmates by creating daily activities. Mrs. Jurdin, in charge of occupational therapy at the Mahelona Memorial Hospital, taught the inmates handcrafts while Dr. Wallace Kawaoka volunteered as a medical advisor. Their efforts highlight the unprecedented awareness that community members had of these inmates and attempts to mitigate the conditions of their imprisonment.

Officials also opened the iron gates and doors so the men could move freely upstairs and into the yard. They encouraged inmates to engage in activities to bide their time and improve their accommodations. While some inmates started knitting under the direction of Mrs. William Groto and Miss McIntyre, others began building beds and furniture out of lumber as part of sanctioned activities, unlike at mainland incarceration centers, where these were unofficial tasks using stolen or repurposed lumber. They also engaged in activities such as lauhala weaving, carving, reading, gardening, and playing games. Authorities sent individuals to the inmates' residences to obtain clothing, toilet articles, and "other equipment that they desired to make their life more comfortable."[24] One of these individuals was likely the Reverend Masao Yamada of the Hanapēpē Japanese Christian Church on the west side, who later became the first American of Japanese ancestry to be commissioned a chaplain in the U.S. Army. Yamada recalled, "I became a messenger for the internees and their families; a receiving station for clothes and bundles to be sent to the camp or the home," and as he tried to comfort the families of the inmates, he recalled, "every visit was tragic."[25] Unlike other incarceration centers in Hawai'i, authorities did not attempt to remove personal property from the detainees. Inmates could hold on to their pocketbooks, money, watches, and knives, and authorities did not report any criminal activity as they "encouraged them to live as normal lives as possible and to be as happy as the circumstances allowed." Later, officials permitted relatives to visit on Sundays and Thursdays from 1 to 3 p.m. under military supervision. These visits helped to increase morale and "it has also assisted materially as laundry could be taken out and in." As a result of these changes, the men began to "brighten up" and took "a keen interest" in the activities at the prison, including improving two blackout rooms for nighttime.[26]

Kaua'i inmates had a surprising level of freedom compared to inmates at other incarceration sites in Hawai'i to improve their living conditions. Soon, authorities began addressing immediate health, food, sanitation, and recreational needs by constructing a two-story dormitory with forty-eight bunks to separate the detainees from the regular prisoners. The Kaua'i County Engineers built a kitchen, an outdoor toilet, a bathhouse with hot water, and new barracks to become the living and sleeping quarters for the detainees. A report states, "It contained two dormitories sleeping twenty-four men each in twelve double decker beds, a twenty-foot square living room, with tables, desks, shelves and benches, and a small dispensary." Along with "modern toilets," the windows were blacked out to adhere to martial law regulations. Inmates, evenly divided in the jail on the upper and lower floors, kept their respective groupings as their leaders tossed a coin for the dormitories.

The inmates also helped run the prison, a practice that would later occur at other sites. Some became "dormitory leaders, clean up leaders, water luna [supervisor], garden superintendent, carpenter supervisor, tool guardian, director of 'K.P.s.,' English teacher." Although officials first hired kitchen staff, the inmates began to organize a kitchen staff and rotating groups to set dishes, prepare vegetables, and wash dishes. The cost of feeding each prisoner was 40 cents per day. Inmates on Kaua'i seem to have played a more active role in running the camp than other sites in Hawai'i, and enjoyed activities provided by outside community organizations, including gardening, carpentry, sewing, knitting, typing, and various sports. An inmate who had worked at a hospital dispensary before his incarceration continued to serve in this capacity, and "to him goes much credit for the fine health record maintained," and a Dr. Kawaoka also visited the jail regularly, sometimes twice a day, to care for the inmates. Authorities kept records on the inmates on a card index, where they "entered special family needs and requirements" as they recognized that many men had families to support. This information was then passed on to a "Miss Bakeman" and the Social Welfare staff to address the needs of family members.

One of the first news items on the status of the inmates was published on December 22, 1941, two weeks after the attack on Pearl Harbor. That day, a letter from an alien incarcerated on Kaua'i appeared in the *Honolulu Star-Bulletin*. According to Hiseki Miyasaki, "contrary to our expectations we have been treated well . . . everything is being done to make our stay comfortable. A paradise has made its appearance in what was believed to be a hell."[27] After praising the improvements made to the camp and the freedoms enjoyed by the inmates, Miyasaki ended his letter by stating: "Finally we wish to thank the authorities . . . for the protection and kind treatment we are receiving here in the Territory of America under the Stars and Stripes. We are deeply touched by the great American spirit of fair play and magnanimity." The detainees reportedly wrote a similar letter in late January to Lieutenant Colonel Fitzgerald, which also shared a positive response to being incarcerated. Despite being "inconvenienced to a certain extent," inmates reportedly were able to "keep up a good spirit and a high morale" due to the freedoms they enjoyed. Inmates could play baseball, bowling, checkers, and cards, and besides tending to a community garden, individuals could attend an English class in the morning.

In summation, this letter stated the inmates were "treated as gentlemen and not as prisoners." It noted, "our sincere hope is that all those who are being detained by the Japanese government are being treated just as well as we are being treated here." Although the integrity of this letter is unknown, Yamada observed a difference in generational responses among the inmates. According to Yamada, "the enemy aliens met the situation far more sanely than the citizens and the younger set of aliens" as they were "quite resigned to the fact that this was war, and they could not help themselves as enemies of the United States."[28] Overall they were "grateful" for the "fair and just treatment accorded them." In contrast, Yamada reported the Nisei were "quite resentful" of their incarceration and added, "the war situation was to them no excuse for their internment without due process of law." Angered by the lack of explanation for their incarceration, they experienced "inner [conflict], depression and rebellion," especially as they were repeatedly interrogated by hearing boards while jailed.

Military Facilities and the Consolidation of Military Authority on Neighbor Islands

Besides appropriating local facilities, military officials also utilized existing facilities built on Kaua'i, Maui, and Hawai'i Island, where inmates were treated like military prisoners. On Kaua'i, officials held residents at the Kalāheo Stockade, which was likely part of a military encampment as it had separate quarters for jailing about fifty members of the Army who had been convicted of a criminal offense or misconduct.[29] Author Patsy Sumie Saiki details how authorities held inmates at the Kalāheo Stockade in one structure large enough to house twenty to twenty-five people, with a mess hall, showers, and latrine.[30] On September 24, 1942, Red Cross representative John Sulzer visited "Kaleo, Kauai." He noted the existence of a camp situated on a hill with nine inmates inhabiting "a barracks of the general type in use in the Islands." Inmates were fed the same food given to Army soldiers, slept on Army cots, and were given three woolen covers.[31] One year later, Swedish Vice-Council G. W. Olson arrived in Maui on September 23, 1943, and reported that Ha'ikū Military Camp was "the best of all the internment camps in the territory," noting that it was a "most delightful place . . . I would have stayed there than return to the hotel in Wailuku."[32] At the time of Olson's visit, there were only four inmates, only one of whom was a Japanese citizen.

The largest military site on the neighbor islands that ultimately housed Japanese inmates was Kīlauea Military Camp on Hawai'i Island. Officials established it in 1916, the same year as the park, as a training ground and recreational camp for sailors and soldiers that stretched over forty-nine acres at a 4,000-foot elevation.[33] By 1937, Kīlauea Military Camp had vacation accommodations for twenty officers and their families, three noncommissioned officers and their families, and about two hundred enlisted men and the fourteen officers and enlisted men of the permanent detachment. The focus of the park staff was to assist the Army as "all personnel and facilities were drawn into the war effort."[34] Park operations would be replaced by efforts to aid the Army and defend the home front, including incarcerating Japanese suspects from the island of Hawai'i. On December 7, 1941, it became the largest incarceration center outside of O'ahu. It would be the only preexisting military site that authorities used to incarcerate Japanese suspects as it was untouched by the Pearl Harbor attack and removed from areas of strategic military importance. Later drawings of the camp would include "six 16-ft-by-60-ft barracks, a mess hall, a post exchange and dayroom, guards quarters, a barbershop, and sentry boxes, surrounding by a double security fence."[35] Thus, unlike Sand Island or Honouliuli, military facilities were already available to incarcerate Japanese suspects and immediately put to use. George Hoshida, who authorities arrested on February 6, 1942, offers one of the most detailed descriptions of the barracks that housed over a hundred people:

> The barrack was set about five or six feet above the gravel-covered ground. . . . A long [veranda] enclosed by wire meshes, ran the full length of the barrack front. A flight of steps led up to the wired porch and then to the main door of the barrack front. . . . The barrack was about a hundred feet long and fifty feet wide. The south-east corner of the barrack was partitioned off to form the office of the guards, and at the center of the opposite wall from the entrance, was a doorway which led into the showers and latrine. A portion of the west was portioned off and a doorway led into a spacious lounge with a fireplace, lounging chairs, and couches. Books and magazines were furnished by the military for the inmates to relax.[36]

Before residents arrived at Kīlauea Military Camp, officials strip-searched them for possible contraband and immediately sent them to the barracks. During his incarceration at Kīlauea Military Camp on Hawai'i Island, Myoshu Sasai (figure 11) recalled that they had to adjust to a life of strict regulation and constant monitoring that extended even to monitoring inmates' bathroom usage with soldiers guarding inmates while they relieved themselves. Despite this embarrassment, both soldiers and prisoners complied with this order.

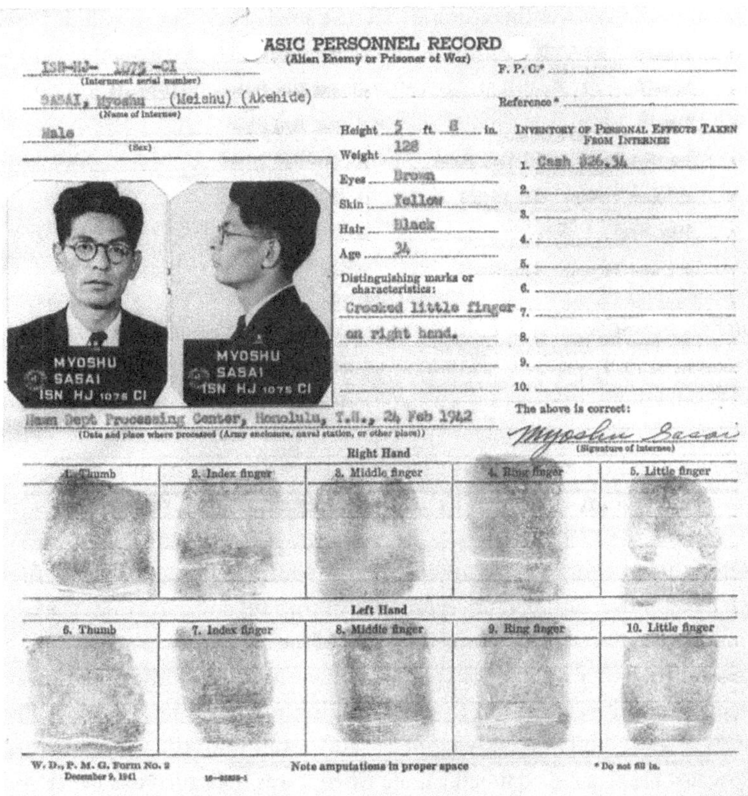

BASIC PERSONNEL RECORD
(Alien Enemy or Prisoner of War)

ISN-HJ- 1075 -CI
(Internment serial number)

SASAI, Myoshu (Meishu) (Akehide)
(Name of Internee)

Male
(Sex)

F. P. C.*

Reference*

MYOSHU SASAI ISN HJ 1075 CI

MYOSHU SASAI ISN HJ 1075 CI

Height 5 ft. 6 in.
Weight 128
Eyes Brown
Skin Yellow
Hair Black
Age 34
Distinguishing marks or characteristics:
Crooked little finger on right hand.

INVENTORY OF PERSONAL EFFECTS TAKEN FROM INTERNEE

1. Cash $26.34
2.
3.
4.
5.
6.
7.
8.
9.
10.

The above is correct:

Myoshu Sasai
(Signature of internee)

Hawn Dept Processing Center, Honolulu, T.H., 24 Feb 1942
(Date and place where processed (Army enclosure, naval station, or other place))

Right Hand

1. Thumb	2. Index finger	3. Middle finger	4. Ring finger	5. Little finger

Left Hand

6. Thumb	7. Index finger	8. Middle finger	9. Ring finger	10. Little finger

W. D., P. M. G. Form No. 2
December 9, 1941

Note amputations in proper space

* Do not fill in.

Figure 11. Incarceration File of Myoshu Sasai. National Archives at College Park, Maryland. RG 494. Record of U.S. Army Forces in the Middle Pacific, 1942–46. Record of the Military Government of the Territory of Hawaii. Alien Processing Center. Internee Case Files. Box 217, Stack Area 290, Row 44, Compartment 6, Shelf 3.

In the morning, soldiers ordered inmates into a building with windows covered in black paper, and they immediately smelled food. Realizing they had reached the mess hall, they were relieved. Hawai'i Island resident Myoshu Sasai recalled his first impressions: "Everything expected was there . . . tables, chairs. There was plenty of food. They had things that we never saw or tasted before. There was plenty of it. Milk, [cereal], eggs, fruits—a lot of food. Japanese are used to having only *chazuke* [tea and rice] for breakfast. We never had the luxury of having a feast for breakfast. They really fed us well." The smell of food also awakened Otokichi Ozaki's appetite, who pragmatically thought, "If they are going to kill us, I may as well have my fill."[37] In reflecting upon his attitude at his first meal at Kīlauea Military Camp, he noted that "perhaps it was this attitude that sustained me during the whole four-year period, or it could be that I am simpleminded. At any rate, I consider myself fortunate that I retained my health and objectivity, while maintaining a positive outlook." The building was about the same size as their barrack, but a portion was partitioned and used as the army canteen where the inmates could purchase a limited amount of necessities.

Sasai and other prisoners were surprised in the mess hall by the bounty of food available to them as "we could eat all that we wanted to. If they ran out of something, all we had to do was to raise our hand."[38] A long serving counter separated the kitchen from the mess hall. Inmates picked up stainless steel serving trays and silverware and walked single file in front of the serving tables. Waiting kitchen personnel served them food as they pushed their trays along the counter before grabbing them to sit at wooden tables and benches. Later the inmates took their trays and threw away their waste into the garbage before placing the trays along the wall near the exit. When they finished eating, they could return to their barracks individually.

After dinner, many headed to the lavatory to take their nightly bath at the back of the barracks. Urinals lined up against a wall without any partitions; wash basins lined another section. Stalls occupied the rest of the room, where four people could take showers together. With hooks at the entrance for their clothes, inmates shared bath facilities and were careful to ration the limited hot water from the kitchen boiler. As a result, the first bathers often had to wait until the water became hot, while the last bathers risked it being gone when it was their turn to shower. A sense of camaraderie developed among the inmates, as noted by Hoshida, who observed that "here, sharing together the same fate in this time of emergency, they were brought together closer as humans on an equal plane and closer comradeship."[39] Unable to sleep the first few days, one prisoner finally got a good night's rest. He recalled, "I was tired and I was told I snored very loudly while I slept. But no one made fun or got angry because they felt everyone had to help each other. Especially since everyone was gathered by the FBI. Some people even grinded their teeth while they slept. But no one said anything."[40] Instead of expressing anger at the personal habits of fellow inmates, they communicated an unspoken agreement of understanding, as they all faced the same uncertain fate.

With their basic needs met, many inmates reported relatively benign treatment by military officials, especially compared to their later experiences in O'ahu at the Immigration Center and Honouliuli. Sasai was particularly impressed with the soldiers' behavior, especially the officer in charge, "a second lieutenant—very serious and young—who was a pleasant person, really took good care of us."[41] Despite this humane treatment, the inmates recognized their incarcerated status as they ate their meals surrounded by armed guards.

As the war progressed, authorities brought additional prisoners into the camp. Inmates greeted each carload with excitement, curious about the newest arrivals. Upon catching sight of the barracks as the car drove through the center, Hoshida observed that "people behind the windows were now waving gleefully at the newcomers as the guard unlocked the doors to herd them into the barrack."[42] As soon as Hoshida went inside, he was "surrounded by outstretched hands and joyous embraces . . . as though to welcome home their separated son or friend."[43] Curious about outside news, Sasai and other inmates asked the new arrivals for recent news and past events. However, Sasai recalls that "the new people were afraid of the situation that they were in and would not tell us anything. They wouldn't talk," as they were afraid of spreading rumors. Isolated from their families and communities and news of the outside world, Sasai notes, "We began living in different worlds; our world was separated from that of the other people on the island of Hawaii. That was the kind of feeling that was going on at that time."[44] One of these later arrivals had a much different experience: "When I first entered, they took notes on my height, weight, job, business and etc. I was welcomed by the rest of the people who were there and they were all eager to hear of any kind of news. So I told them what happened from December 7 up to date. I told them that Japan's navy had attacked Guam. And they all were happy for Japan."[45] New arrivals continued to arrive at the camp, and other inmates, desperate for news, eagerly welcomed them.

Hearing Boards and Suspicions of *Inu*

After two months at Kīlauea Military Camp, Sasai recalls that in February 1942, officials would take groups of four to five to the second floor of the post office in Hilo. Hearing councils consisting of "soldiers, and lawyers and a haole big shot from Hilo" would question them. Officials also conducted hearing boards on Maui, O'ahu, and Kaua'i that were similar to what took place on O'ahu.[46] Sasai recalled they were allowed to call their lawyers, but authorities told them it "would be probably a waste," as they would only be questioned. For Sasai, who was called two to three times, the hearings were of little importance: "The only thing I was happy about was leaving the military camp and seeing the outside world." As the route they traveled was the same as the one he took for his evening sermons, he would always look around for a familiar face, but "no one was out." At the hearings, however, "friends and family would crowd the corridors to peer through the windows to get a view," as hearing boards in Hilo were conducted within the community, reflecting the unique nature of incarceration on Hawai'i Island. Sasai saw his wife and child for the first time in months before being sent back to the barracks at Kīlauea Military Camp, where he and the other inmates would play cards, chess, or Japanese go. Later, when it was warmer, inmates were given basketballs and allowed to play on a court at the northern end of the front grounds. Hoshida recalled that while some "threw balls at each other, or in groups," others strolled around the court or sat on benches sunning themselves and talking.[47] Although this was a nice respite from the barracks, it did not decrease their loneliness. A Red Cross report in September 1942 confirmed that "internees are isolated from the outside" and denied "privileges according to the internees of other camps," including "being authorized to read why they are interned" for periods up to two months.[48]

For many, these hearings broke the monotony of daily camp life. Unable to leave the camp or conduct business or legal affairs, inmates occupied their days reading magazines and books, walking around, or writing letters. For many, letter writing was the only way to communicate with their families and maintain personal ties. Although the military censored letters, cutting out any details of the camp, Hoshida recalled that "letter writing became the main consolation and receiving them was a source of great pleasure to be looked forward to each day."[49] However, letters had to be in English, and most Issei inmates could not read or write English. Thus, Hoshida and others volunteered this service for their fellow inmates.

As their incarceration continued, suspicions soon arose among the inmates about a possible informer in their midst, who they called *inu*—"dogs," who collaborated with the authorities. Within close-knit neighbor island communities, the identity of these individuals became quickly known among the prisoners. According to Hoshida, interviewers questioned prisoners about issues discussed within the camp barracks during these hearing boards. Hoshida pointed out that "they had talked confidentially about things which they thought might be the reason for their detention. Because there couldn't be any possibility of being overheard by [an] outsider, it was apparent that it couldn't be anyone except someone who may have been present with them when they talked."[50] The inmates started looking for a suspect and noticed that one man, an Issei representative of a Honolulu Japanese newspaper who also had been active in Japanese community activities, was called each time FBI agents came to the camp. Hoshida remembered seeing the man in the company of a known FBI agent before the war and remarked that "many people came in later and reported that they had good reasons to believe that they were apprehended because of this informer." As a result of their suspicions, people began to restrict their conversations whenever he was nearby, decreasing his effectiveness as an informer. He was released without apparent reason, confirming suspicions among many. Hoshida recalled, "This informer prospered during the war but misfortune followed after the war and he eventually lost everything, including his [prestige] among the Japanese community."[51] In hindsight, he added, "It is a very unfortunate fact of life resulting from the tragic war which left no one unaffected in this world. This man, sadly, was one of the victims also and should be pitied."

Hoshida's comments are exceptionally forgiving because other inmates in mainland incarceration centers often ostracized and attacked suspected *inu*.[52] In this instance, authorities allegedly used the informer's information to deny other inmates parole and identify other individuals to incarcerate.

Some inmates readily jumped at the chance to inform on their fellow prisoners for the possibility of early release, although their efforts were unsuccessful. On February 22, 1942, Hawai'i Island representative Thomas Sakakihara was arrested "on suspicion of being an alien."[53] However, he was born in Hilo and was named special deputy sheriff to advise Hilo police and act as a liaison between the police and the military after the December 7 attack. While incarcerated at Kīlauea Military Camp, he wrote to FBI officials in Hilo. Sakakihara provided the names, addresses, and occupations of forty-four individuals he believed were "persons who are far more dangerous and whose freedom is detrimental to the internal security of our country and therefore should be taken into protective custody."[54] Sakakihara added, "They are considered not only district and community leaders but persons who have actively worked for the causes of enemy country during peace time and in the case enemy landing would constitute a serious menace to the safety of our defenses." Ironically, he condemned the "filthy, prejudiced and unscrupulous individuals who took advantage of the process or instrument of detention adopted by the authorities," while engaging in this same behavior and praising his own "impartial judgment." Despite offering information on his fellow Japanese in the community, authorities were suspicious of Sakakihara's motives in writing this letter. They noted that he pre-dated it before his incarceration, had named individuals already incarcerated and released, and must have written the letters in camp as officials thoroughly searched him upon entry. In conclusion, authorities noted that "these communications by Sakakihara add up to just one thing—he deliberately pre-dated them in a clumsy attempt to build an alibi." Officials detained Sakakihara at Honouliuli until his release in 1943.[55]

Other Japanese whom authorities approached to become informers refused to collaborate, resulting in their incarceration. During questioning by authorities to determine his loyalty, Hawai'i Island resident Yoshitami (Jack) Tasaka recalled the challenges of answering questions such as "Do you think that it is better for Japan to win this war?"[56] Tasaka understood that answering in the affirmative would result in his incarceration as an enemy alien. But if he replied that he would like America to win, authorities would insist he was lying. Thus, he felt he had no choice but to provide a harmless and inoffensive answer such as "I do not like war. I really hope Japan and America would make peace as soon as possible." Later, authorities asked Tasaka, "Are you willing to work together with us?" which Tasaka clearly understood to mean "if I was willing to make myself a cat's paw for the authority." If he agreed, he knew he would be "allowed to go home and forced to work as an informer." If he refused, they would send him to Honouliuli on O'ahu. Eventually, after numerous rounds of questioning, Tasaka was incarcerated at Honouliuli for being unwilling to become an *inu*.

Besides inmates informing on each other for personal gain, the very experience of incarceration also revealed some unfortunate personality traits among the prisoners who prioritized their own needs above others. Hoshida recalled one businessman who appeared to be very religious, reciting from the Bible and regularly talking about God and Jesus. But when mealtime came, he would rush to be the first person as the kitchen personnel did not monitor the serving proportions and sometimes ran out of food. According to Hoshida, "There was an understanding among the inmates that the older people and people with artificial teeth, who couldn't eat very fast, were to be given priority in the lineup. Despite this, this man, still quite young and with good teeth, would manage to squeeze in among the first in line."[57] Hoshida added, "It was sad to think that his preaching and practices didn't go together," as incarceration brought out the true character of individuals. Others would try to shirk essential housekeeping duties as the inmates cooperated in cleaning up the interior of the barracks every morning. However, according to Hoshida, "there were some who would talk loudly but never actually do much work. This was demonstrated time and time again as they went through their internment life through many camps while the war was going on." For some, their basic needs and desires took precedence over the welfare of others, making them well-known among the other inmates even as authorities continued to arrest and release individuals.

Departure to O'ahu and Mainland Incarceration Sites

On February 15, 1942, authorities on Hawai'i Island announced that immediate families could visit the inmates who would soon be sent to the mainland. The military leaders stated that, under international law, incarcerated aliens could not be kept in a combat zone and relocated to an area where hostilities were unlikely. Thus, they would be sent to incarceration camps on O'ahu or the mainland even though Pearl Harbor had been attacked only two months earlier and had become the center of America's military mobilization in the Pacific. Over 75 families, including at least 270 family members from Hawai'i Island, joined their husbands and fathers in mainland incarceration centers. Some eventually made their way to Jerome, Arkansas. Others departed to Crystal City, Texas, and Ft. Abraham Lincoln (Bismark), North Dakota.[58] Later, some families relocated to other centers, including Tule Lake, California, and Gila River, Arizona. Like their mainland counterparts,

Japanese families from Hawai'i Island had a few days to secure or dispose of their property as they could only bring clothes and necessities.

Authorities permitted each inmate $50 and instructed families and friends to provide that amount and purchase warm clothes. They also allowed a notary public to come to document their business affairs. Hawai'i Island resident Myoshu Sasai recalled that officials gave them a two-day notice when they were about to move. At the same time, a "guy named Richardson from the Hilo Police Department let our families know of our departure," revealing the close personal connections that existed between civil and military authorities.[59] As families frantically scrambled to buy warm clothes for the inmates, Sasai imagined that "the stores in Hilo must have ran out of their stock" of suitcases, hats, gloves, and coats. Richardson, whom other police officers assisted, brought these items to the inmates while families were allowed to come to the barracks and say their farewells. By summer, authorities had relocated most inmates, thus freeing the barracks for military use, although the precise closure date remains unclear.[60] As of September 19, 1942, the Red Cross reported that six inmates were still housed in Hilo, although when they were released remains uncertain.[61]

According to statistics collected by the Japanese Cultural Center of Hawai'i, authorities incarcerated approximately 130 Japanese from Maui, most of whom officials first sent to Sand Island. If authorities sent individuals to the mainland, most were sent to Jerome, Arkansas, or Crystal City, Texas, before being sent to Tule Lake or to return home. Over twenty-nine families from Maui, Lāna'i, and Moloka'i left the Islands to join their fathers or husbands in mainland incarceration centers, ultimately impacting nearly ninety-four children. Some community members ostracized those who decided to stay behind as they feared a similar fate. Robert Kiyoshi Hasegawa, whose father, James Hasegawa, had been incarcerated, recalled that when he returned to Lāna'i from Honolulu to help his mother and his siblings, everything was in a "jumble." His mother was in shock, and to help support the family, Hasegawa began working for the pineapple plantation. However, one day, plantation manager Dexter Fraser, whose testimony was critical in his father's incarceration, called him into the office. Fraser said, "Son, if Uncle Sam can't trust your dad, we cannot trust you either. So I want you to leave the island. Take your family with you."[62] With no other recourse, the family left the island for Maui without the support of their friends and community members as "you couldn't go to any person because if we went to see friends of ours, they would be in trouble now, in view of what's happened to my dad. They were all concerned and scared of the plantation manager." Most people kept the Hasegawas at "arm's length." Although some individuals volunteered to hold household items and heirlooms for the family, none were ever returned. Hasegawa recalled that even on Maui, members of the community shunned them due to the incarceration of his father:

> And Maui, Wailuku, at the time was a small community, like Lāna'i. News goes out fast among the Japanese community. When people found out about my dad's internment and the reason we were on Maui, there were certain things that my mother could not get out of the market owner. My mother told me this some time ago when we were visiting with her, that there were certain cuts of meat that she couldn't get. No merchant would sell to her, but will sell [to] somebody else. She was even being bypassed in line.

Hasegawa recalls "a lot of resentment" that his mother harbored with specific merchants and even with their landlord: "There was a real arm's-length kind of relationship, a 'talk to us if you have to, don't talk to us if you don't need to.' That type, even *aisatsu* [greeting]." Shunned even within the remaining Japanese community, the Hasegawas struggled to survive the war. Unfortunately, other inmate families would also have this experience as selective incarceration created an environment of fear within the remaining Japanese population.

On February 24, 1942, forty-five inmates left the Wailua County Jail under police guard for Nāwiliwili Harbor to be taken to Honolulu, leaving twenty-four detainees on Kaua'i. The jail housed civilian inmates until June 6, 1942, when officials moved them to Sand Island or other incarceration centers or released them. Jukichi Inouye's departure was particularly painful for his wife and their three-year-old daughter, as the families of the inmates knew the date they were leaving and witnessed the inmates leaving the jail. Mrs. Inouye recalled that her daughter "couldn't go to see daddy on the other side. They were dumped into a truck, so we just followed that truck" as it headed to Nāwiliwili Harbor."[63]

According to Kaetsu Furuya, at the time of their departure, "it was impossible to leave without pain and tears," especially in the case of Mrs. Harada. She had two or three young children, about five years or younger, being cared for by her sister.[64] When it was time to leave, Harada's children "wouldn't let her—they couldn't stand to see her go." At that time, a Korean soldier who had witnessed this painful separation of family members took Harada, her sister, and her children to see him for one final farewell. Furuya recalls: "We were all touched by how a Korean, who by rights should despise the Japanese (the Japanese invaded Korea and have been hostile to the Koreans), was so sensitive and thoughtful—all of us who witnessed the incident cried." Their departure was no less painful for other inmates as they and their families were separated. "All we could do was look at each other face to face eye to eye, tears in our eyes," recalled Furuya, as they were not permitted to speak. After leaving Kaua'i, they arrived in Honolulu, where officials first sent them to the Immigration Center for two or three days and then to Sand Island and other incarceration centers.

When at least twenty-eight families comprised of ninety-one family members from Kaua'i learned that authorities would send their husbands and fathers to the mainland, they decided to join them. They quickly packed for travel to incarceration centers in Jerome, Tule Lake, Santa Fe, and Gila River.[65] Two other families went to Crystal City, Texas, and joined other Japanese families from Hawai'i. Janet Tahara Uehara, whose father, Kameo Tahara was a priest and teacher before being incarcerated, recalls the upheaval caused by the short notification before leaving for the mainland:

> Well, we had only (three days)—they told us, "Three days, get ready to leave." You know, they gave us only three days notice and only one suitcase to a person. We cannot bring, you know, a lot of things. Just maybe what you want to bring—belongings. Necessity kind of stuff. So we couldn't bring much. Not much clothes. We didn't have no winter clothes. And we got there, it was January and so cold and freezing, and we didn't have no winter clothes.[66]

Many were not reunited immediately with their husbands and fathers, so they had difficulty adjusting. Some inmates were sent to other camps and joined their families more than a year later. Uehara recalled seeing young mothers, in particular, struggling with adjusting to the move and caring for their children, stating, "You know, babies would cry. I think they really had a hard time."[67] For many family members, incarceration was an adjustment as officials had arrested their husbands and fathers for unknown reasons, and they faced an uncertain future. In response, Uehara's mother adopted an attitude of "*shikata ga nai*" (it cannot be helped) as a reaction to her husband's arrest and the relocation of their family in a fatalistic acceptance of what had occurred as well as what awaited them in the incarceration centers.

Many inmates' removal from their island homes confirmed an inevitable separation from families and communities. With their departure, Hawai'i inmate George Hoshida and others realized that their innocence was irrelevant to the crime of their ethnicity. Hoshida recalled, "we think that our body is ours to do as we please, but here we are being taken away against our will for something which wasn't our fault. But this was life, and this was reality, and such is human life."[68] The inmates and the communities they left behind understood this inevitable outcome of their perceived crimes. They would endure a dual separation, first from their home island and later to mainland incarceration centers.

Although the direct effects of the Pearl Harbor attack were relatively limited on the neighbor islands, all residents of Hawai'i were subject to military regulations under martial law. The plantations, which had dominated the economic and political life of Hawai'i Island, Maui, Moloka'i, Lāna'i, and Kaua'i in the prewar years, facilitated the enactment of martial law as the military appropriated plantation and community structures due to an apparent lack of preparation in the logistics of housing prisoners for an extended time. Thus, officials arrested and confined Japanese suspects in local language schools, jails, and prisons. As many of these sites were within plantation towns, many community members were familiar with incarceration. The prominence of imprisonment on Maui, Kaua'i, Lāna'i, and Moloka'i likely contributed to the mobilization of the Japanese on the neighbor islands. This visibility of incarceration was in contrast to O'ahu, where officials incarcerated prisoners in restricted military areas such as Sand Island and Honouliuli.

Additionally, although officials used military necessity to justify the arrest and detention of individuals, plantation officials seemed to wield unprecedented influence in supporting or preventing individual incarceration. To many, this awareness likely increased the perception of the arbitrariness of imprisonment. It also contributed to community fear and uncertainty within these rural plantation communities.

Authorities also sent residents to military facilities on Maui and Kaua'i, with the largest number to Hawai'i Island. These individuals were placed under armed guard and identified as threats to national security. Thus, neighbor island inmates would experience a diversity of incarceration experiences even as they attempted to navigate the often overlapping claims of authority from civil officials, plantation owners, and the military. While some inmates were treated humanely and could enjoy selective freedoms, others endured life regulated by armed guards who regularly monitored and interrogated them for their alleged disloyalty to America. However, all prisoners shared the same "crime" of being Japanese after the Pearl Harbor attack, following decades of virulent anti-Japanese sentiment on the plantations in Hawai'i and the United States. Officials would eventually transfer many inmates from the neighbor islands to O'ahu, where they would spend the duration of the war at Honouliuli. Like their counterparts in mainland incarceration centers, many inmates reported an easing of restrictions and greater freedom as the war continued and the possibility of another Japanese attack lessened.

Others would be sent to mainland incarceration centers, heightening their separation from their families, communities, and island homes. For many neighbor island inmates, their incarceration on their home island would be the start of a dehumanizing experience designed to have an individual and community-wide impact. The fate of these minorities highlights the fragility of civil liberties in times of war. Still, their continued resistance and agency demonstrate their resiliency in these unprecedented circumstances that only later generations would come to recognize. Yet, in the postwar period, many struggled to reintegrate into a dramatically changed society. Most failed to acknowledge their incarceration. While some successfully navigated the political, economic, and social changes brought by war, others were isolated and silenced by community suspicions that continued in the postwar period. The divergent fate of individuals, even within the same community, highlights the many legacies of the war that still today exclude certain groups within wartime narratives of Japanese American history. Yet, they remain essential in bridging the prewar history of plantations in Hawai'i and the postwar celebratory status of Japanese Americans that remains a critical part of Japanese American identity even today.

5 "Shadows of Their Former Selves" and "A Place in the Sun"

The Legacy of Martial Law and Incarceration for Hawai'i's Japanese Leaders

> *The children suffered. Nobody would play with the children of the internees. . . . My girl was returning home from the library. She was stopped and told, "This is not Japan. This is the United States. I want you to respect it." They stopped her with the intent to punish her. And then, my boy was up in an ohia tree. They didn't bother the other boys, just my boy. They told him the same old stuff. They teased him . . . even me. We had a tough life.*[1]

According to this account by Hisashi Fukuhara, a retired barber from the Kona coast of Hawai'i Island, incarceration affected the inmates and their families as community members treated them with fear and suspicion. Unlike the families of Japanese American veterans of the 442nd Regimental Combat Team, the 100th Infantry Battalion, and the Military Intelligence Service (MIS), a distinct minority of inmates, Issei, and repatriates could not claim to be part of the triumphalist military discourse that has been employed to describe the fortunes of the Japanese community in the postwar period. During the war, while soldiers' families desperately waited for news of the battlefront and the fate of their loved ones, many internee family members anxiously awaited news of the status of the prisoners and an indication of when normal government operations and civilian life would resume. On October 25, 1944, martial law ended with the proclamation of Presidential Order 9489. The Provost Courts were immediately abolished, but other changes made were largely symbolic: The title of Military Governor became Military Commander, and the Office of the Military Governor was designated the Office of Internal Security. The CIC was still granted the authority to continue its investigative jurisdiction over all espionage cases, but it now had to operate through more indirect channels. After October 25, citizens were no longer placed in custodial detention but were immediately evacuated to the mainland. In addition, the Commanding General of the Territory of Hawaii Military Area still possessed the authority to exclude anyone from Hawai'i who was considered dangerous to security for sabotage or espionage reasons.[2] On October 24, 1944, sixty-seven Japanese and fifty aliens remained at the Honouliuli Internment Facility. By November 9, officials sent the sixty-seven Japanese Americans to Tule Lake while they released fifty aliens on parole. The day the war ended, authorities finally allowed the remaining prisoners to leave.

The Postwar Silence on Incarceration

Upon returning to their homes and communities, inmates faced rebuilding their lives. Jukichi Inouye, a former Japanese language school principal, found his entire livelihood gone as the military had disposed of his school and given most of the proceeds to the Salvation Army. "So when I got back," Inouye recalled, "there wasn't anything I could do. Everything was sold or cleaned out. I could sit and do nothing. I couldn't eat then. With a daughter, I wondered what would happen next."[3] Fortunately, his wife had been making a living as a dressmaker while Inouye had been incarcerated, and she could support the family until he found a new job. Inouye's search for new employment proved an enormous challenge as many inmates carried a stigma from their experience, and community members shunned them as unpleasant reminders of the war. A former language school teacher, Kaetsu Furuya, testified about his return by ship to Honolulu: "there were people in Honolulu, other passengers . . . who didn't like to hear about the internees . . . they looked down on us, and ignored us."[4] Many, like Furuya, had lost all their money during the war and were in poor physical shape from the camps, making even low-paying manual labor impossible. Numerous individuals suffered from physical ailments such as ulcers and had lost weight. However, inmates could not report their physical conditions during their incarceration due to military censorship. According to Furuya, "if we wanted to say we lost weight, we'd have to write 'my pants is getting bigger and bigger' or 'my pants is loose'—anyway, we couldn't say, 'I've lost so much weight that my pants is falling down.'"[5] The military restricted their communication while in the camps and censored any full record of the physical and psychological effects of the camp experience.

The emotional and physical scars from the camps lasted long after incarceration was over. Many Hawai'i inmates were ignored by the white community when they returned home. The larger Japanese community also shunned them as they represented the trauma of anti-Japanese sentiment. Several scholars have also noted that while the Japanese community on the West Coast of the United States had been incarcerated, this was a shared burden mitigated by the fact that the entire population, including military volunteers, the elderly, and children, could not all be potentially guilty of treason. However, in Hawai'i, the singling out of specific individuals implied guilt and a clear justification for their incarceration.[6]

Thus, homecoming to Hawai'i was often bittersweet for these former community leaders. Many had lost their physical possessions and the respect and status they had once garnered in the community as prominent Issei. Yoshiko Matsuda, an Issei who arrived in Hawai'i in 1924 following her marriage to Hongwanji Buddhist priest Ryugen Matsuda, described the Issei in the postwar period as "*ranru no gotoku* [tattered rags]."[7] Many would be unable to return to the prominence they had occupied in the prewar period and refused to talk about their wartime experience that had resulted in this dramatic reversal of fortunes. Former U.S. representative Colleen Hanabusa, the granddaughter of inmate Minosuke Hanabusa, explains some of the reluctance inmates had about sharing their incarceration experience with their families: "The people there, like my grandfather, didn't talk about it. If they were activists, you would've expected them to say something or do something about it, but it's their '*shikata ga nai*' [it cannot be helped] attitude, which is a value of how they felt, and I think that's the reason why, and they also wanted it to be behind them."[8]

While mainland Sansei were leading pilgrimages to incarceration sites as part of the larger Asian American civil rights movement during the 1960s, similar trips to locations where Hawai'i prisoners were incarcerated did not occur. While some, like Hanabusa, embraced a fatalistic attitude about their experiences during the war, it still did not make it any easier for them to talk about what had transpired, as there was little to gain from revisiting often painful experiences. Thus, many families of these inmates knew very little about the experience endured by these individuals, echoing an absence in community knowledge about Hawai'i incarceration. Overnight, fathers, and in some cases mothers, disappeared for the duration of the war without explanation, and the children of inmates were left to try to understand unprecedented circumstances without parental guidance. Even those whose parents remained during the war struggled to understand what few adults could comprehend under martial law and military censorship. Thus, unlike their counterparts on the mainland, many Sansei in Hawai'i were confronted by their parents' absence during the war or lacked a direct connection to incarceration. Many were unaware of the details of Hawai'i incarceration that had occurred on a much smaller scale.

Scholar Tetsuden Kashima highlights how the silence surrounding the arrest and incarceration of individuals remains an important distinction between Hawai'i incarceration and the experience on the mainland, as "Martial law and the use of the military-security classification restricted information about the entire wartime episode."[9] Subsequently, incarceration was never elaborated on in detail within wartime Hawai'i due to military censorship, the closure of ethnic presses, and overt silence by civil and military officials. It is also important to note that Hawai'i incarceration was authorized by martial law rather than Executive Order 9066. Except for Honouliuli, which military officials specifically constructed to house inmates and Prisoners of

War (POW), evidence of martial law quickly disappeared after the war's conclusion, even if residents had been continuously faced with the threat of incarceration during the war. The only facility in active use was Kīlauea Military Camp as, after the war, it reverted to its original purpose as a Morale, Welfare, and Recreation facility serving members of the U.S. Armed Forces and their families. However, its usage during the war as an incarceration site was quickly overlooked, and other sites on the neighbor islands were either demolished, repurposed, or entirely forgotten.

The Rise of Nationalistic Groups in the Postwar Period

The Issei "Psychic Epidemic" and "Postwar Delusions"

Adding to their challenges of reintegrating into their communities, many returning inmates were confronted by pro-Japanese nationalistic movements among a select portion of the alien population. Their actions seemed to validate their incarceration and posed considerable obstacles to their acceptance and assimilation into society. Many were outraged by the rise of pro-Japanese movements during and particularly after the war. However, this phenomenon of "postwar delusions" must be understood within the context of the social, political, and economic upheaval experienced by the Japanese community during this period that most drastically affected the Issei population in the Islands, especially those whom authorities had not incarcerated.[10] In researching Japanese incarceration in Hawai'i, scholars Dennis M. Ogawa and Evarts C. Fox Jr. posed an important question: "What happens to a [ethnic] community when its ministers, artists, teachers, writers, and philosophers are taken away?"[11] While Ogawa and Fox directed this question to issues of ethnic identity and cultural continuity within succeeding generations of Japanese Americans in Hawai'i, the wartime removal of cultural leaders resulted in immediate and long-term impacts in both the mainland communities that had been subject to mass removal and the remaining Japanese population in the Islands.

As early as October 26, 1943, an underground movement composed of extremists at Tule Lake organized a series of "educational" lectures that were held regularly in a number of blocks. They expounded Japanese political ideology, emphasized the ideas of the Greater East Asia Co-Prosperity Sphere, and recounted "news items" from Radio Tokyo. They convincingly presented Japan as victorious in Pacific battles and exhorted inmates to be "true Japanese."[12] In August 1944, a group of inmates established an organization called Sokoku Kenkyu Seinen-Dan (Young People's Association for the Study of Ancestral Country) to prepare their members for service to Japan after their repatriation. They encouraged individuals, and in particular young Nisei contemplating repatriation from the United States but unfamiliar with Japan, to study the Japanese language, history, and political ideology. Initially, this radical pro-Japanese organization at Tule Lake targeted younger inmates. Later, leaders of this group organized older inmates into a group called Sokuji Kikoku Hoshidan (Organization to Return Immediately to the Homeland to Serve). According to Vice-President Mojiro Ono, "Our sole loyalty lies with Japan, and as loyal service to our mother country, we . . . are willing to give up everything, both materially and in manpower to devote all of our efforts and be of any assistance to our country, Japan. We have no intention of helping with the national effort of America."[13] At first, organizers gave innocuous lectures on the contribution of the Japanese to the development of California. Gradually, however, they increasingly emphasized and glorified Japan's war aims. Members also participated in early morning outdoor exercises, similar to the radio exercises conducted in Japan, adding to their activities what camp officials considered militaristic features. Organizers purchased bugles and uniforms, and young men wore gray sweatshirts and headbands stamped with the emblem of the Rising Sun. In explaining his motives for participating in these activities, one inmate provided an alternative to Japanese patriotism: "I exercised in the morning with others—calisthenics—to keep physically fit."[14] Questioning the impression of militarism it gave the War Relocation Authority (WRA), he asked, "When did exercising become military training?" According to this inmate, the purpose of wearing "Rising Sun" headbands was "to get them [WRA authorities] to notice us and at least consider our requests." He added that "officials classified us as troublemakers, but they listened to us when we spoke." He noted that we "could only make nuisances of ourselves and thus get attention." Military officials, however, did not consider these actions merely attention-seeking tactics and began closely monitoring burgeoning nationalistic sentiment among mainland inmates and growing support for repatriation to Japan.[15]

For some who remained in Hawai'i during the war, the alienation, discrimination, isolation, and upheaval they experienced proved too much. They became susceptible to rumors connected to a belief in Japan's victory.[16] Following the announcement of Japan's defeat, some Issei were "confused . . . utterly confused," and many "could not eat nor sleep for days."[17] They lost the traditional leadership and status accorded to the older generation overnight and were forbidden from Japanese cultural practices that had provided continuity and stability within the ethnic population. As the government classified the Issei as enemy aliens, their children—the Nisei, who were American citizens by birth—assumed a leadership role in families in what has been described as "a radical disruption of the traditional roles of the members of the family and in a complete change in status between the two generations."[18] Respect and status traditionally accorded to the older generation further declined with the emergence of "victory groups" composed of a small number of

Issei who became vulnerable to notions of Japan's invincibility and refused to believe the news of Japan's unconditional surrender following the dropping of the atomic bombs.[19] As early as 1942 and 1943, various Issei had formed underground *kachigumi* (victory groups) that disputed American "rumors" of Japanese defeats and strove to keep ethnic pride and confidence alive.[20] Even after Japan's official surrender, rumors persisted within the Issei population, such as those concerning the arrival of the Japanese fleet to take over Hawai'i, the impending visit of Prince Nobuhito Takamatsu—the younger brother of Emperor Hirohito—to the Islands, and the transfer of Hawai'i to Japanese control.[21] This notion of Japan's "invincibility" during and after the war was reflected in the extreme shock many experienced upon hearing the news of Japan's defeat. It was also a perception fostered partly by Japanese radio propaganda that revealed a curious inconsistency in American war regulations.[22]

All local Japanese radio and newspapers were restricted from the outbreak of war. However, authorities still permitted direct radio broadcasts from Japan filled with propaganda and news of Japanese victories until February 1942. As many alien Japanese could not read or understand English well, they relied on the Japanese media for information about the war. Subsequently, many refused to accept the censored news of American war activities when the local Japanese press resumed publication on January 8, 1942. One scholar noted that during this critical period early in the war, the prohibitions regarding the use of Japanese in radio and print deprived the Issei of "a most effective means of news dissemination and potential Americanizing influence."[23] In essence, inconsistency in government policy and the upheaval experienced by the Japanese, who were subject to harsh governmental policies and regulations designed to deter these nationalistic activities, inadvertently contributed to the rise of pro-Japanese sentiment.

In place of local Japanese newspapers such as the *Hawaii Hochi* and *Nippu Jiji*, which had been traditional sources of news and events but that officials had suspended as part of the new war restrictions, some individuals became subscribers to mainland Japanese newspapers such as the *Colorado Times*, *Utah Nippo*, and *Rocky Shimpo*. According to scholar Yukiko Kimura, these papers propagated false reports of Japanese victories and celebrated Japan's "invincible tactics" and "fighting spirit."[24] To certain portions of the population, the existence of these papers, like the radio broadcasts from Tokyo that were permitted in an environment where officials restricted the local Japanese media and newspapers, seemed to confirm these stories and sanction pro-Japanese sentiment.

Still, another factor contributing to nationalistic Japanese attitudes was the rise of a religious sect called Seichō-no Ie (House of Growth), which helped promote notions of Japan's invincibility and inevitable victory. Despite its obscure origins in Japan and its small number of converts before the war, this group increased its membership dramatically since it was the only religious group authorized to operate in November 1944 due to its stated objective of providing memorial services for Japanese American service members killed on the battlefield.[25] With the closing of other Japanese religious organizations and the incarceration of traditional religious leaders, many in the community sought other avenues of spiritual support and guidance during this period of chaos and anxiety. This group attracted many followers, given the syncretic nature of Seichō-no Ie, which allowed adherents of different religions to belong to this sect while remaining devoted to their faiths. The activities of Seichō-no Ie similarly increased in popularity among the anxious parents of Nisei soldiers as the organization's leaders provided prayers for Nisei soldiers, along with claims that they could ensure their safety. According to government statistics, by March 1946, an estimated four hundred members belonged to the Honolulu branch of Seichō-no Ie, with over one thousand adherents in the Territory; observers noted that the number was steadily increasing.

At Seichō-no Ie meetings, where between two hundred and five hundred participants gathered, pro-Japanese sentiments were inserted into speeches such as "Demonstrate your Yamato spirit," "We Japanese race," "By the grace of our Emperor," and "Remember our fatherland."[26] Terms and descriptions such as "barbarian" and "inferior" were used to refer to non-Japanese, particularly Americans. The leaders only acknowledged Japanese American war contributions in describing how many had been saved due to prayers by Seichō-no Ie priests.[27] Although it is uncertain if audience members embraced these phrases and ideas, the larger Japanese community considered Seichō-no Ie a pernicious organization propagating anti-American sentiment.

In this atmosphere of heightened anxiety and pro-Japanese sentiment among the Issei population, various victory organizations emerged and encompassed membership from multiple locations on the island. They included Tōbu Dōshi-Kai (東部同志会, Eastern Association of Kindred Spirits) in Waialae, Kōsei-Kai (更生会, Association for Rehabilitation) in Palama, and Hakkō-Kai (八紘会, Association of Brotherhood) in Kalihi.[28] As one member of Tōbu Dōshi-Kai testified, "We are a group of people who retain the Japanese spirit and believe that our fatherland did not lose the war."[29] While disputing claims of Japan's defeat, the primary purpose of this organization was to provide Japanese lunches for prisoners of war every day for nearly two years. "For this we spent almost $10,000," one member claimed, as "we sent our members to all 6 places on the island where they worked every day."[30] Women played a significant role in this endeavor as they "cooked rice and fish and other things and prepared a very palatable lunch." Men who could not cook or did not have wives to assist in food preparation contributed money and materials for this purpose. Many of these members had split from Hawaii Dōshi-Kai (ハワイ同志会, Hawaii Association of Kindred Spirits) and Shosei-Kai (処世会, Holy Righteous Association), which were initially organized to help "bewildered" Japanese during the period of "mental and emotional confusion" following the war. These groups were to help them "pursue the proper course as Japanese and to educate other Japanese following erroneous paths."[31] One of the activities embraced by these organizations was the entertainment of Japanese prisoners of war incarcerated in Hawai'i.[32] As Mr. Inokuchi, an original member of Hawaii Dōshi-kai recalled: "Our group helped the Japanese prisoners of war in Kalihi camp. There were about 1000 Japanese men and officers. We took with us actors and actresses, musicians, etc., sometimes 70 or more of them at a time. We went there early and stayed there till nearly 11 P.M. We were not supposed to stay there too long but in the pretense of making preparations for the stage, etc., we often stayed there quite late."[33]

Although Inokuchi disputed the nationalistic orientation of his organization, he did acknowledge that there were individual members who believed in Japan's victory. The most aggressive group in propagating pro-Japanese notions was Hisshō-Kai (必勝会, Absolute Victory Group), which was known as a "*kattagumi,*" an organization that believed victory had been achieved. According to Tokuzo Shibayama, an advisor to Hisshō-Kai, the organization was "to give comfort and encouragement to the Japanese by telling them the truth."[34] After the end of the war, Shibayama noticed that "there were some who committed suicide, some who went insane and there was a lot of violence." Dismissing these actions as "foolish" as Japan had not lost the war, he and a few others who "knew the true situation decided to form a group and tell others the facts." Shibayama not only dismissed newspaper reports and radio broadcasts as "all false" but argued that San Francisco and San Diego were also under the jurisdiction of Japan while "Pearl Harbor is under the control of the Japanese navy" due to the invasion of Japanese forces in the Islands. Despite widespread criticism of his beliefs, Shibayama remained unshaken in his views:

> The society is topsy-turvy now. We are the only sane ones. Others are crazy and belong at Kaneohe. That picture on the wall was given to me on the 77th birthday by the first battalion of the Japanese army stationed at Schofield. There are three battalions on this island at present. Thousands of Japanese troops are camped at Mokapu. I don't know if you've heard this but MacArthur recently passed away at the Queen's hospital. He sustained serious battle wounds and was convalescing for a while at the Pearl Harbor naval hospital.[35]

Despite these outrageous claims, some Issei did pay membership dues and belonged to this group. Although exact figures are unavailable, the president of Hisshō-Kai claimed that the organization had between 3,500 and 4,000 members.[36] Others have provided more conservative figures of 1,000 total participants, with others holding memberships in other organizations.[37] While only formally disbanded in 1977—thirty-two years after Japan's official surrender—many of Hisshō-Kai's members became discouraged much earlier by the evident lack of truth in the claims espoused by its leaders. Membership declined after exposés by former members, and scathing articles and editorials published by the *Hawaii Times* led to a dramatic drop in membership.[38]

A decline in participation also stemmed from the disorganization and disagreements among the various groups and leaders that resulted in numerous split factions, many of which were left without a purpose after the departure of Japanese prisoners of war.[39] The growth in these organizations was not necessarily reflective of increasing support from the wider Japanese community but instead suggested a growing disillusionment and schisms among the members and leaders. The subsequent arrival in March 1946 of Earl M. Finch, the "patron saint" of Japanese American soldiers, also contributed to the decline of these organizations. All the major newspapers in the Territory—the English and Japanese press—extensively publicized his generosity and kindness to the Nisei from Hawai'i in training at Camp Shelby, Mississippi.[40] Acting governor Gerald R. Corbett and Honolulu mayor Lester Petrie welcomed Finch to 'Iolani Palace and City Hall. Nearly 1,500 veterans and their families feted him at a luau held for his benefit. The celebration surrounding Finch's arrival made it impossible for many individuals—some of whom were parents of veterans or knew families of veterans—to express their gratitude and appreciation while maintaining a pro-Japan stance.[41] Further, the publicity surrounding Finch's visit in both the English and Japanese language press included the first mention among nationalist groups of the merits of Nisei soldiers as opposed to Japanese soldiers fighting for the emperor.[42]

Finally, the arrival of returning inmates and veterans further eroded support for nationalistic movements among the Issei, as these groups expected public criticism of these activities.[43] Some of the incarcerated Buddhist priests found their temples utilized by nationalist leaders who had described them as "Communists," "pro-American," and "Having forgotten the 'On' [obligation] or the grace of their ancestral land and the emperor" to justify their authority over the congregation. Many inmates and their families who experienced discrimination and alienation from the larger Japanese community wondered why authorities had not arrested these fanatical leaders. Most prewar leaders, including businesspeople, newspaper editors, language school teachers, and priests, joined in the criticism of these nationalistic groups. They were seen as damaging to the Japanese community's reputation, the reintegration of the Japanese back into society, and the hard-fought gains made by the Nisei. The latter were also returning to the Islands.[44] Some who had fought in the Pacific theater of the war and who were active during the occupation of Japan—such as the Nisei in the MIS—also brought back newspapers, letters, and magazines from Japan that revealed the "destruction and misery in Japan," clearly contradicting stories of Japan's success.[45]

While most of the Nisei veterans from the European theater returned in small groups, the formal reception for the 442nd and the 100th was held on August 9, 1946, when the last 241 members of those units arrived and were transported in a sixty-car motorcade from the dock to ceremonies at 'Iolani Palace.[46] The return of Nisei veterans marked a fundamental shift in traditional dynamics, as they, not their parents, assumed leadership roles that were once the exclusive domain of the older generation. The postwar ascension of the Nisei was partly due to the efforts of the veterans, who successfully organized themselves into Club 100 and the 442nd Veterans Club, which became mobilized centers of support for returning veterans. These Nisei, having risked their lives and having been exposed to the larger world, were unwilling to return to their second-class status in society. Their rise in public and political life was ironically facilitated by the same government agencies responsible for the relocation and incarceration of the Japanese during the war. In the postwar period, they publicized the accomplishments of Nisei soldiers to ease the transition of returning inmates from the mainland.

Nisei Veterans

"We Wanted Our Place in the Sun"

When the War Department announced in January 1944 that Americans of Japanese ancestry would be called into military service by standard selective service procedures, it listed the "excellent showing" that the 442nd had made in training as a significant factor in this decision. Authorities also cited the "outstanding record" that the 100th had made in battle.[47] During the summer of 1944, the WRA began a campaign to counteract charges against the Japanese American population to enable the peaceful resettlement of inmates in previously restricted areas. To this end, the agency attempted to focus public attention on the essential issues of the program and "bring the full spotlight of publicity on the Nisei units."[48] This campaign was so effective that the WRA later reported that by the early fall of 1944, "it was no longer fashionable over most areas of the country to fling irresponsible accusations at the Japanese American people and to demand further restrictions of their liberties."[49] The WRA began emphasizing the military achievements of Nisei soldiers such as Ben Kuroki, a decorated aerial gunner who flew fifty-eight combat missions over both Europe and the Pacific, to secure acceptance for the West Coast evacuees trying to return home.[50] Kuroki's speeches received extensive positive media coverage, and later, he was profiled in *Time* magazine and featured on singer Ginny Simms's popular radio show.

In the fall of 1944, at WRA's request, the Army assigned Hawai'i-born Lt. Spark M. Matsunaga, one of the original members of the 100th Infantry Battalion, to that agency. Officials then scheduled him for speaking engagements before civic and professional clubs and religious groups in cities where the WRA was trying to find employment, housing, and acceptance for Japanese inmates. Matsunaga, who had been twice wounded and whom Army doctors had declared physically unfit for further combat, regaled audiences with stories of the bravery of Nisei soldiers and asked that their relatives in relocation centers be allowed to return to their homes. Matsunaga's stories deeply impacted his listeners, and one auditor commented that "the lieutenant's talk had inspired more tolerance in thirty minutes than other methods could in thirty years." Another remarked, "In the audience of which he had been a part, many persons had been unable to hold back their tears." A clergyman reported that "after Matsunaga's speech, men of his congregation had come to him to express shame for their previous attitudes toward AJAs."

Five other white officers—one from the 100th Infantry Battalion, three from the 442nd Regimental Combat Team, and one who had supervised the activities of Nisei interpreters in the Pacific theater of operations—were subsequently given similar assignments during the fall of 1944 and the spring of 1945 as increasing numbers of Japanese returned to their home communities on the Pacific coast, sparking widespread protests. The WRA reported that "the anti-evacuee elements of the west coast population employed practically every weapon short of lynching and murder to keep the people of Japanese ancestry from returning to the area."[51] In response to anti-Japanese sentiment, on June 15, 1945, Capt. George H. Grandstaff, then on leave from the 100th Infantry Battalion, wrote to the War Department from his home in Azusa, California, to ask if he could speak against these outrages to audiences throughout his home state. He explained the reason for his request:

> As one of the few white officers who have served with the Japanese American 100th Battalion for some two and a half years, my main interest is to see that the splendid work they have done in combat is called to the attention of the people of the Pacific Coast so that Japanese Americans who desire to return here may receive fair treatment.
>
> The thought in . . . [my] mind . . . was that a white officer who had lived in California most of his life could emphasize their splendid combat

> record as no Japanese American could. Racial prejudice would not enter the minds of the audience where I am concerned.[52]

The WRA reported that these speakers were some of the most effective tools in its campaign to rebuild the status of the incarcerated Japanese. They spoke in school auditoriums, before service club luncheons, and at a few community-wide gatherings. They also talked individually with respected and influential community members, such as chiefs of police, sheriffs, and local newspaper editors. Government officials reported on the success of this endeavor, explaining that "although they certainly did not succeed in eliminating anti-Nisei prejudice from the west coast region, they unquestionably dealt it one of the heaviest and most crippling blows which it has suffered since its birth in the early 1900s." Commenting on this transformation, WRA officials only noted that it "seems a little regrettable that this attitude could not have been expressed in the spring of 1942 and that so much Nisei blood had to be shed on the battlefields of Italy before it could gain widespread acceptance."[53]

White soldiers in outfits who had fought alongside Nisei soldiers contributed to the growing positive sentiment toward returning Japanese inmates as they responded vigorously when news of outbreaks of racial discrimination against evacuees reached them. In August 1945, every man in Company D, 168th Infantry, who had fought alongside the 100th Infantry Battalion from Salerno to the Arno River, signed the following statement:

> From Company D, 168th Regiment, 34th Division to the 100th Infantry Regiment, in appreciation of the heroic and meritorious achievements of our fellow Americans in the 100th Battalion and the 442nd Infantry Regiment, do hereby assert that our help can be counted on to convince the folks back home that you are fully deserving of all the privileges with which we are ourselves bestowed. It is a privilege and honor to acknowledge the members of the 100th Battalion and the 442nd Regiment as fellow Americans. We are duly proud to say "Well done" to you and yours.[54]

While many Nisei veterans from Hawai'i undoubtedly appreciated such sentiments, for most, their primary concern was their return to the Islands and their reentry into civilian life. However, their experiences during the war fundamentally changed these soldiers, and they were unwilling to accept their second-class status within society, particularly in light of the lives lost, to prove the loyalty of the Japanese community. The 100th Infantry Battalion and 442nd Regimental Combat Team accounted for 60 percent of Hawai'i's fighting forces and 80 percent of total casualties. Of the

7,500 men who joined either of these units, 5,000 were awarded medals, approximately 3,600 for battle wounds. Seven hundred died, 700 were maimed, and another 1,000 were seriously wounded.[55]

The Nisei who fought and died on the battlefields of Europe and the Pacific to defend the honor and loyalty of their people learned a great deal about Hawai'i and America in their experiences. Coming from an isolated island chain in the middle of the Pacific, they witnessed firsthand the racial segregation of southern towns while training in areas such as Camp Shelby, Mississippi. They observed the inferior position of poor whites who performed menial labor reserved for non-whites in the Islands and saw the widespread discrimination experienced by African Americans.[56] They also met the better-educated "kotonks," their fellow Nisei from the mainland, who were also in the 100th Infantry Batallion and 442nd Regiment. They heard them describe the opportunities available on the mainland and accompanied them when they visited their incarcerated families. "Most of all," according to one author, "they wondered quietly to themselves if they were fighting for mere acceptance or if, as warriors returning to Hawaii, they could assert their ambitions in politics and business."[57] By fighting and dying on behalf of the United States to prove their loyalty—something no other ethnic group had been asked to do—Japanese American soldiers believed they had earned their rightful place as equals within society. As 442nd Regimental Combat veteran and future Hawai'i senator Daniel Inouye explained:

> Well obviously after going through an experience of that nature where you saw your friends die every day, get wounded every day, keep in mind that we had more purple hearts per capita than any other regiment in the United States Army . . . we received more decorations for valor than any other comparable unit in the United States Army . . . it showed that we were involved in a lot of action . . . and whenever you do involve yourself in action, there is a lot of blood and having spilled that blood . . . we weren't ready to go back to the plantations.[58]

According to Inouye, after having experienced the horrors of war and having sacrificed countless lives to prove their loyalty, many Nisei veterans returned to the Islands with a new perspective and desire for change. "So we knew we were expendable," explained Inouye, "but we knew that we had to pay that price . . . and we were willing to pay that price . . . but once we paid that price we wanted our place in the sun." This desire for political, social, and economic change led many veterans to support the Democratic Party and align themselves with other prominent Nisei. They had emerged as leaders within the Japanese community during World War II. Due to the absence of traditional Issei leaders whom authorities had incarcerated and the war-spawned role reversal of traditional Japanese social patterns, prominent Nisei assumed leadership roles. During the war, they spearheaded organizations such as the Council for Inter-Racial Unity, Morale Committees, and the Emergency Service Committee. The latter organization led the way in demonstrating loyalty and Americanization by encouraging Nisei with dual citizenship to renounce their Japanese citizenship.[59] This group was mainly led by Nisei, including such prominent individuals as Supreme Court Justice Wilfred C. Tsukiyama, University of Hawai'i historian Shunzō Sakamaki, attorney Katsuro Miho, engineer Arthur Y. Akinaka, attorney Masaji Marumoto, and his one-time law partner Robert K. Murakami.[60] They aligned with former police officer John Burns due to his work with the Police Contact Group.

During the war, Burns also attended Emergency Service Committee meetings to assist in coordinating efforts to mobilize the Japanese community and reduce questions about Japanese loyalty. In the process, Burns grew increasingly involved within the Japanese community and made efforts to publicize the military contributions of Japanese Americans who had served in the Varsity Victory Volunteers, the 100th Infantry Battalion, and the 442nd Regimental Combat Team. During the war, Burns established key political alliances and critical community support within the ethnic population, particularly among the Nisei, who were granted new status with the arrest and incarceration of traditional leaders. Consequently, Burns benefited from his wartime activities as his involvement in the arrest and incarceration of Issei was consistent with the promotion of Americanization and his support of the Nisei. Thus, through his efforts within the Japanese community, Burns became acquainted with prominent Nisei. The latter became instrumental in his political aspirations, which came to fruition during the "Revolution of 1954" when Democrats seized control of the Territorial Legislature and ushered in a new era of social and racial equality in Hawai'i. The executive secretary of the Emergency Service Committee was Mitsuyuki "Mits" Kido, who in 1959 ran with Burns as a candidate for lieutenant governor. Kido first met Burns in the early days of the war, and by 1944, Burns, Kido, Edward Murai, Jack Kawano, and politician Chuck Mau met almost weekly to discuss plans for the postwar period. At that time, Kido recalled, "We asked each other, 'What the hell are we going to do when these kids come home.' . . . We said we would stand for equality of opportunity, regardless of race. We wanted acceptance as first-class citizens. Our second goal was to raise the standard of living and the standard of education."[61] They settled on the Democratic Party as the vehicle for challenging the white oligarchy that had maintained its political dominance in Hawai'i through the Republican Party.

After the war ended, Burns resigned from the Police Department, intent on reorganizing a party that had never controlled an elective body in the history of Hawai'i. Key to his success was the alliance Burns formed with a young Nisei veteran, Daniel Inouye, who convinced Dan Aoki, president of the 442nd Veterans Club, that the energies of its members could be used to improve the social and political status of Japanese in Hawai'i.[62] By 1948, after serving six years as O'ahu's Civil Defense director, Burns had gathered enough support to become the O'ahu Chairman of the Democratic Party. In the fall, he entered the nearly impossible race for Delegate to Congress against the popular Republican incumbent, Joseph Farrington. Burns lost, but he had established a core group of supporters: Matsuo Takabuki and Mike Tokunaga, Nisei veterans who had been raised on the plantations and became key party leaders; William Richardson, a part-Hawaiian who envisioned a Japanese-Hawaiian voting bloc to weaken white political control; and Sakae Takahashi, who was a veteran of the 100th Infantry Battalion and who in 1950 won a seat on the Honolulu Board of Supervisors and became the first Japanese American treasurer of the Territory.

As Burns rose from O'ahu chairman to Territorial Chairman of the Democratic Party, his supporters similarly gained in numbers and political positions as they "indefatigably exploited the accumulated resentments of Japanese, Chinese, Hawaiians, and Filipinos against the injustices, real and imagined, of the past."[63] In 1954, thirteen years after the bombing of Pearl Harbor, the now vital Democratic Party achieved victory, securing solid majorities in both houses of the legislature. That same year, Burns ran as a candidate for Delegate to Congress against Joseph Farrington's widow, Elizabeth Farrington, and lost by less than a thousand votes. Two years later, Burns beat Farrington in a landslide to win Hawai'i's most prestigious elective office. As a Democratic delegate in a Democrat-controlled congress, Burns cultivated the support of southern members of Congress, who were the leading opponents to Hawaiian statehood, by working with two influential Texans—House Speaker Sam Rayburn and Senate Majority Leader Lyndon B. Johnson. At risk to his political future, Burns supported the so-called Alaska Strategy, separating the question of statehood for Alaska and Hawai'i and allowing Alaska to go up for a vote first.

In April 1958, both houses of Congress passed a statehood resolution for Alaska, and on January 3, 1959, President Dwight D. Eisenhower signed the bill into law. That same year, the Hawai'i bill came out of committee, passing in the House by a 323 to 89 vote and a 76 to 15 margin in the Senate. At last, eighteen years after Pearl Harbor, Hawai'i's people were official American citizens. In the referendum, Hawai'i voters ratified statehood by an overwhelming margin of 17 to 1. But Burns, who had returned home to run for governor, lost to the incumbent Republican William Quinn by 4,000 votes. Burns bided his time for the next four years while maintaining his public profile. In his last act as a delegate, he introduced the newly elected congressman, Daniel Inouye, to the House, where House Speaker Sam Rayburn immediately took Inouye under his wing. As a Texan, he was "aware that a segregated all-Japanese unit," in which Inouye had served, had "rescued the Lost Battalion of Texans."[64] Rayburn not only extended political support to Inouye, offering to be Inouye's mentor but, as Inouye recalled, "early in my House career, he told me that I would always have a place at 'The Texas Table' in the House Dining Room." While Inouye began establishing his political career, Burns continued working out of Washington, trying to round up state delegations to support Lyndon Johnson's bid for the Democratic presidential nomination.

Two years later, Burns challenged Quinn in a rematch. He was partly helped by James Kealoha, Quinn's lieutenant governor. The latter had turned on Quinn and challenged him in the Republican primary, dividing the already dwindling resources of the Republican Party. This time, Burns won by a landslide. The vote was 114,000 for Burns and 82,000 for Quinn. Burns's victory proved emblematic of the growing political domination in Hawai'i of the Democratic Party and the rise of Japanese American veterans such as Daniel Inouye, Spark Matsunaga, and George Ariyoshi. For many, the 1950s marked a new era dominated by Nisei, who had capitalized on the GI Bill's educational opportunities and had taken advantage of political and economic opportunities.

In the postwar period, many Nisei entered professional occupations. They became teachers, doctors, and lawyers, while others took advantage of the tourism boom in the 1950s to enjoy unprecedented profits from businesses catering to the burgeoning tourist industry.[65] Consequently, destabilizing events, such as problems with recently discharged soldiers, existing military-local tensions, and returning Japanese inmates from mainland incarceration centers and Honouliuli, were strategically "forgotten" in the postwar victory culture. This erasure of Japanese incarceration in Hawai'i is consistent with comments made by media critic Marita Sturken, who argued that the "forgetting of the past in a culture is often highly organized and strategic" to create consensus, coherence, and historical continuity.[66] This need for continuity was particularly relevant in 1945 as the conclusion of World War II marked the beginning of a new era of uncertainty both locally and nationally with the start of the Cold War.[67] Hawai'i would continue to play an essential role in national and international events with the U.S. military expansion into Asia and the Pacific while simultaneously promoting its reputation as a tourist destination and newly granted status as a state. Ironically, the large number of non-whites in the Islands, including Japanese Americans, considered "unfit" and an "impediment" to statehood was recast as an asset. As scholar Christina Klein points out, "It was Hawaii's Asian population that held out the promise of securing access to the markets and resources of Asia," particularly during the Cold War.[68]

Additionally, part of the value of Hawai'i's statehood was that the Island's large Asian American population was considered an intermediary between the historic racial tension between whites and blacks. Scholar Dean Itsuji Saranillio notes how the efforts of Japanese Americans in the 442nd Regimental Combat Team and 100th Infantry Battalion to prove their loyalty and assimilability also helped statehood proponents to "further argue for statehood by working through racial difference, not extinguishing it."[69] Thus, specific members of the Japanese community were celebrated in the postwar era for their military contributions. In contrast, others who had endured wartime incarceration were relegated to a footnote in official wartime histories. Ironically, as the military and tourism industry became cornerstones of Hawai'i's economy, both depended on promoting Hawai'i's military and local culture, minimizing racial conflict that existed in the past, and highlighting the loyalty of the multicultural population who resided in the Islands, particularly the Japanese.

The financial, political, and social mobility of the Nisei during the postwar period and the subsequent rise of the third, fourth, and fifth generations of Japanese Americans stands in sharp contrast to the history of struggle, conflict, resistance, and negotiation that characterized the first century of the history of the Japanese in the Islands. In contrast to the dominant historical narrative that has focused almost exclusively on the military accomplishments of the Nisei that marked their entry into middle-class American respectability, the history of the early years of the Japanese in Hawai'i suggests a counter-narrative far more contentious and complicated. Thus, simply recreating another social history of Japanese cultural achievements and success despite early discrimination and incarceration excludes the possibility of a more detailed understanding of this era and the evolution of Japanese identity.

The postwar period marked a dramatic transformation in the dominant perception of Japanese Americans in Hawai'i, but at the expense of inmates, repatriates from Japan, and even Issei nationalists who did not fit into this unblemished narrative of loyalty and bravery. Yet, these populations highlighted challenges to the authority of white elites and military officials that were consistent with the American ideals of protest and the assertion of personal liberties. Thus, their experiences are crucial to understanding Japanese American struggles for inclusion and equality and highlight the historical agency of individuals from the plantations fields to the incarceration centers in Hawai'i and beyond. It also challenges the assumption of Hawai'i incarceration as a benign alternative to the mass incarceration of Japanese communities on the mainland. Rather, incarceration in Hawai'i should be understood as a targeted strategy of military and civil authorities driven by equally virulent racist fears that emerged from the plantations and allowed them to flourish under the justification of "military necessity" with the outbreak of war. Hawai'i incarceration also mirrored the military roundup of Issei community members on the mainland prior to Executive Order 9066 as a strategy to weaken the ethnic population. Hawai'i incarceration thus reflected past and current racial fears not just in Hawai'i but throughout America of the threat the Japanese allegedly posed to civil authority and military security. These fears ultimately came to "justify" the infringement of their civil liberties and the political, social, and economic disenfranchisement of Japanese in Hawai'i and the mainland. Japanese incarceration thus challenged official proclamations of American ideals of freedom, equality, and justice that were used to counter the ideologies of Nazism and Fascism in wars fought in Europe and the Pacific. Even today, these narratives highlight American exceptionalism in national and international affairs; thus, understanding the experience of minorities during periods of conflict remains critical in reminding and reaffirming civil liberties and rights that are the foundation of a democratic society.

Conclusion

With the evolution of the Japanese American community, which has become increasingly ethnically diverse, Hawaiʻi's incarceration story has begun to take on meaning not just for Japanese Americans but for multiple groups and communities. Understanding the experience of these inmates has become not just a personal story of reconciliation within their families but communities impacted by war. The fact that incarceration occurred in Hawaiʻi is particularly noteworthy as people of Japanese ancestry constituted the largest ethnic group in the Islands and were an integral part of many communities. However their numbers did not protect against racist rhetoric and prewar fears on the plantation that culminated in martial law and the incarceration of community leaders.

Incarceration was not simply a wartime policy to ensure internal security as it originated within the plantations of Hawaiʻi, where Japanese laborers first embarked upon resistance. Workers resisted individually and collectively against planters' efforts to solidify their authority in the "contested terrain" of the plantations. As migrants, Japanese workers were legally Japanese citizens, yet subject to the laws of the kingdom and later Territory of Hawaiʻi. They were also obligated to fulfill the conditions of their labor contracts. These overlapping and sometimes conflicting responsibilities often seemed contrary to the personal aspirations that initially compelled them to leave Japan to seek new opportunities and a better life. In this nebulous legal context, the Japanese encountered a dual justice system that many authors have argued subjected migrants to social, legal, and economic discrimination. Within this biased system, authorities often prosecuted Japanese to the fullest extent of the law, whether or not they had committed the alleged crime. At the same time, whites charged with similar offenses were often never arrested or avoided full punishment for their crimes. Scholars have extensively detailed the vast hardships experienced by these workers. Japanese migrants were essentially indentured servants who worked for little pay, labored under harsh working conditions, and had little legal recourse to protest such discriminatory policies, unfair treatment, and abuse. This argument has generally explained plantation violence, strikes, and sensational crimes involving Japanese residents, such as the Fukunaga kidnapping, Massie case, and incarceration.

However, a closer look at these events and others throughout this period reveals a much more complex and nuanced view that challenges the underlying theme of Japanese victimhood in the face of absolute white authority. Within the unique environment of Hawai'i, populated by a diversity of ethnicities, these migrants were given tantalizing opportunities within the Islands' recently established legal, economic, and social institutions to challenge their oppression to a degree that scholars have recently begun to recognize. This dual system of justice was never wholly established to the satisfaction of whites as migrants were never entirely disenfranchised, nor were whites free from prosecution for their crimes. In this context, it is essential to recognize that the Japanese were not just victims of labor disputes, as the Massie trial and incarceration attested. They were also active agents in their lives, as Nisei soldiers' exploits in Europe and the Pacific indicated. Some Japanese on the plantations perpetrated crimes to resist political, social, and economic oppression. They faced swift punishment for their challenges to white authority within Hawai'i's dual system of justice. Taking a cue from their white oppressors, they resorted to extralegal means of justice, such as beatings of white sympathizers, attacks against plantation authorities, and even murders of whites that demonstrated the weakness of this legal system.

Yet the fact that whites faced trial and other whites collaborated and assisted Japanese and other ethnic groups suggests that this dual system of justice was never fully established and implemented to the satisfaction of elite whites or the military. Within this biased legal system, many expressed outrage at the often blatant miscarriages of justice and fought with considerable effort and dedication on behalf of Japanese defendants. In the process, they risked their political, economic, and social standing. It is important to remember that not all whites sanctioned racial privilege in the law. Some Japanese were even complicit in perpetuating this legal imbalance by testifying against Japanese defendants in exchange for payment and rewards. Many in the Islands did not embrace such a balanced perspective, though. These events collectively spurred repeated calls for American military intervention to protect white interests in Hawai'i as civilian and military elites increasingly aligned with one another over shared interests.

It is important to note that not a single act of espionage was committed by a Japanese in Hawai'i, as numerous studies have indicated, making martial law unnecessary as a matter of objective concerns about security and defense. In addition, the nature of incarceration under martial law was much more authoritarian and restrictive than in the United States. It provided insights into the underlying motives driving martial law and imprisonment in Hawai'i. The enactment of martial law in

Hawai'i represented a crisis in constitutional rights that reflected long-term racial fears among military personnel and select members of the Islands' white elite who shared concerns about the Japanese population.

The twentieth century marked America's entry into two world wars, the building of various military bases on the Islands, including Pearl Harbor, and the establishment of close ties between military officials and elite whites. However, alliances between white leaders and military authorities were unstable as their interests both coalesced and diverged. White elites in the Islands needed to cultivate American political, economic, and military support—particularly as the dual system of justice seemed so unreliable—but they also had their own interests and desired recognition of their authority. White elites saw local labor events such as the 1909 and 1920 strikes involving the Japanese as attacks against planter hegemony. Labor activism also became associated with national threats to America, such as the "Yellow Peril" and the "Red Scare" that renewed calls for military intervention in the Islands. White elites utilized the threatening specter of Japanese criminality and radicalism to support the enactment of discriminatory national legislation such as the Gentlemen's Agreement Act of 1907, the dismissal of Takao Ozawa's petition for citizenship in 1922, and the Immigration Act of 1924 to shore up their authority and control over ethnic workers. Yet, at the same time, they were also critical of threats of commission control during the Massie case and the enactment of martial law in the immediate aftermath of the bombing of Pearl Harbor that dissolved the civil government and threatened their position of social privilege and power in the Islands. Not all whites attempted to marginalize and disenfranchise the Japanese in Hawai'i. Many fought at great personal sacrifice and expense to demand social, legal, and economic rights for the Japanese and to protest against their oppression.

Similarly, the Japanese were never a homogenous entity, and the population was fraught with class, citizenship, and generational differences that often divided them over labor and legal rights, cultural practices, and community authority. However, at the outbreak of war, many ignored these nuances. Authorities regarded the Japanese as inherently dangerous and a threat to the national security of their race. Thus, following the Pearl Harbor attack, military officials targeted the leaders of the Japanese community for incarceration, including newspaper journalists, language school teachers, businesspeople, lawyers, and priests. The purpose was to break the leadership of the community and instill fear in others. While this strategy was a success, it also ushered in a new generation of leaders, the Nisei, who had grown up in fundamentally different circumstances from their Issei parents, having attended American schools, been infused with American values, and being entitled to American citizenship.

During World War II, these Nisei became keenly aware of the contradiction of swearing allegiance and demonstrating loyalty to the country of their birth through military service. At the same time, their Issei parents languished in incarceration centers. Some resisted the military draft and became infamous as "no-no" boys and repatriates, who remain stigmatized by the larger Japanese community today. They represented the most extreme instances of disillusionment and perceived disloyalty, even though they questioned loyalty to a country that demanded acquiescence to injustice. Others, however, such as military veterans of the 100th Infantry Battalion, 442nd Regimental Combat Team, and Military Intelligence Service (MIS), undoubtedly profited from their ties to Japan and the United States. Many brought Japanese and American values with them when they successfully fought on World War II's European and Pacific fronts. On the home front, other Nisei assumed leadership roles during the war that their Issei parents had abandoned with the onset of hostilities and incarceration. In Hawai'i, they spearheaded Americanization campaigns, blood drives, and bond purchases for the American military. While some were coerced and intimidated by martial law and the threat of incarceration, many expressed honest patriotism and sincere sentiments for American victory. Yet the postwar rise of the Nisei and the rights and respect accorded to the second generation came as a result of the heroic efforts and sacrifices made on the home front and battlefield and did so at the expense of the rights and respect traditionally accorded to the older generation—their Issei parents. Their history, however, should not be seen as one of surrender and acceptance but instead as one of struggle and resistance.

These complicated events must also be understood as localized events within an isolated island chain and as part of national and international events affecting Japan, the United States, and Hawai'i. They represent a history fraught with challenges, strife, and struggle, an account that is balanced against and alongside the officially sanctioned history of Japanese American triumph and ethnic harmony. The isolation, marginalization, and alienation experienced by migrants in the prewar period fanned long-standing anxiety over the largest ethnic population that, like the Hawaiian Islands, stood at a critical juncture between East and West. Despite the Nisei proving the allegiance of the Japanese people in Hawai'i through heroic self-sacrifice and effort for the United States, the Japanese did not emerge unscathed as repatriates, inmates, and disillusioned Issei challenged this traditional triumphalist narrative. While many did enjoy their "place in the sun" in the postwar period, others struggled with memories of being "frozen to death in the cold, windy, and barren field" of Sand Island incarceration center.[1]

Notes

Introduction

1. "Mr. Kaetsu Furuya, Japanese Internment and Relocation: The Hawaii Experience," University of Hawai'i, Hamilton Library, Special Collections [JIRHE], Item 233, 2.

2. Yukiko Kimura, "Some Effects of the War Situation Upon the Alien Japanese in Hawaii," *Social Processes in Hawaii* 8 (November 1943): 18.

3. Harry N. Scheiber and Jane L. Scheiber, *Bayonets in Paradise: Martial Law in Hawai'i During World War II* (Honolulu: University of Hawai'i Press, 2016), 4.

4. Scheiber and Scheiber, *Bayonets in Paradise*, 336.

5. Gary Y. Okihiro, *Cane Fires: The Anti-Japanese Movement in Hawaii, 1865–1945* (Philadelphia: Temple University Press, 1991); Claire Sato and Violet Harada, *A Resilient Spirit: The Voice of Hawai'i's Internees* (Honolulu: Japanese Cultural Center of Hawai'i, 2018).

6. Dennis M. Ogawa and Christine Kitano, *Who You? Hawaii Issei* (Honolulu: Japanese Cultural Center of Hawai'i, 2018).

7. Richard Edwards, *Contested Terrain: The Transformation of the Workplace in the Twentieth Century* (New York: Basic Books, Inc., 1979).

8. Edward D. Beechert, *Working in Hawaii: A Labor History* (Honolulu: University of Hawai'i Press, 1985); Ronald Takaki, *Pau Hana: Plantation Life and Labor in Hawaii, 1835–1920* (Honolulu: University of Hawai'i Press, 1983).

9. One of the first large-scale strikes in Hawaiian history involving Japanese workers was the 1909 strike that set an important precedent for white officials to criminally prosecute leaders of a strike in a strategy that would be replicated during World War II. Kelli Y. Nakamura, "'Violence and Press Incendiarism': Media and Labor Conflicts in the 1909 Strike," *Hawaiian Journal of History* 45 (2011): 69–99. For further information on the 1920 strike that had been the largest inter-ethnic strike involving Japanese and Filipino workers see: Masayo Duus, *The Japanese Conspiracy: The Oahu Sugar Strike of 1920* (Berkeley: University of California Press, 1999).

10. United States, Department of the Interior Bureau of Education, *A Survey of Education in Hawaii* 16 (1920): 134.

11. Noriko Asato, *Teaching Mikadoism: The Attack on Japanese Language Schools in Hawaii, California, and Washington, 1919–1927* (Honolulu: University of Hawai'i Press, 2006), 23.

12. Vaughan MacCaughey, "Some Outstanding Educational Problems of Hawaii," *School and Society* 9 (January 1919): 100–101. During this period the Japanese population in Hawai'i was slowly becoming more Americanized despite claims to the contrary. About 29,000 first- and second-generation Japanese registered with the Selective Service out of 71,280 registrants in the Territory following the passage of the Selective Service Draft Act on June 18, 1917. Previously, Japanese had been prohibited from joining the National Guard but that restriction had been modified when Congress lifted the restrictions preventing "friendly aliens" from volunteering. On August 17, 1917, 838 Japanese were accepted into the Japanese Company or "Company D" of the First Regiment of the National Guard of Hawaii. "D" Company did not get a chance to engage in active combat but the *Pacific Commercial Advertiser* reported on their "loyalty to the American flag" and on "the enthusiasm displayed by the Japanese." "New National Guard Unit Will Be Crack Organization, Says Its Captain," *Pacific Commercial Advertiser,* 15 August 1917, 1.

13. Eileen H. Tamura, *Americanization, Acculturation, and Ethnic Identity: The Nisei Generation in Hawaii* (Urbana: University of Illinois Press, 1994), 52.

14. Jonathan Y. Okamura, *Raced to Death in 1920s Hawai'i: Injustice and Revenge in the Fukunaga Case* (Urbana: University of Illinois Press, 2019); David E. Stannard, *Honor Killing: Race, Rape, and Clarence Darrow's Spectacular Last Case* (New York: Penguin, 2006).

15. Shigehiko Shiramizu, "Ethnic Press and Its Society: A Case of Japanese Press in Hawaii," *KEIO Communication Review* 11 (1990): 49–71.

16. Gwenfread Allen, *Hawaii's War Years: 1941–1945* (Honolulu: The Advertiser Publishing Co., Ltd, 1950), 65.

17. Okihiro, *Cane Fires,* 196.

18. Allen, *Hawaii's War Years,* 68.

19. John J. Stephan, *Hawaii Under the Rising Sun: Japan's Plans for Conquest After Pearl Harbor* (Honolulu: University of Hawai'i Press, 1984), 23–24.

20. According to an Army document, the CIC and its predecessor the CIP (Corps of Intelligence Police) had been investigating suspicious activity years before the FBI. By 1942, the CIC was granted complete authority over all investigations through an agreement reached by the CIC, FBI, and Office of Naval Intelligence. "History of the G-2 Section Part II," Japanese Internment and Relocation: The Hawaii Experience, University of Hawai'i, Hamilton Library, Special Collections [JIRHE], Item 230, 23.

21. "History of the G-2 Section Part II," 13.

22. This CIC unit was initially known as the Contact Office; later it operated as the Counter Intelligence Division, first for the Hawaiian Department G-2, then successively

for the Central Pacific Area and Central Pacific Base Command G-2s and MIDPAC. Headquarters for the counterintelligence division were in the Dillingham Building in Downtown Honolulu. There were also branches on the three major outer islands—Hawai'i, Maui, and Kaua'i—and each had two officers and between two to four resident agents. "History of the G-2 Section Part II," 14.

23. "History of the G-2 Section Part I," Item 229, 8.

24. By February 1942, an agreement had been formally reached by the CIC, FBI, and Office of Naval Intelligence (ONI). Under the terms of the agreement, the CIC was given responsibility for the internal security of the Territory. All cases of espionage, treason, sabotage, and other "subversive activities" were made the responsibility of the CIC with the exception of those taking place on naval reservations or in which naval personnel were involved. Investigations of "disaffection cases," cases that resulted in internment, were thus the responsibility of the CIC. "History of the G-2 Section Part II," Item 230, 23.

25. Robert L. Shivers, *Cooperation of the Various Racial Groups with Each Other and with the Constituted Authorities before and after December 7, 1941. Statement Presented before Sub-Committee on Statehood United States House of Representative at Iolani Palace. Honolulu, Hawaii, U.S.A., January 15, 1946* (Honolulu: Chamber of Commerce, 1946), 5.

26. The Morale Section of the Office of the Military Governor had already appointed various racial "morale" committees to work among their respective groups. Authorities delegated the Emergency Service Committee to work among those of Japanese ancestry on O'ahu. Office of the Military Governor, Morale Section, Emergency Service Committee. *Report of the Emergency Service Committee* (Honolulu: N.p., 1944), 1.

27. Andrew Lind, *The Japanese in Hawaii Under War Conditions* (Honolulu: American Council Institute of Pacific Relations, 1943), 30.

28. Allen, *Hawaii's War Years*, 83.

29. Organic Act, Ch. 339, 31 Stat. 141, § 67 (1900), https://www.doi.gov/sites/doi.gov/files/uploads/31_stat_141_hawaiian_organic_act_1900.pdf.

30. J. Garner Anthony, *Hawaii Under Army Rule* (Honolulu: University Press of Hawai'i, 1955), 9.

31. J. Garner Anthony, "Martial Law in Hawaii," *California Law Review* 30.4 (May 1942): 371–396. See also: "Anthony dies—argued against Isle martial law." *Honolulu Advertiser*, November 3, 1982, 16; "Martial Law, Military Government, and the Writ of Habeas Corpus in Hawaii," *California Law Review* 31, no. 5 (December 1943): 477–514; "J.G. Anthony, Martial Law Foe, Is Dead at 82," *Honolulu Star-Bulletin*, November 2, 1982, 1.

32. Harry N. Scheiber and Jane L. Scheiber, "Constitutional Liberty in World War II: Army Rule and Martial Law in Hawaii: 1941–1946," *Western Legal History* 3, no. 2 (1990): 345.

33. Various criticisms were made of the provost courts: that for many months they operated in secret session, except in the city of Honolulu; that the judge was often without legal training; that a copy of the charges was not given to the accused, although the accused was allowed to read the prosecution's copy at the beginning of the trial; that the aid of counsel and cross-examination were discouraged; that the proceedings were summary, a trial rarely exceeding thirty minutes in length; that the defendants were convicted of violating "the spirit of martial law" or "the spirit" of general orders when the text was found inadequate; that one provost judge, appointed on an island exclusively occupied by a large plantation, was the general manager of the plantation. Walter P. Armstrong, "Martial Law in Hawaii," *American Bar Association* 29 (December 1943): 701.

34. Scheiber and Scheiber, "Constitutional Liberty in World War II," 346.

35. Between 1935 and 1937 General George S. Patton Jr. served as Chief of U.S. Army Intelligence in Hawai'i, preparing a secret plan that called for "[the] arrest and intern [of] certain persons of the Orange race who are considered most inimical to American interests, or those whom, due to their position and influence in the Orange community, it is desirable to retain as hostages." By arresting certain individuals Patton hoped to guarantee the quiescence of Hawai'i's 151,000 member Japanese community in the event of war with Japan. Included in this plan was a list of names of certain individuals the military would target with the onset of war as well as their occupation, address, and telephone number. Although the influence of this document on military policy during the war is unknown, it set precedence for Green's own plan based on the military's racial fears of the Japanese. Michael Slackman, "The Orange Race: George S. Patton, Jr.'s Japanese American Hostage Plan," *Biography: An Interdisciplinary Quarterly* 7, no. 1 (Winter 1984): 25.

36. Anthony, *Hawaii Under Army Rule*, 10.

37. Scheiber and Scheiber, "Constitutional Liberty in World War II," 349.

38. Greg Robinson, *A Tragedy of Democracy: Japanese Confinement in North America* (New York: Columbia University Press, 2009), 225–244.

39. "History of the G-2 Section Part II," Item 230, 23.

40. Yukiko Kimura, "Some Effects of the War Situation Upon the Alien Japanese in Hawaii," 18.

41. Dorothy Swaine Thomas, Richard S. Nishimoto, and Jacobus TenBroek, *The Spoilage: Japanese-American Evacuation and Resettlement During World War II* (Berkeley: University of California Press, 1946); Forrest Emmanuel La Violette, *Americans of Japanese Ancestry, a Study of Assimilation in the American Community* (Toronto: Canadian Institute of International Affairs, 1945); Sue Kunitomi Embrey, *The Lost Years, 1942–1946* (Los Angeles: Moonlight Publications, 1972); Leonard Broom and John I. Kitsuse, *The Managed Casualty: The Japanese-American Family in World War II*

(Berkeley: University of California Press, 1973); Dorothy Swaine Thomas, Charles Kikuchi, and James Minoru Sakoda, *The Salvage* (Berkeley: University of California Press, 1975); Michi Weglyn, *Years of Infamy: The Untold Story of America's Concentration Camps* (New York: William Morrow and Company, Inc., 1976).

42. Yukiko Kimura, "Some Effects of the War Situation Upon the Alien Japanese in Hawaii," 18–28; Yuriko Hatanaka and Kimie Kawahara, "The Impact of War on an Immigrant Culture," *Social Process in Hawaii* 8 (November 1943): 36–45.

43. One of the earliest books on Hawaiʻi incarceration was *Hawaii: End of the Rainbow* written by Kazuo Miyamoto (1897–1988), a Nisei doctor and author who was detained at various incarceration camps for the duration of World War II as a result of the publication of his observations during the Second Sino-Japanese War (1937–1945). During his incarceration at Sand Island, Miyamoto began writing *Hawaii: End of the Rainbow*, which took him seventeen years to complete. Although a fictional account of the experiences of Japanese immigrants spanning nearly seventy years from their arrival in the Islands to World War II, it provides key insights from a participant in these important events. Kazuo Miyamoto, *Hawaii: End of the Rainbow* (Rutland, VT: Bridgeway Press [distributed by C. E. Tuttle], 1964).

44. *Honouliuli Special Resource Study, Honolulu, Maui, Hawaii, and Kauai Counties, HI. Interior Department Documents and Publications* (Washington, DC: Federal Information & News Dispatch, LLC), 2011; *Honouliuli Gulch and Associated Sites Special Resource Study* (Honolulu: National Park Service, U.S. Department of the Interior), 2014.

45. Yasutaro Soga, *Life Behind Barbed Wire: The World War II Internment Memoirs of a Hawaiʻi Issei* (Honolulu: University of Hawaiʻi Press, 2007); Gail Honda, ed., *Family Torn Apart: The Internment Story of the Otokichi Muin Ozaki Family* (Honolulu: Japanese Cultural Center of Hawai'i, 2012); George Hoshida and Tamae Hoshida, *Taken from the Paradise Isle: The Hoshida Family Story* (Boulder: University Press of Colorado, 2015); Suikei Furuya, *An Internment Odyssey Haisho Tenten* (Honolulu: Japanese Cultural Center of Hawaiʻi, 2017).

46. Gail Y. Okawa, *Remembering Our Grandfathers' Exile: US Imprisonment of Hawaiʻi's Japanese in World War II* (Honolulu: University of Hawaiʻi Press, 2020); Tom Coffman, *Tadaima! I Am Home: A Transnational Family History* (Honolulu: University of Hawaiʻi Press, 2018); Pamela Rotner Sakamoto, *Midnight in Broad Daylight: A Japanese American Family Caught Between Two Worlds* (New York: HarperCollins, 2016); Hoshida and Hoshida, *Taken from the Paradise Isle.*

47. Gary Y. Okihiro, *Encyclopedia of Japanese American Internment* (Santa Barbara, CA: Greenwood, An Imprint of ABC-CLIO, LLC, 2013), 241.

48. Dennis M. Ogawa, *Kodomo No Tame Ni: For the Sake of the Children: The Japanese American Experience in Hawaii* (Honolulu: University of Hawaiʻi Press, 1978), 283.

Chapter 1: Deconstructing Hawai'i's Racial Paradise

1. Romanzo Adams Social Research Laboratory, *Race Relations in a Plantation Community* (Honolulu: N.p. [1979]), 3.

2. Dennis Ogawa, *Kodomo No Tame Ni: For the Sake of the Children* (Honolulu: University of Hawai'i Press, 1978), 7.

3. Alan Takeo Moriyama, "Imingaisha: Japanese Emigration Companies and Hawaii, 1894–1908" (PhD diss., University of California, Los Angeles, 1982), 35.

4. Andrew Lind, "Assimilation in Rural Hawaii," *American Journal of Sociology* 45, no. 2 (September 1939): 200–214; John F. Embree, "New Local and Kin Groups Among the Japanese Farmers of Kona, Hawaii," *American Anthropologist* 41, no. 3 (July–Sept. 1939): 400–407.

5. John F. Embree, *Acculturation Among the Japanese of Kona, Hawaii* (Menasha, WI: The American Anthropological Association, 1941; repr., New York, Kraus, 1969), 21.

6. Embree, *Acculturation Among the Japanese of Kona, Hawaii,* 31; Larry K. Stephenson and Amy A. Miyashiro, "Rural-Urban Contrasts of *Kumiai's* in Hawaii," *Social Process in Hawaii* 27 (1979): 78–80; "Hawaiian Sugar Plantation History: No. 12—Waiakea Island of Hawaii," *Honolulu Star-Bulletin,* 18 May 1935, Sec. 2, page 8; *Waiakea Town, or, "Yashijima Story": Home of the Waiakea Pirates* (Hilo: N.p., 1994).

7. *Waiakea Town, or, "Yashijima story": Home of the Waiakea Pirates* (Hilo: N.p., 1994).

8. Robert L. Cushing, "The Beginnings of Sugar Production in Hawai'i," *Hawaiian Journal of History* 19 (1985): 29–30.

9. Nancine "Missy" Kamai, William H. Folk, and Hallett H. Hammatt, "Final Archaeological Literature Review and Field Inspection Report for the Po'ipū Road Multi-Modal Improvements Project Kōloa and Weliweli Ahupua'a, Kōloa District, Kaua'i TMKs: multiple 34–36" (Kailua: Cultural Surveys Hawai'i, Inc., April 2021): 34–36.

10. Carol Wilcox, *Sugar Water: Hawaii's Plantation Ditches* (Honolulu: University of Hawai'i Press, 1996), 46.

11. United States Bureau of the Census, *Preliminary Figures on Employment Status, Occupation, and Industry for the Japanese Population of the Territory of Hawaii: 1940* (Washington, DC: Bureau of the Census, [1942]), 2.

12. Tim Klass, *World War II on Kauai: Historical Research by Tim Klass.* Prepared for the Kaua'i Historical Society by the Westland Foundation (Portland, OR: The Westland Foundation, 1970), 8.

13. Klass, *World War II on Kauai,* 9.

14. Hawaiian Sugar Planters' Association, *The Sugar Industry of Hawaii and the Labor Shortage* (Honolulu: HSPA, 1921), 37.

15. Ronald Takaki, *Pau Hana: Plantation Life and Labor in Hawaii, 1835–1920* (Honolulu: University of Hawai'i Press, 1983), 64.

16. Takaki, *Pau Hana,* 65.

17. "Bonus Payments Are Looked Into by Consul Mori," *Honolulu Star-Bulletin,* 27 October 1916, 4.

18. *Pioneer Mill Company: A Maui Sugar Plantation Legacy* (Honolulu: Center for Oral History, Social Science Research Institute, University of Hawai'i at Mānoa, 2003), 254.

19. Rita Goldman, *Every Grain of Rice: Portraits of Maui's Japanese Community* (Virginia Beach: The Donning Company, 2003), 35.

20. This term was likely first used in 1928 by the Japanese press to contrast the trial of Myles Fukunaga—who was tried, convicted, and sentenced for the murder of Gill Jamieson in 1928 within five days—with the experiences of whites who committed similar crimes and who were often acquitted or never charged. During the trial, the *Hawaii Hochi* alleged that "there are two kinds of justice in Hawaii" for ethnics and whites. "A Desperate Expedient," *Hawaii Hochi: The Bee Section,* 20 October 1928, 2; Dennis M. Ogawa, *Jan Ken Po: The World of Hawaii's Japanese* (Honolulu: University of Hawai'i Press, 1973), 145.

21. By 1893, a total of 3,239 foreigners had become naturalized citizens, including 1,105 Americans, 763 Chinese, 596 British, 242 Portuguese, 230 Germans, 47 French, 68 other Europeans, 136 Pacific Islanders, 27 South Americans, 3 Japanese, and 25 of other ancestry. Jon M. Van Dyke, *Who Owns the Crown Lands of Hawai'i* (Honolulu: University of Hawai'i Press, 2008), 140.

22. Gavan Daws, *Shoal of Time: A History of the Hawaiian Islands* (Honolulu: University of Hawai'i Press, 1968), 252. For a copy of the 1887 Constitution consult *Constitutions of Hawaii* (Washington, DC: N.p., 1898), 9–18.

23. Ralph Kuykendall, *The Hawaiian Kingdom,* vol. III: *1874–1893, The Kalakaua Dynasty* (Honolulu: University of Hawai'i Press, 1967), 453.

24. Noel J. Kent, *Hawaii, Islands Under the Influence* (New York: Monthly Review Press, 1983), 60–61.

25. Kuykendall, *The Hawaiian Kingdom,* vol. III, 370, 406–407.

26. United States, Congress, Senate, Committee on Pacific Islands and Porto Rico, *Report of the Subcommittee on Pacific Islands and Porto Rico on General Conditions in Hawaii* (Washington, DC: U.S. Government Printing Office, 1903), 214.

27. The Big Five is the name given to a group of former sugar companies that wielded considerable political power in the Territory of Hawai'i and was associated with the Hawai'i Republican Party. The Big Five was comprised of Castle & Cooke, Alexander & Baldwin, C. Brewer & Co., Amfac, and Theo H. Davies & Co.

28. Okihiro, *Cane Fires,* 58.

29. Thomas C. Hobson, *Hawaiian Almanac and Annual for 1898* (Honolulu: Thomas G. Thrum, 1897), 131–134; Richard Austin Thompson, *The Yellow Peril, 1890–1924* (New York: Arno Press, 1978).

30. Ray Stannard Baker, "Wonderful Hawaii: A World Experiment Station," *American Magazine* 73 (December 1911): 201–214.

31. Peter J. Nelligan and Harry V. Ball, *Ethnic Juries in Hawai'i, 1825–1990* (Honolulu: The Friends of The Judiciary History Center, 1996), 44.

32. Okihiro, *Cane Fires,* 28–29.

33. Sally Engle Merry, *Colonizing Hawai'i: The Cultural Power of Law* (Princeton, NJ: Princeton University Press, 2000), 8.

34. James H. Okahata, ed., *A History of the Japanese in Hawaii* (Honolulu: United Japanese Society of Hawaii, 1971), 123.

35. Hawai'i State Archives, "002 Criminal Case Files of the First Circuit Court Criminal 1430," Series 002, First Circuit Court, 7 May 1890.

36. "Supreme Court—January Term," *Polynesian,* 8 January 1853, 2.

37. Kamehameha III appointed Chief Justice William Little Lee who served as Hawai'i's first chief justice of the Superior Court of Law and Equity from 1848 to 1857. Lee had a profound effect on the development of Hawai'i's political system by establishing the groundwork for the Māhele, drafting the Constitution of 1852, and writing Hawai'i's first comprehensive criminal and civil codes, including the *Masters & Servants Act.* Lee also served as a trustee of Punahou School and was the founder and president of the Royal Hawaiian Agricultural Society.

38. Richard Edwards, *Contested Terrain: The Transformation of the Workplace in the Twentieth Century* (New York: Basic Books, Inc., 1979).

39. Hawaii State Archives, "Island Sheriffs, vol. 5, Hawaii 1889, Police Records," Series 364; Hawaii State Archives, "Letters Received from Sheriff of Hawaii," Series 363, October–December 1889.

40. The community bathhouse and boardinghouse often functioned as gathering places for the early Japanese community. Proprietors of these establishments, who were often educated individuals, served as the letter writers, mailmen, and interpreters for the laborers. These early businessmen also handled legal matters and interpreted American practices. Misako Yamamoto, "Cultural Conflicts and Accommodations of the First and Second Generation Japanese," *Social Process in Hawaii* 4 (May 1938): 41.

41. Okahata, *A History of the Japanese in Hawaii,* 129.

42. Okahata, *A History of the Japanese in Hawaii,* 125.

43. John E. Reineicke, *Labor Disturbances in Hawaii, 1890–1925: A Summary* (Honolulu: N.p., 1966).

44. *Pacific Commercial Advertiser,* 28 July 1866, 1.

45. "Chinese Riot on a Plantation," *Pacific Commercial Advertiser,* 4 October 1879, 3.

46. *Saturday Press,* 12 March 1881, 2.

47. *Maui News,* 18 August 1900, 2.

48. Original accounts of this attack were lost and were reprinted in later editions. "Luna's Abuse Provoked Workers," *Honolulu Record,* 16 October 1952, 8.

49. "Murderous Filipino Attacks His Luna," *Pacific Commercial Advertiser,* 27 June 1915, 1.

50. Gail Miyasaki, "Hole-Hole Bushi: The Only Song of the Japanese in Hawaii," *Hawaii Herald,* 2 February 1973, 5.

51. Edward C. Lydon, *The Anti-Chinese Movement in the Hawaiian Kingdom, 1852–1886* (San Francisco: R and E Research Associates, 1975), 30.

52. United States, Congress, Senate, Committee on Pacific Islands and Porto Rico, *Hawaiian Investigation: Report of Subcommittee on Pacific Islands and Porto Rico on General Conditions in Hawaii, and the Administration of the Affairs Thereof, Part 2* (Washington, DC: U.S. Government Printing Office, 1902), 43.

53. *Pacific Commercial Advertiser,* 13 October 1866, 3.

54. "Coolie Troubles," *Pacific Commercial Advertiser,* 18 November 1865, 2.

55. *Pacific Commercial Advertiser,* 13 October 1866, 3.

56. "Disastrous Fire at Halawa," *Pacific Commercial Advertiser,* 8 June 1867, 2; "More Incendiarism," *Pacific Commercial Advertiser,* 20 August 1870, 3.

57. Hilary Conroy and T. Scott Miyakawa, eds., *East Across the Pacific: Historical and Sociological Studies of Japanese Immigration and Assimilation* (Santa Barbara, CA: American Biographical Center–Clio Press, 1972), 46–47.

58. *Pacific Commercial Advertiser,* 14 August 1880, 3.

59. Yukuo Uyehara, "The Horehore-Bushi: A Type of Japanese Folksong Developed and Sung Among the Early Immigrants in Hawaii," *Social Process in Hawaii* 28 (1980–1981): 116.

60. G. W. Bates, *Sandwich Island Notes* (New York: Harper & Brothers, 1854), 126.

61. Jack Hall, *Kohala's Gay Nineties or the Log of a Luna* (Kohala?: N.p., 1927), 6.

62. Takaki, *Pau Hana,* 131.

63. Isabella L. Bird, *Six Months in the Sandwich Islands* (Tokyo: Charles E. Tuttle Company, 1974), 75.

64. Li Ling Ai, *Life Is for a Long Time: A Chinese Hawaiian Memoir* (New York: Hastings House, 1972), 289–302.

65. Lily Lim-Chong and Harry V. Ball, *Opium and the Law: Hawaii, 1856–1900* (Honolulu: N.p., 1988), 4.

66. "Opium Smoking," *Pacific Commercial Advertiser,* 21 January 1864, 2, 5.

67. Clarence E. Glick, *Sojourners and Settlers: Chinese Migrants in Hawaii* (Honolulu: University of Hawai'i Press, 1980), 38; Bureau of Customs, *Report of the Collector General of Customs, Port of Honolulu, Hawaiian Islands, 1874* (Honolulu: Collector General's Office, 1874).

68. Bird, *Six Months in the Sandwich Islands,* 75.

69. "The Beauties of Opium," *Pacific Commercial Advertiser,* 23 May 1874, 2.

70. M. Forsyth Grant, *Scenes in Hawaii or Life in the Sandwich Islands* (Toronto: Hart & Company, 1888), 64–65.

71. "A Visit to Maui—No. 2," *Pacific Commercial Advertiser,* 24 August 1872, 3.

72. "Early Plantation Life," *Honolulu Record,* 27 October 1949, 8.

73. *The Hawaiian Planters' Monthly* 1, no. 1 (April 1882): 20.

74. "Drink and Work," *Kohala Midget,* 12 July 1911, 1.

75. "Early Plantation Life," *Honolulu Record,* 8.

76. "Chinaman Disappears," *Pacific Commercial Advertiser,* 4 January 1897, 6.

77. "Ha'alele Hana," *Honolulu Record,* 1 January 1953, 8.

78. "Attempt at Arson," *Polynesian,* 3 December 1859, 2.

79. "Want to Get Thousands of Japanese," *Hawaiian Star,* 17 March 1906, 1.

80. *Laws of the Territory of Hawaii Passed by the Legislature at its Regular and Extra Sessions 1905* (Honolulu: The Bulletin Publishing Co., Ltd., 1905), 115.

81. Hawaii State Archives, U.S. President, Executive Orders, Sept 1903–Oct 1918 (no. 225/2978).

82. Jonathan Y. Okamura, "Race Relations in Hawai'i During World War II: The Non-internment of Japanese Americans," *Amerasia* 26, no. 2 (2000): 133.

83. United States, Congress (56th, 1st session: 1899–1900), *Versions of the Hawaii organic act, Senate bill 222, To provide a government for the Territory of Hawaii, 56th Congress, first session, 1899–1900* (Washington, DC: Senate of the United States, 1899–1900); United States, *The Hawaiian Organic Act Including Amendments Up To December 1955* (Honolulu: Legislative Reference Bureau, University of Hawai'i, 1955).

84. "Looking Backward," *Honolulu Record,* 12 August 1948, 8.

85. "Labor," *Hawaiian Star,* 20 June 1900, 4.

86. *Report of the Commissioner of Labor on Hawaii, 1901* (Washington, DC: U.S. Government Printing Office, 1902), 114.

87. *Report of the Governor of the Territory of Hawaii to the Secretary of the Interior, 1900* (Washington, DC: U.S. Government Printing Office, 1900), 16.

88. *Report of the Governor of the Territory of Hawaii to the Secretary of the Interior, 1901* (Washington, DC: U.S. Government Printing Office, 1900), 63.

89. John E. Reinecke, *Labor Disturbances In Hawaii, 1890–1925,* 6.

90. Ernest K. Wakukawa, *A History of the Japanese People in Hawaii* (Honolulu: The Toyo Shoin, 1938), 169; Helen Geracimos Chapin, *Shaping History: The Role of Newspapers in Hawai'i* (Honolulu: University of Hawai'i Press, 1996), 118–119.

91. Kelli Y. Nakamura, "'Violence and Press Incendiarism': Media and Labor Conflicts in the 1909 Strike," *Hawaiian Journal of History* 45 (2011): 69–99.

92. According to historian Ernest Wakukawa, "the labor disputes and the free migration of laborers resulted in suspicion and misunderstandings and anti-Japanese

actions and attitudes on the part of privileged classes in Hawaii. Wakukawa, *A History of the Japanese People in Hawaii,* 219; "Bloodshed in Lahaina," *Honolulu Record,* 22 November 1951, 8.

93. U.S. Bureau of the Census, *Preliminary Figures on Employment Status, Occupation, and Industry for the Japanese Population of the Territory of Hawaii: 1940* (Washington, DC: Bureau of the Census, [1942]), 1–3.

94. "'A'ala: Once a Thriving Japanese Community," *Oral History Recorder* 14, 2 (Summer 1997): 1–14.

95. See Helen Chapin's *Guide to Newspapers of Hawai'i, 1834–2000* through the Hawaiian Historical Society, http://www.hawaiianhistoricalsociety.org/ref/chapin multisearch.php.

96. The Imperial Diet revised these regulations in 1924 whereby Nisei born after December 1, 1924 could nullify their Japanese citizenship by submitting a formal notification accompanied by appropriate documentation to the Home Minister. Those born after that date would lose their Japanese citizenship within two weeks of birth unless their parents registered them at a Japanese consulate. John J. Stephan, *Hawaii Under the Rising Sun: Japan's Plans for Conquest After Pearl Harbor* (Honolulu: University of Hawai'i Press, 1984), 23–24.

97. Stephan, *Hawaii Under the Rising Sun,* 30–31.

98. Stephan, *Hawaii Under the Rising Sun,* 22.

99. United States Office of Education, *A Survey of Education in Hawaii, Made Under the Direction of the Commissioner of Education* (Washington, DC: U.S. Government Printing Office, 1920), 134.

100. Stephan, *Hawaii Under the Rising Sun,* 24.

101. Linda Nishigawa and Ernest Oshiro, "Reviving the Lotus: Japanese Buddhism and World War II Internment," *Social Process in Hawai'i* 45 (Honolulu: University of Hawai'i Press, 2014), 176–177.

102. Vaughan MacCaughey, "Some Outstanding Educational Problems of Hawaii," *School and Society* 9 (January 1919): 100–101.

103. The murder of Gill Jamieson by Myles Fukunaga also garnered national interest. The details of the case were published in two books by Edward Dean Sullivan in 1932, *The Snatch Racket* and *This Kidnapping Business.* Edward Dean Sullivan, *The Snatch Racket* (New York: Vanguard Press, 1932), 71.

104. "Letter Sent Jamieson Demands $10,000 For Return of Young Son," *Honolulu Star Bulletin,* 19 September 1928, 1.

105. R. P. White, "Boy Committed Crime to Bring Happiness to Poor Parents, He Says," *Honolulu Star Bulletin,* 24 September 1928, 1.

106. In 1907, Fort Shafter became the first permanent post for federal troops in Hawai'i, and 234 men were stationed there. Two years later, Schofield Barracks was established near Wahiawa, and the number of troops stationed there rose to about 600

men. During World War I, the number of solders increased to as many as 12,463. After the armistice, the size of the force was reduced to fewer than 5,000 men. Bob Dye, ed., *Hawai'i Chronicles III: World War Two In Hawai'i From the Pages of Paradise of the Pacific* (Honolulu: University of Hawai'i Press, 2000), 11.

107. Jadelyn J. Moniz Nakamura, "Up in Arms! The Struggle to Preserve the Legacy of the National Park Service During Wartime," *Hawaiian Journal of History* 47 (2013): 179–209; Hawai'i Volcanoes National Park (HAVO) Archives, *Superintendent Report, 1927–1945;* Frances Jackson, "Military Use of Haleakalā National Park," *Hawaiian Journal of History* (1972): 129–141; United States Senate, *Investigation of the Pearl Harbor Attack, Report of the Joint Committee on the Investigation of the Pearl Harbor Attack Congress of the United States,* Senate Document 244, 2d Session, 79th Congress (Washington, DC: U.S. Government Publishing Office, 1946); Erwin N. Thompson, *Pacific Ocean Engineers: History of the U.S. Army Corps of Engineers in the Pacific, 1905–1980* (Washington, DC: U.S. Government Printing Office, 1985); William H. Dorrance, "The U.S. Army on Kauai, 1909–1942," *Hawaiian Journal of History* 32 (1998): 155–169; George F. Nellist, *The Story of Hawaii and Its Builders* (Honolulu: Honolulu Star-Bulletin, 1925).

108. Yates Stirling, *Sea Duty: The Memoirs of a Fighting Admiral* (New York: G.P. Putnam's Sons, 1939), 245; Chuck Frankel, "'Pressured' in Massie Case, Says Ex-Governor," *Honolulu Star Bulletin,* 13 February 1967, A-1; Lawrence M. Judd, *Lawrence M. Judd and Hawaii: An Autobiography* (Tokyo: Charles E. Tuttle Company, Inc., 1971), 216.

109. Walter F. Dillingham, *A Memorandum* (Honolulu: N.p., 1932), 10. Walter Dillingham had a close relationship with Gen. George S. Patton Jr., who served as Chief of U.S. Army Intelligence in Hawai'i. On one occasion, both he and Frank Baldwin, another prominent local white, intervened and prevented General Drum from removing Patton as captain of the Army polo team after Patton cursed in the presence of some women who were observing a hard-fought polo match. Michael Slackman, "The Orange Race: George S. Patton, Jr.'s Japanese American Hostage Plan," *Biography: An Interdisciplinary Quarterly* 7, no. 1 (Winter 1984): 5.

110. Jonathan Y. Okamura, "Race Relations in Hawai'i During World War II," 133.

111. "Memorandum for the Officer in Charge: Subject: Kibei," F6-Item17–1942-04-Memo Re Kibei-Blake, 442nd Veterans Club Collection, Archives & Manuscripts Department, University of Hawai'i at Mānoa Library. Estimates on the number of Kibei vary with reports from the Ministry of Foreign Affairs and the the Home Ministry in Japan estimating in 1932 that the number of U.S.-born Nisei in Japan remained consistently between 20,000 and 30,000 in any given year since 1929. The statistics I cite from Military Intelligence specifically address Hawai'i-born Kibei in 1940 although numbers may be much higher. Michael R. Jin, *Citizens, Immigrants, and the Stateless: A Japanese American Diaspora in the Pacific* (Stanford, CA: Stanford University Press, 2022), 49.

112. Michi Weglyn, *Years of Infamy: The Untold Story of America's Concentration Camps* (Seattle: University of Washington Press, 1996), 34.

113. Curtis B. Munson, "Japanese on the West Coast," in *American Concentration Camps,* vol. 1: *July, 1940—December 31, 1941,* edited with an introduction by Roger Daniels (New York: Garland Publishing, 1989).

114. Ogawa, *Kodomo No Tame Ni,* 303.

115. "Memorandum for the Officer in Charge: Subject: Kibei."

116. Dan Boylan and T. Michael Holmes, *John A Burns: The Man and His Times* (Honolulu: University of Hawai'i Press, 2000), 31.

117. "Memorandum for the Officer in Charge: Subject: Kibei."

118. Lawrence H. Fuchs, *Hawaii Pono: A Social History* (New York: Harcourt, Brace & World, Inc.), 129.

119. Mark K. Santoki, "Iwao Mizuta: Reflection on the McKinley Class of '34 and the Legacy of Miles Cary," *Hawaii Herald,* 1 November 1991, 1.

120. Fuchs, *Hawaii Pono,* 129.

121. "New National Guard Unit Will Be Crack Organization, Says Its Captain," *Pacific Commercial Advertiser,* 15 August 1917, 1.

122. Stephan, *Hawaii Under the Rising Sun,* 24.

123. *Takao Ozawa v. United States,* 260 U.S. 178 (1922).

Chapter 2: Community Mobilization and Surveillance under Martial Law

1. "Balch Says Japs Will Dominate Islands Unless Many Removed," *Honolulu Star-Bulletin,* 24 June 1943, 1.

2. Balch further elaborated his claims in a pamphlet where he argued that "it is my contention that if the Japanese are left in their present numbers as the largest racial group in Hawaii the position of all other racial groups and that of their descendants will be jeopardized, and as these people gain even greater political and economic control we shall be forced out of our jobs and our homes." John Adrian Balch, *Shall the Japanese Be Allowed to Dominate Hawaii?* (Honolulu: N.p., 1943), 5.

3. Dorothy Ochiai Hazama and Jane Okamoto Komeiji, *Okage Same De: The Japanese in Hawai'i 1885–1985* (Honolulu: Bess Press, 1986), 137–138.

4. Greg Robinson, *By Order of the President: FDR and the Internment of Japanese* (Cambridge, MA: Harvard University Press, 2001), 147. In February 1942, Emmons was also focused on the transportation of white civilians from the danger zone and argued that since it was impossible to identify all potential disloyal Japanese, the War Department would have to transport one hundred thousand people, logistically impossible under the circumstances.

5. J. Garner Anthony, *Hawaii Under Army Rule* (Honolulu: University Press of Hawai'i, 1955), 9.

6. Various criticisms were made of the provost courts: that for many months they operated in secret session, except in the city of Honolulu; that the judge was often without legal training; that a copy of the charges was not given to the accused, although the accused was allowed to read the prosecution's copy at the beginning of the trial; that the aid of counsel and cross-examination were discouraged; that the proceedings were summary, a trial rarely exceeding thirty minutes in length; that the defendants were convicted of violating "the spirit of martial law" or "the spirit" of general orders when the text was found inadequate; that one provost judge, appointed on an island exclusively occupied by a large plantation, was the general manager of the plantation. Walter P. Armstrong, "Martial Law in Hawaii," *American Bar Association* 29 (December 1943): 701.

7. Between 1935 and 1937 Gen. George S. Patton Jr. served as Chief of U.S. Army Intelligence in Hawai'i, preparing a secret plan that called for "[the] arrest and intern [of] certain persons of the Orange race who are considered most inimical to American interests, or those whom, due to their position and influence in the Orange community, it is desirable to retain as hostages." By arresting certain individuals Patton hoped to guarantee the quiescence of Hawai'i's 151,000-member Japanese community in the event of war with Japan. Included in this plan was a list of names of certain individuals the military would target with the onset of war as well as their occupation, address, and telephone number. Although the influence of this document on military policy during the war is unknown, it set precedence for Green's own plan based on the military's racial fears of the Japanese. Michael Slackman, "The Orange Race: George S. Patton, Jr.'s Japanese American Hostage Plan," *Biography: An Interdisciplinary Quarterly* 1, no. 1 (Winter 1984): 25.

8. Anthony, *Hawaii Under Army Rule*, 10.

9. *The War Record of Civilian and Industrial Hawaii. A Documentary History of the Assistance Extended to the Armed Forces by the Civilian Community and the Sugar Plantations* (Honolulu: N.p., 1945), 2.

10. Yasutaro Soga, *Life Behind Barbed Wire* (Honolulu: University of Hawai'i Press, 2008), 23.

11. Suikei Furuya, *An Internment Odyssey–Haisho Tenten* (Honolulu: Japanese Cultural Center of Hawai'i, 2017), 7.

12. Hawaii Nikkei History Editorial Board, ed., *Japanese Eyes, American Heart: Personal Reflections of Hawaii's World War II Nisei Soldiers* (Honolulu: Tendai Educational Foundation, 1998), 86.

13. *Japanese Eyes, American Heart*, 36.

14. Allan Beekman, *The Niihau Incident: The true story of the Japanese fighter pilot who, after the Pearl Harbor attack, crash landed on the Hawaiian Island of Niihau and terrorized the residents* (Honolulu: Heritage Press of the Pacific, 1982), 83.

15. "Hawaiian Who Killed Japanese Aviator on Niihau Isle Honored," *Honolulu Advertiser,* 7 June 1943, 2.

16. While Beekman provided a more negative portrayal of Harada's motives, other authors have argued "the actions of Harada and Shintani stemmed more from fear of the pilot than from loyalty to the emperor." The exact motives of these two men, however, remain unclear. Bob Dye, ed., *Hawai'i Chronicles: Island History from the Pages of Honolulu Magazine* (Honolulu: University of Hawai'i Press, 1996), 255.

17. Dorothy Matsuo, *Boyhood to War: History and Anecdotes of the 442nd RCT* (Korea: Mutual Publishing of Honolulu, 1992), 27.

18. Matsuo, *Boyhood to War,* 25.

19. Matsuo, *Boyhood to War,* 24.

20. *Japanese Eyes American Heart,* 26.

21. *Japanese Eyes American Heart,* 27.

22. *Japanese Eyes American Heart,* 95.

23. *Japanese Eyes American Heart,* 96; Franklin Odo, *No Sword to Bury: Japanese Americans in Hawai'i During World War II* (Philadelphia: Temple University Press, 2004), 41–44; Roland Kotani, *The Japanese In Hawaii: A Century of Struggle* (Honolulu: The Hawaii Hochi, Ltd., 1985), 88–90.

24. Odo, *No Sword to Bury,* 120; Harry N. Scheiber and Jane L. Scheiber, *Bayonets in Paradise: Martial Law in Hawai'i During World War II* (Honolulu: University of Hawai'i Press, 2016), 28.

25. Robert L. Shivers, *Cooperation of the Various Racial Groups with Each Other and with the Constituted Authorities before and after December 7, 1941, Statement Presented before Sub-Committee on Statehood United States House of Representative at Iolani Palace Honolulu, Hawaii, U.S.A., January 15, 1946* (Honolulu: Chamber of Commerce, 1946), 5.

26. Shivers, *Cooperation of the Various Racial Groups with Each Other and with the Constituted Authorities before and after December 7, 1941,* 9.

27. The roots of the Emergency Service Committee can be traced to the Hawaiian Japanese Civic Association in 1927. The purpose of the Hawaiian Japanese Civic Association was to promote educational, cultural, and political efforts. In 1938, it campaigned to persuade dual citizens to expatriate. During a two-week drive, one thousand Nisei took the first steps to make themselves full American citizens. The same organization made similar efforts in 1939, 1940, and 1941. In November 1940, the leaders of the association drew up a petition to present to Secretary of State Cordell Hull, which described the existing expatriation process as "complicated and cumbersome, entailing involved correspondence and long waiting." It many cases, it stated, "the technical difficulties are appalling, and in numerous instances more than a year elapses before the action is at long last completed." Some citizens had deferred taking the necessary steps, not only for these reasons, but also because they were unwilling to recognize a claim upon them by any other government than the United States. The whole

situation brought much "undeserved and unwarranted" suspicion of Americans of Japanese ancestry by other citizens. In addition to an expatriation drive, the *Honolulu Star-Bulletin* reported that the association also sponsored discussions of "civil and economic problems facing American citizens of Japanese ancestry." "Service Group, Civic Club Merge," *Honolulu Advertiser,* 24 July 1942, 7; "Campaign for Simpler Form of Expatriation Opens Here," *Honolulu Star-Bulletin,* 8 November 1940, 3; "Civic Club Is Planning Active Year," *Honolulu Star-Bulletin,* 8 August 1939, 9.

28. Gwenfread Allen, *Hawaii's War Years: 1941–1945* (Honolulu: The Advertiser Publishing Co., Ltd., 1950), 144.

29. Yukiko Kimura, *Issei: Japanese Immigrants in Hawaii* (Honolulu: University of Hawai'i Press, 1988), 227; Hawaii, Office of the Military Governor, Morale Section, Emergency Service Committee, *Final Report of the Emergency Service Committee* (Honolulu: N.p., 1946), 48–49.

30. Shivers, *Cooperation of the Various Racial Groups with Each Other and with the Constituted Authorities before and after December 7, 1941,* 10.

31. *Final Report of the Emergency Service Committee,* 19.

32. *Final Report of the Emergency Service Committee,* 22.

33. Allen, *Hawaii's War Years,* 91.

34. Michael John Gordon, "Suspects in Paradise: Looking for Japanese 'Subversives' in the Territory of Hawaii, 1939–1945" (Master's thesis, University of Iowa, 1983), 10.

35. Emergency Service Committee, *The AJA—Their Present and Future* (Honolulu: N.p., [1940?]), 9.

36. "Sanji Abe's Case," *Honolulu Advertiser,* 8 October 1940, editorial page; "Un-American Reasoning," *Honolulu Advertiser,* 11 October 1940, editorial page; "Hawaii, U.S.A.," *Honolulu Advertiser,* 2 November 1940, editorial page; "Sanji Abe's Expatriation," *Honolulu Advertiser,* 5 November 1940, editorial page.

37. Kei Suzuki, "Sanji Abe," *Hawaii Herald,* 17 October 2008, B-3; Bob Dye, "The Case of Sanji Abe," *Honolulu Magazine* 37, no. 5 (November 2002): 38; Allen, *Hawai'i's War Years,* 350; "Sanji Abe, 87; First AJA in Isle Senate," Abe, Sanji, University of Hawai'i at Mānoa, Microfiche D98050 Biographical.

38. Kauai Morale Committee, *The Final Report of the Kauai Morale Committee* (Lihue: The Committee, 1945), 10.

39. *The Final Report of the Kauai Morale Committee,* 41.

40. *The Final Report of the Kauai Morale Committee,* 35–36.

41. The Romanzo Adams Social Research Laboratory (RASRL), Box 12 / Folder No: 20–24 Ka Kaua'i / Index, 10–26, "How the Kauai Candidates Withdrew," 1.

42. Klass, *World War II on Kauai: Historical Research by Tim Klass,* prepared for the Kaua'i Historical Society by the Westland Foundation (Portland, OR: The Westland Foundation, 1970), 59–60.

43. Clarice B. Taylor, "Kauai Is Out on a Limb," *Garden Island,* 13 October 1942, 6.

44. RASRL, "How the Kauai Candidates Withdrew," 7.

45. "Gov. Stainback Praises Patriotic Candidates Who Quit Politics," *Garden Island,* 20 October 1942, 1.

46. "Kahului, Maui, Shelled by Enemy," *Maui News,* 16 December 1941, 1; "Maui Port Shelled by Sub No Casualties in Attack," *Honolulu Advertiser,* 17 December 1941, 3; "Submarines Attack Maui, Kauai, Hawaii," *Honolulu Star-Bulletin,* 31 December 1941, 1.

47. "No Casualties In [Maui's] First Actual Bombardment," *Maui News,* 17 December 1941, 1.

48. "24 Lost on January 28 in Sub Attack; 36 Survive," *Maui News,* 11 February 1942, 1.

49. *Pioneer Mill Company,* 418.

50. Maya M. Hara, *An Oral History on Issei in Lahaina* (N.p.: West Maui Cultural Council, 1991), 44.

51. Maui Historical Society, *World War II's Impact on Maui County: A Social History* (Wailuku: Maui Historical Society, 1992), 3.

52. *Pioneer Mill Company,* 454.

53. Maui County, Police Department, & Maui County, *Annual Report, Police Department 1941* (Territory of Hawaii: County of Maui, 1941), 5.

54. *Pioneer Mill Company,* 15.

55. Allen, *Hawai'i's War Years,* 136.

56. Hawai'i Volcanoes National Park (HAVO) Archives, *Superintendent Report, 1941,* 2.

57. HAVO Archives, *Superintendent Report, 1941,* 3.

58. Allen, *Hawai'i's War Years,* 144. The Emergency Service Committee on O'ahu was formed in February 1942, the Kaua'i Morale Committee shortly after in May 1942, the Maui Emergency Service Committee in August, and the Lāna'i Emergency Service Committee in January 1943.

59. The Romanzo Adams Social Research Laboratory Confidential Research Files, 1942–1959, Inventory box 13 / 10–11, Ko Kona / 10–19, 1942–1952, "Life in Kona," 7.

60. Allen, *Hawai'i's War Years,* 65.

61. Gary Okihiro, *Cane Fires: The Anti-Japanese Movement in Hawaii, 1865–1945* (Philadelphia: Temple University Press, 1991), 196.

62. Allen, *Hawai'i's War Years,* 68.

63. "History of the G-2 Section Part I." Japanese Internment and Relocation: The Hawaii Experience, University of Hawai'i, Hamilton Library, Special Collections [JIRHE], Item 229; "History of the G-2 Section Part II," Japanese Internment and Relocation: The Hawaii Experience, University of Hawai'i, Hamilton Library, Special Collections [JIRHE], Item 230, 13.

64. John Anthony Burns, *John A. Burns Oral History Project,* Tape No. 4, p. 1.

65. Honolulu Police Department, *Annual Report: Police Department, City and County of Honolulu, Territory of Hawaii 1941*, "Police," 31.01, Romanzo Adams Social Research Laboratory Confidential Research Files [RASRL].

66. "General Information, Richard C. Miller Espionage Bureau, December 3 1941," Romanzo Adams Social Research Laboratory Confidential Research Files [RASRL].

67. Dan Boylan and T. Michael Holmes, *John A. Burns: The Man and His Times* (Honolulu: University of Hawai'i Press, 2000), 31.

68. "Address given by Chief of Police W.A. Gabrielson, Honolulu, to the Annual Convention of the International Association of Chiefs of Police, held in Detroit, Michigan, August 9–12, 1943," 31.01, p. 1, Romanzo Adams Social Research Laboratory Confidential Research Files [RASRL].

69. "Address given by Chief of Police W.A. Gabrielson," 16.

70. Members of the Oahu Citizens Committee for Home Defense who helped to identify "beat leaders" of certain districts included "Dr. [Shunzo] Sakamaki, Jack Wakayama, Lt. [Yoshio] Hasegawa, Mr. W. Amioka, Mr. G. Eguchi, Mr. Masatoshi Katagiri, Mr. M. Maneki, Mr. S. Higashino, Mr. Paul Morihara, Mr. Shigeo Yoshida, and Mr. Clifton Yamamoto." "Honolulu Police Department Contact Group," pg. 1. Romanzo Adams Social Research Laboratory Confidential Research Files [RASRL].

71. *John A. Burns Oral History Project*, Tape No. 4, pp. 5–6.

72. John Anthony Burns, *John A. Burns Oral History Project*, Tape No. 2, p. 8.

73. *John A. Burns Oral History Project*, Tape No. 2, p. 8; *John A. Burns Oral History Project*, Tape No. 4, p. 2.

74. *John A. Burns Oral History Project*, Tape No. 4, p. 2.

75. *John A. Burns Oral History Project*, Tape No. 4, pp. 2, 3.

76. *John A. Burns Oral History Project*, Tape No. 4, p. 4.

77. *John A. Burns Oral History Project*, Tape No. 4, p. 2.

78. Boylan and Holmes, *John A. Burns*, 17.

79. *John A. Burns Oral History Project*, Tape No. 4, p. 6.

80. *John A. Burns Oral History Project*, Tape No. 4, p. 8.

81. However, this surveillance would not come at the expense of regular police duties as there would be a dramatic growth in the ranks of HPD with the hiring of more than two hundred reserve officers, all of whom would be equipped courtesy of the U.S. Army with a steel helmet and gas mask. Additionally, "it furnished rifles and shotguns to stock up a large police arsenal." "Letter to Mayor Lester Petrie from W.A. Gabrielson, January 29, 1943," Romanzo Adams Social Research Laboratory Confidential Research Files [RASRL].

82. National Archives and Records Administration, San Francisco, RG 181 Records of Naval Districts and Shore Establishments, Naval Shipyard, Pearl Harbor, Hawaii Office of the Commandant, General Correspondence (Formerly Classified), 1940–1946 ARC 296911, NN 373–91 (FRC Accession No. 181–58–3404A), Box 51, 62, 63.

83. "FBI Course for Police Opens Here," *Honolulu Star-Bulletin*, 8 January 1942, 1; "Police Take FBI Course," *Honolulu Star-Bulletin*, 9 January 1942, 3.

84. James Dulaney and Eichi Hongo, "Special Detail, 11–17–42," November 17, 1942, p. 1, Romanzo Adams Social Research Laboratory Confidential Research Files [RASRL]; Ansley N. Neptune and Eichi Hongo, "Tour of Duty—Special Detail #2," July 15, 1942, p. 1, Romanzo Adams Social Research Laboratory Confidential Research Files [RASRL].

85. Ansley N. Neptune and Eichi Hongo, "Tour of Duty—Special Detail #2," July 15, 1942, p. 1, Romanzo Adams Social Research Laboratory Confidential Research Files [RASRL].

86. "Policemen Can Search Homes," *Honolulu Advertiser*, 2 March 1942, 1.

87. Ansley N. Neptune and Eichi Hongo, "Tour of Duty—Special Detail #2," No date, p. 1, Romanzo Adams Social Research Laboratory Confidential Research Files [RASRL].

88. Ernest Nowell and Eichi Hongo, "Tour of Duty—Special Detail #2," July 29, 1942, p. 1, Romanzo Adams Social Research Laboratory Confidential Research Files [RASRL]; Ernest Nowell and Eichi Hongo, "Tour of Duty—Special Detail #2," August 11, 1942, p. 1, Romanzo Adams Social Research Laboratory Confidential Research Files [RASRL].

89. Ernest Nowell and Eichi Hongo, "Tour of Duty—Special Detail #2," August 18, 1942, p. 2, Romanzo Adams Social Research Laboratory Confidential Research Files [RASRL].

90. Ansley N. Neptune and Eichi Hongo, "Tour of Duty—Special Detail #2," July 25, 1942, p. 1, Romanzo Adams Social Research Laboratory Confidential Research Files [RASRL].

91. James Dulaney and Eichi Hongo, "Special Detail 10-20-42," October 20, 1942, p. 1, Romanzo Adams Social Research Laboratory Confidential Research Files [RASRL].

92. Ansley N. Neptune and Eichi Hongo, "Tour of Duty—Special Detail #2," July 17, 1942, p. 1, Romanzo Adams Social Research Laboratory Confidential Research Files [RASRL].

93. James Dulaney and Eichi Hongo, "Special Detail," October 17, 1942, p. 3, Romanzo Adams Social Research Laboratory Confidential Research Files [RASRL].

94. Ansley N. Neptune and Eichi Hongo, "Tour of Duty—Special Detail #2," June 5, 1942, p. 2, Romanzo Adams Social Research Laboratory Confidential Research Files [RASRL].

95. Ernest Nowell and Eichi Hongo, "Tour of Duty—Special Detail #2," August 10, 1942, p. 2, Romanzo Adams Social Research Laboratory Confidential Research Files [RASRL].

96. Ernest Nowell and Eichi Hongo, "Tour of Duty—Special Detail #2," July 31, 1942, p. 1, Romanzo Adams Social Research Laboratory Confidential Research Files [RASRL].

97. John L. Upton and Eichi Hongo, "Tour of Duty—Special Detail #2," July 26, 1942, p. 1, Romanzo Adams Social Research Laboratory Confidential Research Files [RASRL].

98. Ernest Nowell and Eichi Hongo, "Tour of Duty—Special Detail #2," July 28, 1942, p. 1, Romanzo Adams Social Research Laboratory Confidential Research Files [RASRL].

99. Ansley N. Neptune and Eichi Hongo, "Tour of Duty—Special Detail #2," June 9, 1942, p. 1, Romanzo Adams Social Research Laboratory Confidential Research Files [RASRL].

100. James Dulaney and Eichi Hongo, "Special Detail, 11-3-42," November 3, 1942, p. 3, Romanzo Adams Social Research Laboratory Confidential Research Files [RASRL].

101. Dulaney and Hongo, "Special Detail, 11-3-42," p. 1.

102. Ernest Nowell and Eichi Hongo, "Supplement—Tour of Duty—Special Detail #2," August 7, 1942, p. 1, Romanzo Adams Social Research Laboratory Confidential Research Files [RASRL].

103. Nowell and Hongo, "Supplement—Tour of Duty—Special Detail #2," August 7, 1942, p. 1.

104. James Dulaney and Eichi Hongo, "Special Detail, 10-19-42," October 19, 1942, p. 1, Romanzo Adams Social Research Laboratory Confidential Research Files [RASRL].

105. James Dulaney and Eichi Hongo, "Special Detail, 11-12-42," November 12, 1942, p. 1, Romanzo Adams Social Research Laboratory Confidential Research Files [RASRL]; James Dulaney and Eichi Hongo, "Special Detail, 12-8-42," December 9, 1942, p. 1, Romanzo Adams Social Research Laboratory Confidential Research Files [RASRL].

106. James Dulaney and Eichi Hongo, "Check of a Rumor in Kaheka Lane," October, 23, 1942, p. 1, Romanzo Adams Social Research Laboratory Confidential Research Files [RASRL].

107. Ernest Nowell and Eichi Hongo, "Tour of Duty—Special Detail #2," August 13, 1942, p. 1, Romanzo Adams Social Research Laboratory Confidential Research Files [RASRL].

108. "Honolulu Police Department Contact Group," p. 1, Romanzo Adams Social Research Laboratory Confidential Research Files [RASRL].

109. Hawaii, Office of the Military Governor, Morale Section, Emergency Service Committee, *Final Report of the Emergency Service Committee* (Honolulu: N.p., 1946), 49–50.

110. James Dulaney and Eichi Hongo, "Special Detail," October 27, 1942, p. 1, Romanzo Adams Social Research Laboratory Confidential Research Files [RASRL].

111. Dulaney and Hongo, “Special Detail,” October 27, 1942, p. 1.

112. Nowell and Hongo, “Tour of Duty—Special Detail #2,” August 13, 1942, p. 2.

113. Ernest Nowell and Eichi Hongo, “Tour of Duty—Special Assignment #2,” August 18, 1942, p. 2, Romanzo Adams Social Research Laboratory Confidential Research Files [RASRL].

114. As the Emergency Service Committee was organizing meetings on Oʻahu, Hans L’Orange, manager of Oʻahu Sugar’s plantation at Waipahu refused to allow Burns to organize any meetings on the premises believing that it would be disruptive to his workers. Both Burns and military intelligence felt that Waipahu, “a virtual Japanese ghetto,” strategically located next to Pearl Harbor, had to participate in the program. After personally approaching L’Orange, who remained intransigent, Burns went to the Hawaii Sugar Planters’ Association (HSPA) and urged them to encourage L’Orange to participate. Within days, the HSPA notified Burns that L’Orange was more than happy to participate in the program. Boylan and Holmes, *John A. Burns,* 63–64.

115. Boylan and Holmes, *John A. Burns,* 64; Kotani, *The Japanese In Hawaii,* 99.

116. United States, Commission on Wartime Relocation and Internment of Civilians, *Personal Justice Denied: Report of the Commission on Wartime Relocation and Internment of Civilians* (Washington, DC: Civil Liberties Public Education Fund; Seattle: University of Washington Press, 1997), 179–180.

117. Nowell and Hongo, “Tour of Duty—Special Detail #2,” August 7, 1942, p. 2.

118. James Dulaney and Eichi Hongo, “Special Detail, 10-17-42,” October 17, 1942, p. 3, Romanzo Adams Social Research Laboratory Confidential Research Files [RASRL].

119. Yuriko Hatanaka and Kimie Kawahara, “The Impact of War on an Immigrant Culture,” *Social Processes in Hawaii* 8 (November 1943): 42.

120. James Dulancy and Eichi Hongo, “Special Detail, 11-21-42,” November 21, 1942, p. 1, Romanzo Adams Social Research Laboratory Confidential Research Files [RASRL].

121. William G. Ross and Eichi Hongo, “Tour of Duty—Special Detail #2,” June 20, 1942, p. 1, Romanzo Adams Social Research Laboratory Confidential Research Files [RASRL].

122. “ʻAʻala: Once a Thriving Japanese Community,” *Oral History Recorder* 14, no. 2 (Summer 1997): 1–14.

123. “Anti-Japanese Sentiment of Naval Commander,” Japanese Internment and Relocation: The Hawaii Experience, University of Hawaiʻi, Hamilton Library, Special Collections [JIRHE], Item 361.

124. Hatanaka and Kawahara, “The Impact of War on an Immigrant Culture,” 40.

125. Yukiko Kimura, “The Effects of the War Situation Upon the Alien Japanese in Hawaii,” *Social Process in Hawaii* 8 (November 1943): 18–19.

126. James Dulaney and Eichi Hongo, "Special Detail, 11-30-42," November 30, 1942, p. 1, Romanzo Adams Social Research Laboratory Confidential Research Files [RASRL].

127. James Dulaney and Eichi Hongo, "Special Detail, 11-11-42," November 11, 1942, p. 1, Romanzo Adams Social Research Laboratory Confidential Research Files [RASRL].

128. Dulaney and Hongo, "Special Detail," October 21, 1942, p. 3.

129. Ernest Nowell and Eichi Hongo, "Tour of Duty—Special Detail #2," August 17, 1942, p. 2. Romanzo Adams Social Research Laboratory Confidential Research Files [RASRL].

130. James Dulaney and Eichi Hongo, "Special Detail, 12-8-42," December 8, 1942, p. 1, Romanzo Adams Social Research Laboratory Confidential Research Files [RASRL].

131. Dulaney and Hongo, "Special Detail, 12-8-42," December 8, 1942, p. 3.

132. James Dulaney and Eichi Hongo, "Special Detail," September 17, 1942, p. 2, Romanzo Adams Social Research Laboratory Confidential Research Files [RASRL].

133. Hazama and Komeiji, *Okage Same De,* 130.

134. "Police Say No Evidence of Parachutists," *Honolulu Star-Bulletin,* 8 December 1941, 2; "Police Probe Reports of Parachutists," *Honolulu Star-Bulletin,* 8 December 1941, 2; "City Water Is Safe To Drink, Ohrt Announces," *Honolulu Star-Bulletin,* 8 December 1941, 2; "Sabotage Reported in Waikiki Area," *Honolulu Star-Bulletin,* 7 December 1941, 3.

135. Hazama and Komeiji, *Okage Same De,* 132.

136. James Dulaney and Eichi Hongo, "Special Detail," October 27, 1942, p. 2.

137. James Dulaney and Eichi Hongo, "Special Detail, 12-10-42," December 10, 1942, p. 1, Romanzo Adams Social Research Laboratory Confidential Research Files [RASRL].

138. James Dulaney and Eichi Hongo, "Special Detail, 12-11-42," December 11, 1942, p. 1, Romanzo Adams Social Research Laboratory Confidential Research Files [RASRL].

139. Neptune and Hongo, "Tour of Duty—Special Detail #2," July 17, 1942, p. 1.

140. Robinson, *By Order of the President,* 146.

Chapter 3: "They Even Checked Our Assholes"

1. "Soga, Translations of My Life behind Barbed Wire (Fukuhara)," Japanese Internment and Relocation: The Hawaii Experience, University of Hawai'i, Hamilton Library, Special Collections [JIRHE], Item 263, 6.

2. Yukiko Kimura, "Some Effects of the War Situation Upon the Alien Japanese in Hawaii," *Social Processes in Hawaii* 8 (November 1943): 18.

3. Duncan R. Williams, "Complex Loyalties: Issei Buddhist Ministers during the Wartime Incarceration," *Pacific World*, 3rd ser., no. 5 (Fall 2003): 261; National Archives at San Francisco, USIS (RG 566) series: *Alien Case Files*, File: Mitsumyo Tottori: #A2071200 in Box 110.

4. H.S. Burr, U.S. Navy Reserve, District Intelligence Officer, U.S. Navy, "Naval Intelligence Manual for Investigating Japanese Cases in Hawaii," RG: 389: Record of the Office of the Provost Marshal General, 1941–, Japanese Internment and Relocation: Hawaii Experience [JIRHE], University of Hawai'i, Hamilton Library, Special Collections, Box 3, A-40, pp. 50–51.

5. Kelli Y. Nakamura, "Bishop Mitsumyo Tottori: Patriotism Through Buddhism During World War II," *Hawaiian Journal of History* 51 (2017): 115–145. Besides Tottori, his colleague the Reverend Shindo Wasai was also not incarcerated but very little information is currently known about him or his World War II experiences. The Reverend Yoshiko Shimabukuro who was the priest of the Jōdo Shinshū at 'Ele'ele Hongwanji on Kaua'i was also not incarcerated, although FBI officials did fingerprint, photograph, and question her at Kaua'i County Building. As the only Buddhist priest on Kaua'i, she conducted funeral, memorial, and Obon services along with weddings during the war and believes that she was not incarcerated as "maybe they felt sorry for me because I was handicapped. But I don't know." As a breach baby, she lost her left arm at birth but that did not prevent her from becoming the first Nisei Okinawan American woman to serve as a Jōdo Shinshū minister in Hawai'i. Tetsuei Katoda, *The Fiftieth Anniversary of the Establishment of the Shingon Sect Mission of Hawaii* (Honolulu: The Mission, 1966), 58; Roy Kodani, "Yoshiko Shimabukuro," *Hawaii Herald*, 4 July 2003, A-10.

6. "Soga, Translations of My Life behind Barbed Wire (Fukuhara)," 1.

7. University of Hawai'i at Mānoa. Center for Oral History, *Unspoken Memories: Oral Histories of Hawai'i Internees at Jerome, Arkansas* (Honolulu: Center for Oral History, Social Science Research Institute, University of Hawai'i at Mānoa, 2014), 88.

8. *Unspoken Memories*, 89.

9. "Col. William F. Steer," AR 19, Box 21, Folder 26, p. 9, Japanese Cultural Center of Hawai'i Resource Room.

10. Jack Y. Tasaka, *Confidential Stories at Honouliuli Internment Camp*, trans. Ari Uchida ([Honolulu]: N.p., 1980), manuscript, Japanese Cultural Center of Hawai'i, 8.

11. Harry N. Scheiber and Jane L. Scheiber, *Bayonets in Paradise: Martial Law in Hawai'i During World War II Honolulu* (Honolulu: University of Hawai'i Press, 2016), 158.

12. "Mr. Minosuke Hanabusa, TR-3," 4.

13. "Soga, Translations of My Life behind Barbed Wire (Fukuhara)," 4. These sentiments were also echoed by other inmates. "Mr. Minosuke Hanabusa, TR-3," 6.

14. Yasutaro Soga, *Life Behind Barbed Wire: The World War II Internment Memoirs of a Hawai'i Issei* (Honolulu: University of Hawai'i Press, 2008), 27–28.

15. Shigehiko Shiramizu, "Ethnic Press and Its Society: A Case of Japanese Press in Hawaii," *KEIO Communication Review* 11 (1990): 63; Helen Geracimos Chapin, *Shaping History: The Role of Newspapers in Hawai'i* (Honolulu: University of Hawai'i Press, 1996), 140–147.

16. "Mr. Hisashi Fukuhara, TR-1," Japanese Internment and Relocation: The Hawaii Experience, University of Hawai'i, Hamilton Library, Special Collections [JIRHE], Item 232, 5.

17. "Transfer of Quarantine Station RG 407," Japanese Internment and Relocation: The Hawaii Experience, University of Hawai'i, Hamilton Library, Special Collections [JIRHE], Item 305.

18. "Mr. Minosuke Hanabusa, TR-3," 5.

19. "Mr. Myoshu Sasai," Japanese Internment and Relocation: The Hawaii Experience, University of Hawai'i, Hamilton Library, Special Collections [JIRHE], Item 239, 4.

20. "Soga, Translations of my Life Behind Barbed Wire (Fukuhara)," 9.

21. "Soga, Translations of My Life behind Barbed Wire (Fukuhara)," 6.

22. "Furuya, Suikei (translation) Haisho Ten-ten," Japanese Internment and Relocation: The Hawaii Experience, University of Hawai'i, Hamilton Library, Special Collections [JIRHE], Item 257, 4.

23. Gail Honda, ed., *Family Torn Apart: The Internment Story of the Otokichi Muin Ozaki Family* (Honolulu: Japanese Cultural Center of Hawai'i, 2012), 44.

24. Honda, *Family Torn Apart,* 44.

25. "Furuya, Suikei (translation) Haisho Ten-ten," 7.

26. "S-27 Internee Treatment," Japanese Internment and Relocation: The Hawaii Experience, University of Hawai'i, Hamilton Library, Special Collections [JIRHE], Item 416, 1.

27. Honda, *Family Torn Apart,* 42.

28. Mistakes that appear in the spelling exist in the original and are reproduced for authenticity. "Furuya, Suikei (translation) Haisho Ten-Ten," 4.

29. "Furuya, Suikei (translation) Haisho Ten-ten," 75.

30. "S-28 Treatment of Civilian Internees at Sand Island," Japanese Internment and Relocation: The Hawaii Experience, University of Hawai'i, Hamilton Library, Special Collections [JIRHE], Item 417, 3.

31. "Mr. Hisashi Fukuhara," 5.

32. "Soga, Keiho (trans.) My Life Behind Barbed Wire," Japanese Internment and Relocation: The Hawaii Experience, University of Hawai'i, Hamilton Library, Special Collections [JIRHE], Item 264, 4.

33. "Soga, Keiho (trans.) My Life Behind Barbed Wire," 2.

34. "Mr. Jukichi Inouye TR-5," 5.

35. "Soga, Keiho (trans.) My Life Behind Barbed Wire," 4.

36. "Soga, Keiho (trans.) My Life Behind Barbed Wire," 5.

37. "Furuya, Suikei (translation) Haisho Ten-ten," 5.

38. "Furuya, Suikei (translation) Haisho Ten-ten," 5.

39. "Soga, Keiho (trans.) My Life Behind Barbed Wire," 4.

40. "Mr. Minosuke Hanabusa, TR-3," 6.

41. "Soga, Translations of My Life Behind Barbed Wire (Fukuhara)," 9.

42. "Furuya, Suikei (translation) Haisho Ten-ten," 3.

43. Honda, *Family Torn Apart,* 44–45.

44. "History of the G-2 Section Part II," Japanese Internment and Relocation: The Hawaii Experience, University of Hawai'i, Hamilton Library, Special Collections [JIRHE], Item 230, 26.

45. "Soga, Keiho (trans.) My Life Behind Barbed Wire," 5.

46. "DETENTION CAMP: SAND ISLAND," Japanese Internment and Relocation: The Hawaii Experience, University of Hawai'i, Hamilton Library, Special Collections [JIRHE], p. 3.

47. Dennis M. Ogawa and Evarts C. Fox Jr., "Japanese Internment and Relocation: The Hawaii Experience" (paper presented at the International Conference of Relocation and Redress: The Japanese-American Experience, March 1983), 4.

48. "History of the G-2 Section Part II," 24. For more information about Hearing Boards consult: Scheiber and Scheiber, *Bayonets in Paradise,* 157–170.

49. "Enclosure (B): Factors to Be Considered in Investigations of Japanese Subjects," Japanese Internment and Relocation: The Hawaii Experience, University of Hawai'i, Hamilton Library, Special Collections [JIRHE], p. 7.

50. "Mr. Myoshu Sasai," 3.

51. "Col. S.H. Spillner Correspondence with Michael Gordon," AR 19 Japanese American Relocation and Internment: The Hawai'i Experience, Box 21: The Research Process, Japanese Cultural Center of Hawai'i Resource Room.

52. National Park Service, U.S. Department of the Interior, *Honouliuli Gulch and Associated Sites: Draft Special Resource Study and Environmental Assessment, May 2014* (Washington, DC: U.S. Department of the Interior, 2014), 23.

53. Masanori Nakahodo, "The POW Camp in Hawai'i: On the Yasuo Kayo 'Islands of captives,'/ ハワイの捕虜収容所一嘉陽安男「捕虜たちの島」をめくって" *Bulletin of the Faculty of Law and Letters University of the Ryukyus/日本東洋文化論集琉球大学本文部紀要* (March 2014): 49.

54. National Park Service, U.S. Department of the Interior, *Honouliuli Gulch and Associated Sites Draft,* xii.

55. Nakahodo, "The POW Camp in Hawai'i," 49.

56. Tasaka, *Confidential Stories at Honouliuli Internment Camp*, 21.

57. "Toso Haseyama 2," National Park Service, World War II Valor in the Pacific, accessed June 11, 2018, pg. 13. https://www.nps.gov/valr/learn/historyculture/oral-history-interviews.htm.

58. Dan Toru Nishikawa, From the Patsy Saiki archival collection (AR 18, Box 2, Folder 9), 3.

59. Dan Toru Nishikawa, 4.

60. "Toso Haseyama 2," National Park Service, p. 13.

61. "Toso Haseyama 2," National Park Service, p. 14.

62. "Memoir #2 by Dan Toru Nishikawa," p. 4, Japanese Cultural Center of Hawai'i Resource Room.

63. "Toso Haseyama 2," National Park Service, p. 14.

64. "Harry Urata," National Park Service, World War II Valor in the Pacific, accessed June 11, 2018, p. 5, https://www.nps.gov/valr/learn/historyculture/oral-history-interviews.htm.

65. "Harry Urata," National Park Service, p. 6.

66. "Toso Haseyama 2," National Park Service, p. 13.

67. Tasaka, *Confidential Stories at Honouliuli Internment Camp*, 5.

68. Tasaka, *Confidential Stories at Honouliuli Internment Camp*, 25.

69. Dan Toru Nishikawa, 8.

70. Tasaka, *Confidential Stories at Honouliuli Internment Camp*, 19.

71. Tasaka, *Confidential Stories at Honouliuli Internment Camp*, 19.

72. "Toso Haseyama 2," National Park Service, p. 15.

73. Tasaka, *Confidential Stories at Honouliuli Internment Camp*, 29–30.

74. "Toso Haseyama 2," National Park Service, p. 16.

75. Tasaka, *Confidential Stories at Honouliuli Internment Camp*, 14.

76. Tasaka, *Confidential Stories at Honouliuli Internment Camp*, 14.

77. Tasaka, *Confidential Stories at Honouliuli Internment Camp*, 24.

78. Tasaka, *Confidential Stories at Honouliuli Internment Camp*, 14.

79. Tatsumi Hayashi, JCCH Hawai'i Japanese Internee Database, XLS (Honolulu: Japanese Cultural Center of Hawai'i, n.d.).

80. Japanese Cultural Center of Hawai'i Resource Room. AR 19: Japanese American Relocation and Internment: The Hawaii Experience, Box 12—Articles and Manuscripts, 1942–1949, Folder 25: Chapter IX: Prisoners of War and Internees, circa 1945, p. 2.

81. Japanese Cultural Center of Hawai'i Resource Room. AR 19: Japanese American Relocation and Internment: The Hawaii Experience, Box 9, Folder 30. Vital Statistics.

82. Dan Toru Nishikawa, 5.

83. Dan Toru Nishikawa, 5.

84. Dan Toru Nishikawa, 6.

85. Nishikawa, 4.

86. Tasaka, *Confidential Stories at Honouliuli Internment Camp*, 7.

87. Tasaka, *Confidential Stories at Honouliuli Internment Camp*, 13.

88. Nishikawa, 7.

89. "Memoir #2 by Dan Toru Nishikawa," Japanese Cultural Center of Hawai'i Resource Room, p. 4.

90. Abe, Sanji, "Consideration for Release from Internment," Letter to Lt. Gen. Robert C. Richardson, Jr., 11 Jan. 1944, MS, Honouliuli Internment Camp, Honolulu, Territory of Hawaii; *The Untold Story: The Internment of Japanese Americans in Hawai'i*, Web, March 23, 2018.

91. Tasaka, *Confidential Stories at Honouliuli Internment Camp*, 7.

92. "Harry Urata," National Park Service, p. 7.

93. Dan Toru Nishikawa, 4.

94. Tasaka, *Confidential Stories at Honouliuli Internment Camp*, 22.

95. Dan Toru Nishikawa, 4–5.

96. Tasaka, *Confidential Stories at Honouliuli Internment Camp*, 12.

97. Robinson, *A Tragedy of Democracy: Japanese Confinement in North America* (New York: Columbia University Press, 2009), 232.

Chapter 4: The Extension of Military Control on the Neighbor Islands and the Arrest, Criminalization, and Incarceration of Japanese Residents

Parts of this chapter were originally published in Kelli Y. Nakamura, "'Into the Dark Cold I Go, the Rain Gently Falling': Hawai'i Island Incarceration," *Pacific Historical Review* 86, no. 3 (August 2017): 407–442, https://doi.org/10.1525/phr.2017.86.3.407.

1. "Mr. Myoshu Sasai," Japanese Internment and Relocation: The Hawaii Experience, University of Hawai'i, Hamilton Library, Special Collections [JIRHE], Item 239, p. 2.

2. Alan Rosenfeld, "'An Everlasting Scar': Civilian Internment on Wartime Kaua'i," *Hawaiian Journal of History* 45 (2011): 124.

3. Most incarceration sites fall into these eight categories: Concentration Camps, Temporary Assembly Centers, Immigration Detention Station, Department of Justice Internment Camp, U.S. Army Internment Camp, Citizen Isolation Center, Additional Facility, and U.S. Federal Prison.

4. Ronald Takaki, *Pau Hana: Plantation Life and Labor in Hawaii, 1835–1920* (Honolulu: University of Hawai'i Press, 1983), 64.

5. Japanese Cultural Center of Hawai'i Resource Room, AR 18, Box 2 Folder 5, "Paul Muraoka—Interview Notes (1 card) (Kauai)."

6. HSPA Plantation Archives, Lihue Plantation Company, Box R-3/1–5 (Roll Box).

7. John R. K. Clark, *The Beaches of Maui County* (Honolulu: University of Hawai'i Press, 1985), 7.

8. "Paul Muraoka—Interview Notes (1 card) (Kauai)."

9. Lāna'i Culture and Heritage Center, "2008 Lāna'i City Hongwanji Excerpts"; Mason Architects, *Historic Architecture Assessment of Four Buildings at the Police Station/ Courthouse/ Jail Complex in Lanai City* (Honolulu: N.p., 2006).

10. "Ha'alele Hana," *Honolulu Record,* 1 January 1953, 8.

11. United States, Congress, Senate, Committee on Pacific Islands and Porto Rico, *Report of the Subcommittee on Pacific Islands and Porto Rico on General Conditions in Hawaii* (Washington, DC: U.S. Government Printing Office, 1903), 214.

12. Julia Neal, "Wailua Hilton," *Garden Island,* 30 July 1975, 7. Despite efforts to save parts of the jail for historic and commercial purposes, it was demolished in 1978 to make way for the new State Kaua'i Community Correctional Center/ Kaua'i Intake Service Center. "Wailua Jail Now History," *Garden Island,* 9 January 1978, 1.

13. Allan Beekman, *The Niihau Incident: The true story of the Japanese fighter pilot who, after the Pearl Harbor attack, crash landed on the Hawaiian Island of Niihau and terrorized the residents* (Honolulu: Heritage Press of the Pacific, 1982).

14. Japanese Cultural Center of Hawai'i Resource Room, AR 19: Box 10, Folder 12, "An American Experiment, re: detention of detainees on Kauai, n.d., source covered up"; *Garden Island,* 15 July 1974, 2.

15. "Mr. Kaetsu Furuya TR-2," Japanese Internment and Relocation: The Hawaii Experience, University of Hawai'i, Hamilton Library, Special Collections [JIRHE], Item 233, 1.

16. Curtis Wong, "Seeing the Wailua Jail From the Inside-Out," *Garden Island,* 15 July 1974, 2.

17. Curtis Wong, "Sharing Life with Mice, Flies, Roaches—and Many Mosquitoes," *Garden Island,* 22 July 1974, 5.

18. "Mr. Kaetsu Furuya TR-2," 1.

19. Wong, "Sharing Life with Mice, Flies, Roaches—and Many Mosquitoes."

20. "Janet Chieko Uehara," JCCH Oral History, p. 4.

21. Curtis Wong, "Mosquitoes Feast on the Prisoners," *Garden Island,* 5 August 1974, 3.

22. "Mr. Kaetsu Furuya TR-2," 1–2.

23. "Mr. Kaetsu Furuya TR-2," 2.

24. "An American Experiment, re: detention of detainees on Kauai, n.d., source covered up."

25. "'Struggling Within a Struggle,' Japanese American Evacuation and Resettlement Records," UC Berkeley, Bancroft Library, BANC MSS 67/14 c, folder W2.463, p. 7.

26. "An American Experiment, re: detention of detainees on Kauai, n.d., source covered up."

27. Hiseki Miyasaki, "Aliens Grateful for Treatment," *Honolulu Star Bulletin,* 22 December 1941, 1.

28. "Struggling Within a Struggle," 7.

29. *Honouliuli Gulch and Associated Sites: Final Special Resource Study and Environmental Assessment* (Washington, DC: U.S. Department of the Interior, National Park Service, 2015), 33.

30. Patsy Sumie Saiki, *Ganbare!: An Example of Japanese Spirit* (Honolulu: Mutual Publishing, 2004), 61.

31. "DETENTION CAMP—KALEO, KAUAI," Japanese Internment and Relocation: The Hawaii Experience, University of Hawai'i, Hamilton Library, Special Collections [JIRHE], p. 1.

32. "Honouliuli, Haiku, Kalaheo Report," Japanese Internment and Relocation: The Hawaii Experience, University of Hawai'i, Hamilton Library, Special Collections [JIRHE], 249.

33. AGF Hawai'i 1945, untitled manuscript prepared by Army Garrison Force, Hawai'i, Central Pacific Base Command, dated October 20, 1945, Ephemeral property # 0186, U.S. Army Museum of Hawai'i, Fort DeRussy, Honolulu, p. III-133.

34. Jadelyn J. Moniz Nakamura, "Up in Arms! The Struggle to Preserve the Legacy of the National Park Service During Wartime," *Hawaiian Journal of History* 47 (2013): 191.

35. Jeffrey F. Burton and Mary M. Farrell, *World War II Japanese American Internment Sites in Hawai'i* (Tucson: N.p., 2007), 15.

36. George Hoshida, *Life of a Japanese Immigrant Boy in Hawaiian America: From Birth Through World War II, 1907–1945,* Japanese Internment and Relocation: The Hawaii Experience, University of Hawai'i, Hamilton Library, Special Collections [JIRHE], 255–256; Heidi Kathleen Kim, ed., *Taken from the Paradise Isle: The Hoshida Family Story* (Boulder: University Press of Colorado).

37. Gail Honda, ed., *Family Torn Apart: The Internment Story of the Otokichi Muin Ozaki Family* (Honolulu: Japanese Cultural Center of Hawai'i, 2012), 20.

38. "Mr. Myoshu Sasai," 2.

39. Hoshida, *Life of a Japanese Immigrant Boy in Hawaiian America,* 256.

40. "Sueda: (Transl) Internment Notes," Japanese Internment and Relocation: The Hawaii Experience, University of Hawai'i, Hamilton Library, Special Collections [JIRHE], Item 265, 22.

41. "Mr. Myoshu Sasai," 2.

42. Hoshida, *Life of a Japanese Immigrant Boy in Hawaiian America,* 255.

43. Hoshida, *Life of a Japanese Immigrant Boy in Hawaiian America,* 256.

44. "Mr. Myoshu Sasai," 3.

45. "Sueda: (Transl) Internment Notes," 22.

46. "Mr. Myoshu Sasai," 3.

47. Hoshida, *Life of a Japanese Immigrant Boy in Hawaiian America,* 264.

48. “S-23 Red Cross Report,” Japanese Internment and Relocation: The Hawaii Experience, University of Hawai‘i, Hamilton Library, Special Collections [JIRHE], Item 412.

49. Hoshida, *Life of a Japanese Immigrant Boy in Hawaiian America,* 265.

50. Hoshida, *Life of a Japanese Immigrant Boy in Hawaiian America,* 263.

51. Hoshida, *Life of a Japanese Immigrant Boy in Hawaiian America,* 263–264.

52. Dorothy Swaine Thomas, Richard Nishimoto, and Jacobus TenBroek, *The Spoilage* (Berkeley: University of California Press, 1969), 261–282.

53. “Thomas Sakakihara, Former Magistrate,” *Honolulu Advertiser,* 2 March 1989, 7.

54. “Sakakihara, Thomas,” Vertical file (Internment biographies): R-S, Japanese Cultural Center of Hawai‘i Resource Center.

55. Hank Sato, “Honouliuli: Oahu’s Little-Known World War II Internment Camp,” *Honolulu Star-Bulletin,* 18 March 1976, 1–8.

56. Jack Y. Tasaka, *Confidential Stories at Honouliuli Internment Camp*, trans. Ari Uchida ([Honolulu], 1980), MS, Japanese Cultural Center of Hawai‘i. Print.

57. Hoshida, *Life of a Japanese Immigrant Boy in Hawaiian America,* 266.

58. Tatsumi Hayashi, JCCH Hawaii Japanese Internee Database (Honolulu: Japanese Cultural Center of Hawaii, n.d.), XLS.

59. “Mr. Myoshu Sasai,” 3.

60. Burton and Farrell, *World War II Japanese American Internment Sites in Hawai‘i,* 15.

61. “S-23 Red Cross Report.”

62. Michi Kodama-Nishimoto, Warren S. Nishimoto, and Cynthia A. Oshiro, *Talking Hawai‘i’s Story: Oral Histories of an Island People* (Mānoa: Published for the Biographical Research Center by the University of Hawai‘i Press, 2009), 98.

63. “Mr. Jukichi Inouye TR-5,” 5.

64. “Mr. Kaetsu Furuya TR-2,” 2.

65. Hayashi, JCCH Hawaii Japanese Internee Database.

66. *Unspoken Memories: Oral Histories of Hawai‘i Internees at Jerome, Arkansas,* ([Honolulu]: Center for Oral History, Social Science Research Institute, University of Hawai‘i at Mānoa, 2014), 207.

67. *Unspoken Memories,* 214.

68. Hoshida, *Life of a Japanese Immigrant Boy in Hawaiian America,* 284.

Chapter 5: "Shadows of Their Former Selves" and "A Place in the Sun"

1. “Mr. Hisashi Fukuhara,” Japanese Internment and Relocation: The Hawaii Experience, University of Hawai‘i, Hamilton Library, Special Collections [JIRHE], Item 232, 6.

2. "History of the G-2 Section Part II," Japanese Internment and Relocation: The Hawaii Experience, University of Hawai'i, Hamilton Library, Special Collections [JIRHE], Item 230, 26.

3. "Mr. Jukichi Inouye TR-5," Japanese Internment and Relocation: The Hawaii Experience, University of Hawai'i, Hamilton Library, Special Collections [JIRHE], Item 236, 1.

4. "Mr. Kaetsu Furuya TR-2," Japanese Internment and Relocation: The Hawaii Experience, University of Hawai'i, Hamilton Library, Special Collections [JIRHE], Item 233, 7.

5. "Mr. Kaetsu Furuya TR-2," 6.

6. Jeff Burton, Mary Farrell, Lisa Kaneko, Linda Maldonato, and Kelly Altenhofen, "Hell Valley: Uncovering a Prison Camp in Paradise," *Social Process in Hawai'i* 45 (2014): 47.

7. Jiro Nakano, "Yoshiko Matsuka, Tanka Poetess of Hawaii," *Hawaii Herald,* 17 May 1991, A-8.

8. "74 Years Later: How Recalling Honouliuli's Dark Past Is Forging Its Future" (Honolulu: Hawai'i News Now, 2017), television interview.

9. Tetsuden Kashima, *Judgement Without Trial: Japanese American Imprisonment during World War II* (Seattle: University of Washington Press, 2003), 85.

10. "Some Older Japanese Here Said Gripped By 'Psychic Epidemic,'" *Honolulu Advertiser,* 4 March 1946, 1; "Postwar Delusions of Old Japanese Here Studied By UH Research Unit," *Honolulu Star Bulletin,* 9 March 1946, 16.

11. Dennis M. Ogawa and Evarts C. Fox Jr., "Japanese Internment and Relocation: The Hawaii Experience," paper presented at the International Conference of Relocation and Redress: The Japanese-American Experience, March 1983, p. 10.

12. Gladys Ishida, "The Japanese American Renunciants of Okayama Prefecture: Their Accommodation and Assimilation to Japanese Culture" (PhD diss., University of Michigan, 1955), 89.

13. National Archives and Records Administration, Records of the War Relocation Authority Headquarters, Subject-Classified General Files, 36.239 (12) to 36.310 (1), Box 248, Stack Area 17002, Row 2, Compartment 3, Shelf 4–5, Entry #16 File 36.300–36.31, Boxes 248–251, 36.310 Repatriation and Expatriation (Japanese) January 1 to April 29th, 1943.

14. Clifford Uyeda, "International Implication of Internment: WWII Story of Japanese Hawaiians, Japanese Peruvians, Japanese Canadians, and Aleuts" *Nikkei Heritage* 4, no. 1 (Winter 1992): 5.

15. Edward Holland Spicer, et al. *Impounded People: Japanese-Americans in the Relocation Centers* (Washington, DC: U.S. Government Printing Office, 1946), 182–194.

16. Yukiko Kimura, "Rumor Among the Japanese" *Social Process in Hawaii* 11 (May 1947): 84–92. A University of Hawai'i Research Unit extensively studied this phenomenon among the Issei population in Hawai'i after authorities charged Jisho Yamazaki, a thirty-three-year-old Japanese priest, with six counts of disloyalty for allegedly propagating messages where he expressed concern for people who "talk bad" about Japan. "Alien Priest Now Under Indictment Upset By 'Bad Talk' About Japan," *Honolulu Star Bulletin,* 6 March 1946, 11; "Japanese Indicted Under Disloyalty Law of 1918," *Honolulu Star Bulletin,* 5 March 1946, 7.

17. The Romanzo Adams Social Research Laboratory (RASRL), A-1989: 006, Box 10–11, "Interview with Mr. A. and Mr. B who are two of the officers of the Shosei-Kai (the original group of the Hawaii Doshi-Kai) at Mr. A's hat store on Beretania Street on May 16, 1946."

18. Yukiko Kimura, "Some Effects of the War Situation Upon the Alien Japanese in Hawaii," *Social Process in Hawaii* 8 (November 1943): 21.

19. One scholar estimates that only 3 percent of the entire Issei population, which dwindled to 1 or 1.5 percent in the course of eight months, were unwilling to accept news of Japan's defeat as a fact. Yukiko Kimura, "A Comparative Study of the Collective Adjustment of the Issei, the First Generation Japanese, in Hawaii and the Mainland United States Since Pearl Harbor" (PhD diss., University of Chicago, 1952), 351.

20. John J. Stephan, *Hawaii Under the Rising Sun: Japan's Plans for Conquest After Pearl Harbor* (Honolulu: University of Hawai'i Press, 1984), 172.

21. Yukiko Kimura, "Rumor Among the Japanese," *Social Process in Hawaii* 11 (May 1947): 84–85.

22. Yukiko Kimura, "A Sociological Analysis of Types of Social Readjustment of Alien Japanese in Hawaii Since the War" (Master's thesis, University of Hawai'i at Mānoa, 1947), 29; Yukiko Kimura, "A Comparative Study of the Collective Adjustment of the Issei, the First Generation Japanese, in Hawaii and the Mainland United States Since Pearl Harbor," 330.

23. Andrew W. Lind, *The Japanese in Hawaii Under Wartime Conditions* (Honolulu and New York: American Council, Institute of Pacific Relations, 1943), 21.

24. The editor of the *Colorado Times* estimated that there were approximately one thousand subscribers in Hawai'i. However, the total readership is estimated to be much larger as "the same copy was passed around among a number of friends and relatives." One scholar notes that "the number of readers was several times larger than the number of subscribers and consequently the effects of those papers were 'far reaching.'" Yukiko Kimura, "A Sociological Analysis of Types of Social Readjustment of Alien Japanese in Hawaii Since the War," 51, 202, 207.

25. Yukiko Kimura, "A Sociological Analysis of Types of Social Readjustment of Alien Japanese in Hawaii Since the War," 65. Masaharu Taniguchi founded Seichō-No Ie in 1930 as a nondenominational movement based on the belief that all religions emanate

from one universal God. It was introduced to Hawai'i around 1935, and its adherents disseminated its holy scripture, *Seimei-no Jisso* (The reality of life) and its monthly publication called *Seichō-no Ie.*; *What People in Hawaii are Saying and Doing, War Research Laboratory, University of Hawai'i, March 1, 1946 Report No. 8* (Honolulu: N.p., 1952).

26. Yukiko Kimura, "A Comparative Study of the Collective Adjustment of the Issei, the First Generation Japanese, in Hawaii and the Mainland United States Since Pearl Harbor," 356.

27. Yukiko Kimura, "A Comparative Study of the Collective Adjustment of the Issei, the First Generation Japanese, in Hawaii and the Mainland United States Since Pearl Harbor," 356–357.

28. The Romanzo Adams Social Research Laboratory (RASRL), A-1989: 006, Box 10–11, "Mr. Y., Waialae Ave., April 11, 1947," 3. According to a member of Tōbu Dōshi-Kai, his organization had about three hundred members while Kōsei-Kai had about two hundred and Hakkō-Kai one hundred members. The translation for Hakkō-Kai could possibly have a more nationalistic orientation. According to one scholar, the word 八紘 (Hakkō) comes from the saying 八紘一宇 (Hakkō-ichiu), which has two meanings: "universal brotherhood" or "all eight corners of the world under one roof," meaning under the control of Japan. Yukiko Kimura, "A Sociological Analysis of Types of Social Readjustment of Alien Japanese in Hawaii Since the War," 136.

29. RASRL, "Mr. Y., Waialae Ave., April 11, 1947," 1.

30. RASRL, "Mr. Y., Waialae Ave., April 11, 1947," 3.

31. The Romanzo Adams Social Research Laboratory (RASRL), A-1989: 006, Box 10–11, "A Former Hissho-Kai Leader Aiding Relief Projects for Japan: Exposes Inner Activities of 'Katta-To,'" 22 July 1948, 1. This split between various organizations is detailed in Yukiko Kimura, "A Sociological Analysis of Types of Social Readjustment of Alien Japanese in Hawaii Since the War," 134.

32. The Romanzo Adams Social Research Laboratory (RASRL), A-1989: 006, Box 10–11, "Mr. Inokuchi, Hawaii Doshi-kai, April 8, 1947," 1.

33. RASRL, "Mr. Inokuchi, Hawaii Doshi-kai, April 8, 1947," 1.

34. The Romanzo Adams Social Research Laboratory (RASRL), A-1989: 006, Box 10–11, "Interview with Mr. Tokuzo Shibayama—advisor of Hissho Kai," 9 July 1948, 1.

35. RASRL, "Interview with Mr. Tokuzo Shibayama—advisor of Hissho Kai," 9 July 1948, 1.

36. The Romanzo Adams Social Research Laboratory (RASRL), A-1989: 006, Box 10–11, "MEMBERSHIP FEE OF HISSHO-KAI IS $10.00—4,000 PAID-UP MEMBERS," 26 July 1948.

37. Yukiko Kimura, "A Sociological Analysis of Types of Social Readjustment of Alien Japanese in Hawaii Since the War," 126.

38. On November 17, 1977, Hisshō-Kai secretary Seiichi Masuda announced the formal disbanding of the organization in an announcement published in the *Hawaii*

Hochi. "ハワイ島必勝会解解の辞," *Hawaii Hochi,* 17 November 1977, 4; The Romanzo Adams Social Research Laboratory (RASRL), A-1989: 006, Box 10–11, "KAHALUU MEMBER OF HISSHO-KAI EVICTED FROM FARM: Refused to Re-new Lease Because He Believed Rumours," 9 July 1948; The Romanzo Adams Social Research Laboratory (RASRL), A-1989: 006, Box 10–11, "HISSHO-KAI SHOULD DISBAND—PAU: We Should All Try to Get Along Happily," 30 June 1948; The Romanzo Adams Social Research Laboratory (RASRL), A-1989: 006, Box 10–11, "A FORMER HISSHO-KAI LEADER AIDING RELIEF PROJECTS FOR JAPAN: Exposes Inner Activities of 'Katta-to,'" 22 July 1948. Many members of Hisshō-Kai eventually left because of its radical nature and created their own groups. Nearly seventy individuals formed a faction organization known as Sekisei-Kai (Association of the faithful) whose objective was "not to assert to the outsiders our belief in Japanese victory but it is primarily to keep our Japanese spirit unwavered" in the turmoil of the postwar period. The Romanzo Adams Social Research Laboratory (RASRL), A-1989: 006, Box 10–11, "Mr. K. H[igashi], Waipio, April 6, 1947."

39. By April 1947 there were at least eight known groups on O'ahu alone that were very similar in nature: Hawaii Dōshi-kai, Shosei-kai, Hisshō-Kai, Tōbu Dōshi-kai, Kōsei-kai, Hakkō-kai, Sekisei-kai, and the short-lived Bansai Club. Yukiko Kimura, "A Sociological Analysis of Types of Social Readjustment of Alien Japanese in Hawaii Since the War," 136.

40. "Earl Finch Given Rousing Reception," *Honolulu Star Bulletin,* 5 March 1946, 1.

41. Elizabeth Jones, "AJAs Fete Finch At Luau In Palama Auditorium," *Honolulu Advertiser,* 7 March 1946, 1; "Earl Finch Given Honorary Life Membership in C of C," *Honolulu Advertiser,* 26 March 1946, 1.

42. Yukiko Kimura, "A Sociological Analysis of Types of Social Readjustment of Alien Japanese in Hawaii Since the War," 139.

43. "Nisei Officer Shocked at Local Skepticism on Japan Defeat," *Honolulu Advertiser,* 6 December 1946, 6.

44. Yukiko Kimura, "A Comparative Study of the Collective Adjustment of the Issei, the First Generation Japanese, in Hawaii and the Mainland United States Since Pearl Harbor," 367–369.

45. Yukiko Kimura, "A Sociological Analysis of Types of Social Readjustment of Alien Japanese in Hawaii Since the War," 142–143.

46. "241 Officers, Men of 442nd Regiment Land," *Honolulu Star Bulletin,* 9 August 1946, 8; "241 Officers and Men To Be Given Iolani Reception," *Honolulu Advertiser,* 9 August 1946, 1.

47. Radford Mobley, "Plans Made to Call Japanese American Troops," *Honolulu Star Bulletin,* 21 January 1944, 6.

48. *WRA: A Story of Human Conservation* (Washington, DC: U.S. Government Printing Office, n.d.), 121.

49. *WRA: A Story of Human Conservation*, 123.

50. "An Oral History with Ben Kuroki," interviewed by Arthur A. Hansen, October 17, 1994, Ojai, California, pp. 46–51, Center for Oral and Public History, California State University, Fullerton, Japanese American Oral History Project, OH 2385, http://digitalcollections.archives.csudh.edu/digital/collection/p16855coll4/id/12092/rec/3; *Most Honorable Son*, documentary produced by KDN Films, written and directed by Bill Kubota, 2007, 57 min., http://www.pbs.org/mosthonorableson/.

51. *WRA: A Story of Human Conservation*, 129–130.

52. *WRA: A Story of Human Conservation*, 129–130.

53. *WRA: A Story of Human Conservation*, 124.

54. "GIs in Italy Promise Full Aid to Nisei American Veterans Upon Return to Civilian Life," *Pacific Citizen*, 25 August 1945, 1.

55. Lawrence H. Fuchs, *Hawaii Pono: A Social History* (New York: Harcourt, Brace & World Inc., 1961), 306.

56. Andrew W. Lind, "Some Problems of Veteran Adjustment in Hawaii," *Social Process in Hawaii* 12 (August 1948): 67.

57. Lawrence H. Fuchs, *Hawaii Pono: A Social History*, 306–307.

58. *From Bullets to Ballots.*

59. According to one prominent Nisei official, of the approximately 113,000 American citizens of Japanese ancestry in Hawai'i, 60,000 had been born after December 1, 1924. By an imperial ordinance that became effective December 1, 1924, the government of Japan declared that in the future it would claim no American-born child of Japanese parents as a citizen unless the parents registered the infant's name with a Japanese consulate within fourteen days of its birth. Dual citizenship would result only when the parents strongly desired that their children share the same citizenship. Procedures for formal renunciation of Japanese citizenship through registration with imperial government agencies were also made somewhat less complicated. They could be used by those born before December 1, 1924, as well as by any born after that date who might as they grew older wish to deny the Japanese citizenship registered for them by their parents. Kiyosue Inui, *The Unsolved Problem of the Pacific: A Survey of International Contacts, Especially in Frontier Communities, with Special Emphasis upon California and An Analytic Study of the Johnson Report to the House of Representatives* (Tokyo: The Japan Times, 1925), 258–261, 313, 320.

60. "Katagiri Due for Presidency of Civic Group," *Honolulu Star Bulletin*, 27 June 1940, 2; "New Citizen Conference Concluded," *Honolulu Star Bulletin*, 21 July 1941, 3; "Civic Group Will Install New Officers," *Honolulu Star Bulletin*, 11 July 1942, 9.

61. Tom Coffman, *Catch a Wave: Hawaii's New Politics* (Honolulu: Honolulu Star-Bulletin, 1972), 19.

62. Dennis M. Ogawa, *Kodomo no tame ni: For the Sake of the Children* (Honolulu: University of Hawai'i Press, 1985), 381.

63. Lawrence H. Fuchs, *Hawaii Pono: A Social History*, 318.

64. Daniel K. Inouye, "Correspondence, 8 May 2007," private collection of author.

65. For more information on the postwar rise of the Nisei, consult Dorothy Ochiai Hazama and Jane Okamoto Komeiji, *Okage Sama De: The Japanese in Hawaii 1885–1985* (Honolulu: Bess Press, 1986), 177–218.

66. Marita Sturken, *Tangled Memories: The Vietnam War, the Aids Epidemic, and the Politics of Remembering* (Berkeley: University of California Press, 1997), 7.

67. Tom Engelhardt, *The End of Victory Culture: Cold War America and the Disillusioning of a Generation* (New York: Basic Books, 1995), 10.

68. Christina Klein, *Cold War Orientalism: Asia in the Middlebrow Imagination, 1945–1961* (Berkeley: University of California Press, 2004), 192.

69. Dean Itsuji Saranillio, *Unsustainable Empire: Alternative Histories of Hawaiʻi Statehood* (Durham, NC: Duke University Press, 2018), 140.

Conclusion

1. "Soga, Translations of My Life behind Barbed Wire (Fukuhara)," Japanese Internment and Relocation: The Hawaii Experience, University of Hawaiʻi, Hamilton Library, Special Collections [JIRHE], Item 263, 6.

Bibliography

Primary Sources

"24 Lost on January 28 in Sub Attack; 36 Survive." *Maui News,* 11 February 1942, 1.

"74 years Later: How Recalling Honouliuli's Dark Past Is Forging Its Future." Honolulu: Hawai'i News Now, 2017. Television interview.

"241 Officers and Men To Be Given Iolani Reception." *Honolulu Advertiser,* 9 August 1946, 1.

"241 Officers, Men of 442nd Regiment Land." *Honolulu Star-Bulletin,* 9 August 1946, 8.

Abe, Sanji. "Consideration for Release from Internment." Letter to Lt. Gen. Robert C. Richardson, Jr., 11 Jan. 1944. MS. Honouliuli Internment Camp, Honolulu, Territory of Hawaii. *The Untold Story: The Internment of Japanese Americans in Hawai'i.* Web. March 23, 2018.

"Address given by Chief of Police W.A. Gabrielson, Honolulu, to the Annual Convention of the International Association of Chiefs of Police, held in Detroit, Michigan, August 9–12, 1943," 31.01, p. 1. Romanzo Adams Social Research Laboratory Confidential Research Files [RASRL].

AGF Hawai'i 1945, untitled manuscript prepared by Army Garrison Force, Hawai'i, Central Pacific Base Command, dated October 20, 1945. Ephemeral property # 0186, U.S. Army Museum of Hawai'i, Fort DeRussy, Honolulu, p. III-133.

"Alien Priest Now Under Indictment Upset By 'Bad Talk' About Japan." *Honolulu Star-Bulletin,* 6 March 1946, 11.

"Anthony Dies—Argued against Isle Martial Law." *Honolulu Advertiser.* November 3, 1982, 6.

Anthony, J. Garner. "Martial Law in Hawaii." *California Law Review* 30, no. 4 (May 1942): 371–396.

Anthony, J. Garner. "Martial Law, Military Government, and the Writ of Habeas Corpus in Hawaii." *California Law Review* 31, no. 5 (December 1943): 477–514.

"Anti-Japanese Sentiment of Naval Commander." Japanese Internment and Relocation: The Hawaii Experience, University of Hawai'i, Hamilton Library, Special Collections [JIRHE], Item 361.

Armstrong, Walter P. "Martial Law in Hawaii." *American Bar Association* 29 (Dec. 1943): 698–701.

"Attempt at Arson." *Polynesian,* 3 December 1859, 2.

Balch, John Adrian. *Shall the Japanese Be Allowed to Dominate Hawaii?* Honolulu: N.p., 1943.

"Balch Says Japs Will Dominate Islands Unless Many Removed." *Honolulu Star-Bulletin,* 24 June 1943, 1.

Baker, Ray Stannard. "Wonderful Hawaii: A World Experiment Station." *American Magazine* 73 (December 1911): 201–214.

"The Beauties of Opium." *Pacific Commercial Advertiser,* 23 May 1874, 2.

"Bloodshed in Lahaina." *Honolulu Record,* 22 November 1951, 8.

"Bonus Payments Are Looked Into by Consul Mori." *Honolulu Star-Bulletin,* 27 October 1916, 4.

Bureau of Customs. *Report of the Collector General of Customs, Port of Honolulu, Hawaiian Islands, 1874.* Honolulu: Collector General's Office, 1874.

Burns, John Anthony. *John A. Burns Oral History Project.* Tape No. 2.

Burns, John Anthony. *John A. Burns Oral History Project.* Tape No. 4.

"Campaign for Simpler Form of Expatriation Opens Here." *Honolulu Star-Bulletin,* 8 November 1940, 3.

"Chairman Spalding's Protest In Behalf of Sanji Abe and the Advertiser's Answer." *Honolulu Advertiser,* 4 November 1940, editorial page.

"Chinaman Disappears." *Pacific Commercial Advertiser,* 4 January 1897, 6.

"Chinese Riot on a Plantation." *Pacific Commercial Advertiser,* 4 October 1879, 3.

"City Water Is Safe To Drink, Ohrt Announces." *Honolulu Star-Bulletin,* 8 December 1941, 2.

"Civic Club Is Planning Active Year." *Honolulu Star-Bulletin,* 8 August 1939, 9.

"Civic Group Will Install New Officers." *Honolulu Star-Bulletin,* 11 July 1942, 9.

"Col. S.H. Spillner Correspondence with Michael Gordon." AR 19 Japanese American Relocation and Internment: The Hawai'i Experience, Box 21: The Research Process, Japanese Cultural Center of Hawai'i Resource Room.

"Col. William F. Steer." AR 19, Box 21, Folder 26, p. 9. Japanese Cultural Center of Hawai'i Resource Room.

Constitutions of Hawaii. Washington, DC: N.p., 1898.

"Coolie Troubles." *Pacific Commercial Advertiser,* 18 November 1865, 2.

Dan Toru Nishikawa. From the Patsy Saiki archival collection (AR 18, Box 2, Folder 9), 3.

"A Desperate Expedient." *Hawaii Hochi: The Bee Section,* 20 October 1928, 2.

"DETENTION CAMP—KALEO, KAUAI." Japanese Internment and Relocation: The Hawaii Experience, University of Hawai'i, Hamilton Library, Special Collections [JIRHE], p. 1.

"DETENTION CAMP: SAND ISLAND." Japanese Internment and Relocation: The Hawaii Experience, University of Hawai'i, Hamilton Library, Special Collections [JIRHE].

Dillingham, Walter F. *A Memorandum*. Honolulu: N.p., 1932.

"Disastrous Fire at Halawa." *Pacific Commercial Advertiser,* 8 June 1867, 2.

"Drink and Work." *Kohala Midget,* 12 July 1911, 1.

Dulaney, James, and Eichi Hongo. "Check of a Rumor in Kaheka Lane." October 23, 1942, p. 1. Romanzo Adams Social Research Laboratory Confidential Research Files [RASRL].

Dulaney, James, and Eichi Hongo. "Special Detail." October 17, 1942, p. 3. Romanzo Adams Social Research Laboratory Confidential Research Files [RASRL].

Dulaney, James, and Eichi Hongo. "Special Detail, 10-19-42." October 19, 1942, p. 1. Romanzo Adams Social Research Laboratory Confidential Research Files [RASRL].

Dulaney, James, and Eichi Hongo. "Special Detail 10-20-42." October 20, 1942, p. 1. Romanzo Adams Social Research Laboratory Confidential Research Files [RASRL].

Dulaney, James, and Eichi Hongo. "Special Detail." October 21, 1942, p. 3. Romanzo Adams Social Research Laboratory Confidential Research Files [RASRL].

Dulaney, James, and Eichi Hongo. "Special Detail." October 27, 1942, p. 1. Romanzo Adams Social Research Laboratory Confidential Research Files [RASRL].

Dulaney, James, and Eichi Hongo. "Special Detail, 11-3-42." November 3, 1942, p. 3. Romanzo Adams Social Research Laboratory Confidential Research Files [RASRL].

Dulaney, James, and Eichi Hongo. "Special Detail, 11-7-42." November 8, 1942, p. 1. Romanzo Adams Social Research Laboratory Confidential Research Files [RASRL].

Dulaney, James, and Eichi Hongo. "Special Detail, 11-11-42." November 11, 1942, p. 1. Romanzo Adams Social Research Laboratory Confidential Research Files [RASRL].

Dulaney, James, and Eichi Hongo. "Special Detail, 11-12-42." November 12, 1942, p. 1. Romanzo Adams Social Research Laboratory Confidential Research Files [RASRL].

Dulaney, James, and Eichi Hongo. "Special Detail, 11-17-42." November 17, 1942, p. 1. Romanzo Adams Social Research Laboratory Confidential Research Files [RASRL].

Dulaney, James, and Eichi Hongo. "Special Detail, 11-21-42." November 21, 1942, p. 1. Romanzo Adams Social Research Laboratory Confidential Research Files [RASRL].

Dulaney, James, and Eichi Hongo. "Special Detail, 11-30-42." November 30, 1942, p. 1. Romanzo Adams Social Research Laboratory Confidential Research Files [RASRL].

Dulaney, James, and Eichi Hongo. "Special Detail, 12-8-42." December 9, 1942, p. 1. Romanzo Adams Social Research Laboratory Confidential Research Files [RASRL].

Dulaney, James, and Eichi Hongo. "Special Detail, 12-10-42." December 10, 1942, p. 1. Romanzo Adams Social Research Laboratory Confidential Research Files [RASRL].

Dulaney, James, and Eichi Hongo. "Special Detail, 12-11-42." December 11, 1942, p. 1. Romanzo Adams Social Research Laboratory Confidential Research Files [RASRL].

"Earl Finch Given Honorary Life Membership in C of C." *Honolulu Advertiser,* 26 March 1946, 1.

"Earl Finch Given Rousing Reception." *Honolulu Star-Bulletin,* 5 March 1946, 1.

"Early Plantation Life." *Honolulu Record,* 27 October 1949, 8.

Emergency Service Committee. *The AJA—Their Present and Future,* Honolulu: N.p., [1940?].

"Enclosure (B): Factors to Be Considered in Investigations of Japanese Subjects." Japanese Internment and Relocation: The Hawaii Experience, University of Hawai'i, Hamilton Library, Special Collections [JIRHE], p. 7.

"FBI Course for Police Opens Here." *Honolulu Star-Bulletin,* 8 January 1942, 1.

Frankel, Chuck. "'Pressured' in Massie Case, Says Ex-Governor." *Honolulu Star-Bulletin,* 13 February 1967, 1.

Furuya, Suikei. *An Internment Odyssey—Haisho Tenten.* Honolulu: Japanese Cultural Center of Hawai'i, 2017.

"Furuya, Suikei (translation) Haisho Ten-ten." Japanese Internment and Relocation: The Hawaii Experience, University of Hawai'i, Hamilton Library, Special Collections [JIRHE], Item 257.

Garden Island, 15 July 1974, 2.

"General Information, Richard C. Miller Espionage Bureau, December 3 1941." Romanzo Adams Social Research Laboratory Confidential Research Files [RASRL].

"GIs in Italy Promise Full Aid to Nisei American Veterans Upon Return to Civilian Life." *Pacific Citizen,* 25 August 1945, 1.

"Gov. Stainback Praises Patriotic Candidates Who Quit Politics." *Garden Island,* 20 October 1942, 1.

Grant, M. Forsyth. *Scenes in Hawaii or Life in the Sandwich Islands.* Toronto: Hart & Company, 1888.

"Ha'alele Hana." *Honolulu Record,* 1 January 1953, 8.

Hall, Jack. *Kohala's Gay Nineties or the Log of a Luna.* Kohala?: N.p., 1927.

"Harry Urata." National Park Service, World War II Valor in the Pacific, p. 5. https://www.nps.gov/valr/learn/historyculture/oral-history-interviews.htm. Accessed June 11, 2018.

Hawaii, Office of the Military Governor, Morale Section, Emergency Service Committee. *Final Report of the Emergency Service Committee.* Honolulu: N.p., 1946.

Hawaii, Office of the Military Governor, Morale Section, Emergency Service Committee. *Report of the Emergency Service Committee.* Honolulu: N.p., 1945.

"Hawaii, U.S.A." *Honolulu Advertiser,* 2 November 1940, editorial page.

"ハワイ島必勝会解の辞" [Hawaishima hisshō-kai kai no ji]. *Hawaii Hochi,* 17 November 1977, 4.

Hawai'i State Archives. "002 Criminal Case Files of the First Circuit Court Criminal 1430." Series 002, First Circuit Court, 7 May 1890.

Hawai'i State Archives. "Island Sheriffs, Vol. 5, Hawaii 1889, Police Records." Series 364.

Hawai'i State Archives. "Letters Received from Sheriff of Hawai'i." Series 363, October–December 1889.

Hawai'i State Archives. U.S. President. Executive Orders. Sept 1903–Oct 1918 (no. 225/2978).

Hawai'i Volcanoes National Park (HAVO) Archives. HAVO 17707 Image Collection; Box 16, Folder 1.

Hawai'i Volcanoes National Park (HAVO) Archives. HAVO 17707 Image Collection; Box 43, Folder 1.

Hawai'i Volcanoes National Park (HAVO) Archives. *Superintendent Report, 1927–1945.*

Hawai'i Volcanoes National Park (HAVO) Archives. *Superintendent Report, 1941,* 2.

The Hawaiian Planters' Monthly 1, no. 1 (April 1882): 20.

"Hawaiian Sugar Plantation History: No. 12—Waiakea Island of Hawaii." *Honolulu Star-Bulletin,* 18 May 1935, Sec. 2, p. 8.

Hawaiian Sugar Planters' Association. *The Sugar Industry of Hawaii and the Labor Shortage.* Honolulu: HSPA, 1921.

"Hawaiian Who Killed Japanese Aviator on Niihau Isle Honored." *Honolulu Advertiser,* 7 June 1943, 2.

"History of the G-2 Section Part I." Japanese Internment and Relocation: The Hawaii Experience, University of Hawai'i, Hamilton Library, Special Collections [JIRHE], Item 229.

"History of the G-2 Section Part II." Japanese Internment and Relocation: The Hawaii Experience, University of Hawai'i, Hamilton Library, Special Collections [JIRHE], Item 230.

Hobson, Thomas C. *Hawaiian Almanac and Annual for 1898.* Honolulu: Thomas G. Thrum, 1897.

Honolulu Police Department. *Annual Report: Police Department, City and County of Honolulu, Territory of Hawaii 1941,* "Police," 31.01. Romanzo Adams Social Research Laboratory Confidential Research Files [RASRL].

"Honolulu Police Department Contact Group," p. 1. Romanzo Adams Social Research Laboratory Confidential Research Files [RASRL].

"Honouliuli, Haiku, Kalaheo Report." Japanese Internment and Relocation: The Hawaii Experience, University of Hawai'i, Hamilton Library, Special Collections [JIRHE], Item 249.

Hoshida, George. *Life of a Japanese Immigrant Boy in Hawaiian America: From Birth Through World War II, 1907–1945.* Japanese Internment and Relocation: The Hawaii Experience, University of Hawai'i, Hamilton Library, Special Collections [JIRHE].

H.S. Burr, U.S. Navy Reserve, District Intelligence Officer, U.S. Navy. "Naval Intelligence Manual for Investigating Japanese Cases in Hawaii." RG: 389: Record of the Office of the Provost Marshal General, 1941–. Japanese Internment and Relocation: Hawaii Experience [JIRHE], University of Hawai'i, Hamilton Library, Special Collections, Box 3, A-40, pp. 50–51.

HSPA Plantation Archives. Lihue Plantation Company, Box R-3/1–5 (Roll Box). https://www.doi.gov/sites/doi.gov/files/uploads/31_stat_141_hawaiian_organic_act_1900.pdf.

Inouye, Daniel K. "Correspondence, 8 May 2007." Private collection of author.

Irwin, Edwin P. "The Hand Across the Sea." *Honolulu Advertiser,* 30 January 1920, 4.

"Janet Chieko Uehara." Japanese Cultural Center of Hawai'i Resource Room, Oral History.

Japanese Cultural Center of Hawai'i Resource Room. AR 18, Box 2, Folder 5. "Paul Muraoka—Interview Notes (1 card) (Kauai)."

Japanese Cultural Center of Hawai'i Resource Room. AR 19: Japanese American Relocation and Internment: The Hawaii Experience, Box 9, Folder 30, Vital Statistics.

Japanese Cultural Center of Hawai'i Resource Room. AR 19: Box 10, Folder 12, "An American Experiment, re: detention of detainees on Kauai, n.d., source covered up."

Japanese Cultural Center of Hawai'i Resource Room. AR 19: Japanese American Relocation and Internment: The Hawaii Experience, Box 12—Articles and Manuscripts, 1942–1949, Folder 25: Chapter IX: Prisoners of War and Internees, circa 1945.

Japanese Cultural Center of Hawai'i Resource Room. Otokichi Ozaki Collection. #606 "Otokichi Ozaki."

Japanese Cultural Center of Hawai'i Resource Room. R.H. Lodge photographer, #910. "Honouliuli Internment & POW Camp—barracks and tents." AR 19 Archival Collection.

Japanese Cultural Center of Hawai'i Resource Room. R.H. Lodge photographer, #2137. "Honouliuli Internment & POW Camp—barracks and tents." Hawai'i's Plantation Village Collection.

Japanese Cultural Center of Hawai'i Resource Room. R.H. Lodge photographer, #2466. "Honouliuli internee barracks." Hawai'i's Plantation Village Collection.

"Japanese Indicted Under Disloyalty Law of 1918." *Honolulu Star-Bulletin,* 5 March 1946, 7.

"Kahului, Maui, Shelled by Enemy." *Maui News,* 16 December 1941, 1.

"Katagiri Due for Presidency of Civic Group." *Honolulu Star-Bulletin,* 27 June 1940, 2.

Kaua'i Historical Society. "Photo 03–300.JPG." From the Hofgarrd photo album in possession of Kekaha Plantation.

Kaua'i Historical Society. "Wailua Jail 2001055134."

Kauai Morale Committee. *The Final Report of the Kauai Morale Committee.* Lihue: The Committee, 1945, 10.

Kodani, Roy. "Yoshiko Shimabukuro." *Hawaii Herald,* 4 July 2003, 10.

"Labor." *Hawaiian Star,* 20 June 1900, 4.

Laws of the Territory of Hawaii Passed by the Legislature at its Regular and Extra Sessions 1905. Honolulu: The Bulletin Publishing Co., Ltd., 1905.

"Letter Sent Jamieson Demands $10,000 For Return of Young Son." *Honolulu Star-Bulletin,* 19 September 1928, 1.

"Letter to Mayor Lester Petrie from W.A. Gabrielson, January 29, 1943." Romanzo Adams Social Research Laboratory Confidential Research Files [RASRL].

Lind, Andrew. "The Japanese in Hawaii Under War Conditions." Paper presented at the Eighth Conference of the Institute of Pacific Relations, Honolulu, 1942.

"Looking Backward." *Honolulu Record,* 12 August 1948, 8.

"Luna's Abuse Provoked Workers." *Honolulu Record,* 16 October 1952, 8.

MacCaughey, Vaughan. "Some Outstanding Educational Problems of Hawaii." *School and Society* 9 (January 1919): 100–101.

Maui County, Police Department, & Maui County. *Annual Report. Police Department 1941.* Territory of Hawaii: County of Maui, 1941.

Maui News, 18 August 1900, 2.

"Maui Port Shelled by Sub No Casualties in Attack." *Honolulu Advertiser,* 17 December 1941, 3.

"Memoir #2 by Dan Toru Nishikawa." Japanese Cultural Center of Hawai'i Resource Room.

"Memorandum for the Officer in Charge: Subject: Kibei." F6-Item17–1942–04-Memo Re Kibei-Blake, 442nd Veterans Club Collection, Archives & Manuscripts Department, University of Hawai'i at Mānoa Library.

Miyasaki, Hiseki. "Aliens Grateful for Treatment." *Honolulu Star-Bulletin,* 22 December 1941, 1.

Mobley, Radford. "Plans Made to Call Japanese American Troops." *Honolulu Star-Bulletin,* 21 January 1944, 6.

"More Incendiarism." *Pacific Commercial Advertiser,* 20 August 1870, 3.

"Mr. Hisashi Fukuhara, TR-1." Japanese Internment and Relocation: The Hawaii Experience, University of Hawai'i, Hamilton Library, Special Collections [JIRHE], Item 232.

"Mr. Jukichi Inouye TR-5." Japanese Internment and Relocation: The Hawaii Experience, University of Hawai'i, Hamilton Library, Special Collections [JIRHE], Item 236.

"Mr. Kaetsu Furuya." Japanese Internment and Relocation: The Hawaii Experience, University of Hawai'i, Hamilton Library, Special Collections [JIRHE], Item 233.

"Mr. Minosuke Hanabusa, TR-3." Japanese Internment and Relocation: The Hawaii Experience, University of Hawai'i, Hamilton Library, Special Collections [JIRHE], Item 234.

"Mr. Myoshu Sasai." Japanese Internment and Relocation: The Hawaii Experience, University of Hawai'i, Hamilton Library, Special Collections [JIRHE], Item 239.

Munson, Curtis B. "Japanese on the West Coast." In *American Concentration Camps*, vol. 1: *July, 1940—December 31, 1941*, edited with an introduction by Roger Daniels. New York: Garland Publishing, 1989.

"Murderous Filipino Attacks His Luna." *Pacific Commercial Advertiser*, 27 June 1915, 1.

Nakano, Jiro. "Yoshiko Matsuka, Tanka Poetess of Hawaii." *Hawaii Herald*, 17 May 1991, 8.

National Archives and Records Administration, College Park, Maryland. RG 494. Record of U.S. Army Forces in the Middle Pacific, 1942–46. Record of the Military Government of the Territory of Hawaii. Alien Processing Center. Internee Case Files. Box 217, Stack Area 290, Row 44, Compartment 6, Shelf 3.

National Archives and Records Administration. Records of the War Relocation Authority Headquarters. Subject—Classified General Files, 36.239 (12) to 36.310 (1). Box 248, Stack Area 17002, Row 2, Compartment 3, Shelf 4–5. Entry #16 File 36.300–36.310 Boxes 248–251. 36.310 Repatriation and Expatriation (Japanese) January 1 to April 29, 1943.

National Archives and Records Administration, San Francisco. RG 181 Records of Naval Districts and Shore Establishments, Naval Shipyard, Pearl Harbor, Hawaii Office of the Commandant, General Correspondence (Formerly Classified), 1940–1946 ARC 296911, NN 373–91 (FRC Accession No. 181–58–3404A), Box 51, 62, 63.

National Archives and Records Administration, San Francisco. USIS (RG 566) series: *Alien Case Files*. File: Mitsumyo Tottori: #A2071200 in Box 110.

National Park Service, U.S. Department of the Interior. *Honouliuli Gulch and Associated Sites: Draft Special Resource Study and Environmental Assessment, May 2014*. Washington DC: U.S. Department of the Interior, 2014.

Neal, Julia. "Wailua Hilton." *Garden Island*, 30 July 1975, 7.

Neptune, Ansley N., and Eichi Hongo. "Tour of Duty—Special Detail #2." June 5, 1942, p. 2. Romanzo Adams Social Research Laboratory Confidential Research Files [RASRL].

Neptune, Ansley N., and Eichi Hongo. "Tour of Duty—Special Detail #2." June 9, 1942, p. 1. Romanzo Adams Social Research Laboratory Confidential Research Files [RASRL].

Neptune, Ansley N., and Eichi Hongo. "Tour of Duty—Special Detail #2." July 15, 1942, p. 1. Romanzo Adams Social Research Laboratory Confidential Research Files [RASRL].

Neptune, Ansley N., and Eichi Hongo. "Tour of Duty—Special Detail #2." July 17, 1942, p. 1. Romanzo Adams Social Research Laboratory Confidential Research Files [RASRL].

Neptune, Ansley N., and Eichi Hongo. "Tour of Duty—Special Detail #2." No date, p. 1. Romanzo Adams Social Research Laboratory Confidential Research Files [RASRL].

"New Citizen Conference Concluded." *Honolulu Star-Bulletin*, 21 July 1941, 3.

"New National Guard Unit Will Be Crack Organization, Says Its Captain." *The Pacific Commercial Advertiser,* 15 August 1917, 1.

"Nisei Officer Shocked at Local Skepticism on Japan Defeat." *Honolulu Advertiser,* 6 December 1946, 6.

"No Casualties in [Maui's] First Actual Bombardment." *Maui News,* 17 December 1941, 1.

Nowell, Ernest, and Eichi Hongo. "Supplement—Tour of Duty—Special Detail #2, 8-7-42." August 5, 1942, p. 1. Romanzo Adams Social Research Laboratory Confidential Research Files [RASRL].

Nowell, Ernest, and Eichi Hongo. "Tour of Duty—Special Detail #2." July 28, 1942, p. 1. Romanzo Adams Social Research Laboratory Confidential Research Files [RASRL].

Nowell, Ernest, and Eichi Hongo. "Tour of Duty—Special Detail #2." July 29, 1942, p. 1. Romanzo Adams Social Research Laboratory Confidential Research Files [RASRL].

Nowell, Ernest, and Eichi Hongo. "Tour of Duty—Special Detail #2." July 31, 1942, p. 1. Romanzo Adams Social Research Laboratory Confidential Research Files [RASRL].

Nowell, Ernest, and Eichi Hongo. "Tour of Duty—Special Detail #2." August 7, 1942, p. 2. Romanzo Adams Social Research Laboratory Confidential Research Files [RASRL].

Nowell, Ernest, and Eichi Hongo. "Tour of Duty—Special Detail #2." August 10, 1942, p. 2. Romanzo Adams Social Research Laboratory Confidential Research Files [RASRL].

Nowell, Ernest, and Eichi Hongo. "Tour of Duty—Special Detail #2." August 11, 1942, p. 1. Romanzo Adams Social Research Laboratory Confidential Research Files [RASRL].

Nowell, Ernest, and Eichi Hongo. "Tour of Duty—Special Detail #2." August 13, 1942, p. 1. Romanzo Adams Social Research Laboratory Confidential Research Files [RASRL].

Nowell, Ernest, and Eichi Hongo. "Tour of Duty—Special Detail #2." August 17, 1942, p. 2. Romanzo Adams Social Research Laboratory Confidential Research Files [RASRL].

Nowell, Ernest, and Eichi Hongo. "Tour of Duty—Special Detail #2." August 18, 1942, p. 2. Romanzo Adams Social Research Laboratory Confidential Research Files [RASRL].

"Opium Smoking." *Pacific Commercial Advertiser,* 21 January 1864, 2.

Organic Act. Ch. 339, 31 Stat. 141, § 67 (1900).

Pacific Commercial Advertiser, 14 August 1880, 3.

Pacific Commercial Advertiser, 28 July 1866, 1.

Pacific Commercial Advertiser, 13 October 1866, 3.

"Police Probe Reports of Parachutists." *Honolulu Star-Bulletin,* 8 December 1941, 2.

"Police Say No Evidence of Parachutists." *Honolulu Star-Bulletin,* 8 December 1941, 2.

"Police Take FBI Course." *Honolulu Star-Bulletin*, 9 January 1942, 3.

"Policemen Can Search Homes." *Honolulu Advertiser*, 2 March 1942, 1.

"Postwar Delusions of Old Japanese Here Studied by UH Research Unit." *Honolulu Star-Bulletin*, 9 March 1946, 16.

Report of the Commissioner of Labor on Hawaii, 1901. Washington, DC: U.S. Government Printing Office, 1902.

Report of the Governor of the Territory of Hawaii to the Secretary of the Interior, 1900. Washington, DC: U.S. Government Printing Office, 1900.

Report of the Governor of the Territory of Hawaii to the Secretary of the Interior, 1901. Washington, DC: U.S. Government Printing Office, 1901.

The Romanzo Adams Social Research Laboratory Confidential Research Files, 1942–1959. Inventory Box 13 / 10–11, Ko Kona / 10–19, 1942–1952, "Life in Kona."

The Romanzo Adams Social Research Laboratory (RASRL). A-1989: 006, Box 10–11, "A FORMER HISSHO-KAI LEADER AIDING RELIEF PROJECTS FOR JAPAN: Exposes Inner Activities of 'Katta-to,'" 22 July 1948.

The Romanzo Adams Social Research Laboratory (RASRL). A-1989: 006, Box 10–11, "HISSHO-KAI SHOULD DISBAND—PAU: We Should All Try to Get Along Happily," 30 June 1948.

The Romanzo Adams Social Research Laboratory (RASRL). A-1989: 006, Box 10–11, "Interview with Mr. A. and Mr. B who are two of the officers of the Shosei-Kai (the original group of the Hawaii Doshi-Kai) at Mr. A's hat store on Beretania Street on May 16, 1946."

The Romanzo Adams Social Research Laboratory (RASRL). A-1989: 006, Box 10–11, "Interview with Mr. Tokuzo Shibayama—advisor of Hissho Kai," 9 July 1948.

The Romanzo Adams Social Research Laboratory (RASRL). A-1989: 006, Box 10–11, "KAHALUU MEMBER OF HISSHO-KAI EVICTED FROM FARM: Refused to Re-new Lease Because He Believed Rumours," 9 July 1948.

The Romanzo Adams Social Research Laboratory (RASRL). A-1989: 006, Box 10–11, "MEMBERSHIP FEE OF HISSHO-KAI IS $10.00—4,000 PAID-UP MEMBERS," 26 July 1948.

The Romanzo Adams Social Research Laboratory (RASRL). A-1989: 006, Box 10–11, "Mr. Inokuchi, Hawaii Doshi-kai, April 8, 1947."

The Romanzo Adams Social Research Laboratory (RASRL). A-1989: 006, Box 10–11, "Mr. K. H[igashi], Waipio, April 6, 1947."

The Romanzo Adams Social Research Laboratory (RASRL). A-1989: 006, Box 10–11, "Mr. Y., Waialae Ave., April 11, 1947."

The Romanzo Adams Social Research Laboratory (RASRL). Box 12 / Folder No: 20–24 Ka Kaua'i / Index, 10–26, "How the Kauai Candidates Withdrew."

The Romanzo Adams Social Research Laboratory (RASRL). *Race Relations in a Plantation Community.* Honolulu: N.p., [1979].

Rosenfeld, Alan. "'An Everlasting Scar': Civilian Internment on Wartime Kaua'i." *Hawaiian Journal of History* 45 (2011): 123–145.

Ross, William G., and Eichi Hongo. "Tour of Duty-Special Detail #2." June 20, 1942, p. 1. Romanzo Adams Social Research Laboratory Confidential Research Files [RASRL].

"S-23 Red Cross Report." Japanese Internment and Relocation: The Hawaii Experience, University of Hawai'i, Hamilton Library, Special Collections [JIRHE], Item 412.

"S-27 Internee Treatment." Japanese Internment and Relocation: The Hawaii Experience, University of Hawai'i, Hamilton Library, Special Collections [JIRHE], Item 416.

"S-28 Treatment of Civilian Internees at Sand Island." Japanese Internment and Relocation: The Hawaii Experience, University of Hawai'i, Hamilton Library, Special Collections [JIRHE], Item 417.

"Sabotage Reported in Waikiki Area." *Honolulu Star-Bulletin,* 7 December 1941, 3.

"Sakakihara, Thomas." Vertical file (Internment biographies): R–S, Japanese Cultural Center of Hawai'i Resource Center.

"Sanji Abe's Case," *Honolulu Advertiser,* 8 October 1940, editorial page.

"Sanji Abe's Expatriation," *Honolulu Advertiser,* 5 November 1940, editorial page.

Santoki, Mark K. "Iwao Mizuta: Reflection on the McKinley Class of '34 and the Legacy of Miles Cary." *Hawaii Herald,* 1 November 1991, 1.

Sato, Hank. "Honouliuli: Oahu's Little-Known World War II Internment Camp." *Honolulu Star-Bulletin,* 18 March 1976, 1–8.

Saturday Press, 12 March 1881, 2.

"Service Group, Civic Club Merge." *Honolulu Advertiser,* 24 July 1942, 7.

Shivers, Robert L. *Cooperation of the Various Racial Groups with Each Other and with the Constituted Authorities before and after December 7, 1941. Statement Presented before Sub-Committee on Statehood United States House of Representative at Iolani Palace. Honolulu, Hawaii, U.S.A., January 15, 1946.* Honolulu: Chamber of Commerce, 1946.

"Soga, Keiho (trans.) My Life Behind Barbed Wire." Japanese Internment and Relocation: The Hawaii Experience, University of Hawai'i, Hamilton Library, Special Collections [JIRHE], Item 264.

"Soga, Translations of My Life behind Barbed Wire (Fukuhara)." Japanese Internment and Relocation: The Hawaii Experience, University of Hawai'i, Hamilton Library, Special Collections [JIRHE], Item 263.

Soga, Yasutaro. *Life Behind Barbed Wire: The World War II Internment Memoirs of a Hawai'i Issei.* Honolulu: University of Hawai'i Press, 2007.

"Some Older Japanese Here Said Gripped By 'Psychic Epidemic.'" *Honolulu Advertiser,* 4 March 1946, 1.

Spicer, Edward Hollan, et al. *Impounded People: Japanese-Americans in the Relocation Centers.* Washington, DC: U.S. Government Printing Office, 1946.

Stirling, Yates. *Sea Duty: The Memoirs of a Fighting Admiral.* New York: G.P. Putnam's Sons, 1939.

"Struggling Within a Struggle." Japanese American Evacuation and Resettlement Records, UC Berkeley, Bancroft Library, BANC MSS 67/14 c, Folder W2.463.

"Submarines Attack Maui, Kauai, Hawaii." *Honolulu Star-Bulletin,* 31 December 1941, 1.

"Sueda: (Transl) Internment Notes." Japanese Internment and Relocation: The Hawaii Experience, University of Hawai'i, Hamilton Library, Special Collections [JIRHE], Item 265.

"Supreme Court—January Term." *Polynesian,* 8 January 1853, 2.

Takao Ozawa v. United States. 260 U.S. 178 (1922).

Tasaka, Jack Y. *Confidential Stories at Honouliuli Internment Camp,* translated by Ari Uchida. [Honolulu]: n.p.: 1980, manuscript, Japanese Cultural Center of Hawaiʻi.

Taylor, Clarice B. "Kauai Is Out on a Limb." *Garden Island,* 13 October 1942, 6.

"Thomas Sakakihara, Former Magistrate." *Honolulu Advertiser,* 2 March 1989, 7.

"Toso Haseyama 2." National Park Service, World War II Valor in the Pacific, p. 13. https://www.nps.gov/valr/learn/historyculture/oral-history-interviews.htm. Accessed June 11, 2018.

"Transfer of Quarantine Station RG 407." Japanese Internment and Relocation: The Hawaii Experience, University of Hawaiʻi, Hamilton Library, Special Collections [JIRHE], Item 305.

"Un-American Reasoning," *Honolulu Advertiser,* 11 October 1940, editorial page.

United States. *The Hawaiian Organic Act Including Amendments Up to December 1955.* Honolulu: Legislative Reference Bureau, University of Hawaiʻi, 1955.

United States, Bureau of the Census. *Preliminary Figures on Employment Status, Occupation, and Industry for the Japanese Population of the Territory of Hawaii: 1940.* Washington, DC: Bureau of the Census, [1942].

United States, Commission on Wartime Relocation and Internment of Civilians. *Personal Justice Denied: Report of the Commission on Wartime Relocation and Internment of Civilians.* Washington DC: Civil Liberties Public Education Fund; Seattle: University of Washington Press, 1997.

United States, Congress. Senate. Committee on Pacific Islands and Porto Rico. *Hawaiian Investigation: Report of Subcommittee on Pacific Islands and Porto Rico on General Conditions in Hawaii, and the Administration of the Affairs Thereof, Part 2.* Washington, DC: U.S. Government Printing Office, 1902.

United States, Congress. Versions of the Hawaii organic act, Senate bill 222, To provide a government for the Territory of Hawaii, 56th Congress, first session, 1899–1900. Washington, DC: Senate of the United States, 1899–1900.

United States, Department of the Interior Bureau of Education. *A Survey of Education in Hawaii* 16 (1920): 1–408.

United States, Office of Education. *A Survey of Education in Hawaii, Made Under the Direction of the Commissioner of Education.* Washington, DC: U.S. Government Printing Office, 1920.

United States, Senate. *Investigation of the Pearl Harbor Attack, Report of the Joint Committee on the Investigation of the Pearl Harbor Attack Congress of the United States,* Senate Document 244, 2d Session, 79th Congress. Washington, DC: U.S. Government Publishing Office 1946.

Upton, John L., and Eichi Hongo. "Tour of Duty—Special Detail #2." July 26, 1942, p. 1. Romanzo Adams Social Research Laboratory Confidential Research Files [RASRL].

"A Visit to Maui—No. 2." *Pacific Commercial Advertiser,* 24 August 1872, 3.

"Wailua Jail Now History." *Garden Island,* 9 January 1978, 1.

"Want to Get Thousands of Japanese." *Hawaiian Star,* 17 March 1906, 1.

The War Record of Civilian and Industrial Hawaii. A Documentary History of the Assistance Extended to the Armed Forces by the Civilian Community and the Sugar Plantations. Honolulu: N.p., 1945.

What People in Hawaii are Saying and Doing, War Research Laboratory, University of Hawaii, March 1, 1946, Report No. 8. [Honolulu]: N.p., 1952.

White, R. P. "Boy Committed Crime to Bring Happiness to Poor Parents, He Says." *Honolulu Star-Bulletin,* 24 September 1928, 1.

Wong, Curtis. "Mosquitoes Feast on the Prisoners." *Garden Island,* 5 August 1974, 3.

Wong, Curtis. "Seeing the Wailua Jail From the Inside-Out." *Garden Island,* 15 July 1974, 2.

Wong, Curtis. "Sharing Life with Mice, Flies, Roaches—and Many Mosquitoes." *Garden Island,* 22 July 1974, 5.

WRA: A Story of Human Conservation. Washington, DC: U.S. Government Printing Office, n.d.

Secondary Sources

"'A'ala: Once a Thriving Japanese Community." *Oral History Recorder* 14, no. 2 (Summer 1997): 1–14.

Ai, Li Ling. *Life Is for a Long Time: A Chinese Hawaiian Memoir.* New York: Hastings House, 1972.

Allen, Gwenfread. *Hawaii's War Years.* Westport, CT: Greenwood Press, 1971.

Anthony, J. Garner. *Hawaii Under Army Rule.* Honolulu: University Press of Hawai'i, 1955.

Asato, Noriko. *Teaching Mikadoism: The Attack on Japanese Language Schools in Hawaii, California, and Washington, 1919–1927.* Honolulu: University of Hawai'i Press, 2006.

Bates, G. W. *Sandwich Island Notes.* New York: Harper & Brothers, 1854.

Beechert, Edward D. *Working in Hawaii: A Labor History.* Honolulu: University of Hawai'i Press, 1985.

Beekman, Allan. *The Niihau Incident: The true story of the Japanese fighter pilot who, after the Pearl Harbor attack, crash landed on the Hawaiian Island of Niihau and terrorized the residents.* Honolulu: Heritage Press of the Pacific, 1982.

Bird, Isabella L. *Six Months in the Sandwich Islands.* Tokyo: Charles E. Tuttle Company, 1974.

Boylan, Dan, and T. Michael Holmes. *John A Burns: The Man and His Times.* Honolulu: University of Hawai'i Press, 2000.

Broom, Leonard, and John I. Kitsuse. *The Managed Casualty: The Japanese-American Family in World War II.* Berkeley: University of California Press, 1973.

Burton, Jeffrey F., and Mary M. Farrell. *World War II Japanese American Internment Sites in Hawai'i.* Tucson, Arizona: n.p., 2007.

Burton, Jeffrey F., Mary Farrell, Lisa Kaneko, Linda Maldonato, and Kelly Altenhofen. "Hell Valley: Uncovering a Prison Camp in Paradise," *Social Process in Hawai'i* 45 (2014): 43–79.

Chapin, Helen Geracimos. *Guide to Newspapers of Hawaii: 1834–2000.* Honolulu: Hawaiian Historical Society, 2000.

Chapin, Helen Geracimos. *Shaping History: The Role of Newspapers in Hawai'i.* Honolulu: University of Hawai'i Press, 1996.

The Civil Liberties Public Education Fund. *Personal Justice Denied: Report of the Commission on Wartime Relocation and Internment of Citizens.* Seattle: University of Washington Press, 1997.

Clark, John R. K. *The Beaches of Maui County.* Honolulu: University Press of Hawai'i, 1985.

Coffman, Tom. *Catch a Wave: Hawaii's New Politics.* Honolulu: Honolulu Star-Bulletin, 1972.

Coffman, Tom. *Tadaima! I Am Home: A Transnational Family History.* Honolulu: University of Hawai'i Press, 2018.

Conroy, Hilary, and T. Scott Miyakawa, eds. *East Across the Pacific: Historical and Sociological Studies of Japanese Immigration and Assimilation.* Santa Barbara, CA: American Biographical Center–Clio Press, 1972.

Curtis, Dorothe, et al. *Recommendations to the Molokai Task Force for the Historical and Cultural Resources of Molokai.* Hawai'i: N.p., 1973.

Cushing, Robert L. "The Beginnings of Sugar Production in Hawai'i," *Hawaiian Journal of History* 19 (1985): 29–30.

Daws, Gavan. *Shoal of Time: A History of the Hawaiian Islands.* Honolulu: University of Hawai'i Press, 1968.

Dorrance, William H. "The U.S. Army on Kauai, 1909–1942." *Hawaiian Journal of History* 32 (1998): 155–169.

Duus, Masayo. *The Japanese Conspiracy: The Oahu Sugar Strike of 1920.* Berkeley, CA: University of California Press, 1999.

Dye, Bob. "The Case of Sanji Abe," *Honolulu Magazine* 37, no. 5 (November 2002): 38.

Dye, Bob, ed. *Hawai'i Chronicles: Island History from the Pages of Honolulu Magazine.* Honolulu: University of Hawai'i Press, 1996.

Dye, Bob, ed. *Hawai'i Chronicles III: World War Two In Hawai'i From the Pages of Paradise of the Pacific.* Honolulu: University of Hawai'i Press, 2000.

Edwards, Richard. *Contested Terrain: The Transformation of the Workplace in the Twentieth Century.* New York: Basic Books, Inc., 1979.

Embree, John F. *Acculturation Among the Japanese of Kona, Hawaii.* Menasha, WI: The American Anthropological Association, 1941; New York: Kraus Reprint, 1969.

Embree, John F. "New Local and Kin Groups Among the Japanese Farmers of Kona, Hawaii." *American Anthropologist* 41, no. 3 (July–Sept. 1939): 400–407.

Embrey, Sue Kunitomi. *The Lost Years, 1942–1946.* Los Angeles: Moonlight Publications, 1972.

Engelhardt, Tom. *The End of Victory Culture: Cold War America and the Disillusioning of a Generation.* New York: Basic Books, 1995.

From Bullets to Ballots. Produced by the Japanese American National Museum. 24 min. 1997. Videocassette.

Fuchs, Laurence. *Hawaii Pono: A Social History.* New York: Harcourt, Brace & World, 1961.

Glick, Clarence E. *Sojourners and Settlers: Chinese Migrants in Hawaii.* Honolulu: University Press of Hawai'i, 1980.

Goldman, Rita. *Every Grain of Rice: Portraits of Maui's Japanese Community.* Virginia Beach: The Donning Company, 2003.

Gordon, Michael John. "Suspects in Paradise: Looking for Japanese 'Subversives' in the Territory of Hawaii, 1939–1945." Master's thesis, University of Iowa, 1983.

Hara, Maya M. *An Oral History on Issei in Lahaina.* N.p.: West Maui Cultural Council, 1991.

"Harry Urata." National Park Service, World War II Valor in the Pacific, p. 5. https://www.nps.gov/valr/learn/historyculture/oral-history-interviews.htm. Accessed June 11, 2018.

Hatanaka, Yuriko, and Kimie Kawahara. "The Impact of War on an Immigrant Culture." *Social Processes in Hawaii* 8 (Nov. 1943): 36–45.

Hawaii Nikkei History Editorial Board, ed. *Japanese Eyes, American Heart: Personal Reflections of Hawaii's World War II Nisei Soldiers.* Honolulu: Tendai Educational Foundation, 1998.

Hayashi, Tatsumi. JCCH Hawai'i Japanese Internee Database, XLS. Honolulu: Japanese Cultural Center of Hawai'i, n.d.

Hazama, Dorothy Ochiai, and Jane Okamoto Komeiji. *Okage Same De: The Japanese in Hawaii 1885–1985.* Honolulu: Bess Press, 1986.

Honda, Gail, ed., *Family Torn Apart: The Internment Story of the Otokichi Muin Ozaki Family.* Honolulu: Japanese Cultural Center of Hawai'i, 2012.

Honouliuli Gulch and Associated Sites Special Resource Study. Honolulu: National Park Service, U.S. Department of the Interior, 2014.

Honouliuli Special Resource Study, Honolulu, Maui, Hawaii, and Kauai Counties, HI. Interior Department Documents and Publications. Washington, DC: Federal Information & News Dispatch, LLC, 2011.

Hoshida, George, and Tamae Hoshida. *Taken from the Paradise Isle: The Hoshida Family Story.* Edited by Heidi Kim. Boulder: University Press of Colorado, 2015. http://www.100thbattalion.org/history/veterans/chaplains/masao-yamada/.

Inui, Kiyosue. *The Unsolved Problem of the Pacific: A Survey of International Contacts, Especially in Frontier Communities, with Special Emphasis upon California and An Analytic Study of the Johnson Report to the House of Representatives.* Tokyo: The Japan Times, 1925.

Ishida, Gladys. "The Japanese American Renunciants of Okayama Prefecture: Their Accommodation and Assimilation to Japanese Culture." PhD diss., University of Michigan, 1955.

"J.G. Anthony, Martial Law Foe, Is Dead at 82." *Honolulu Star-Bulletin*, 2 November 1982, 1.

Jackson, Frances. "Military Use of Haleakalā National Park." *Hawaiian Journal of History* (1972): 102–107.

Jin, Michael R. *Citizens, Immigrants, and the Stateless: A Japanese American Diaspora in the Pacific.* Stanford, CA: Stanford University Press, 2022.

Jones, Elizabeth. "AJAs Fete Finch at Luau in Palama Auditorium." *Honolulu Advertiser,* 7 March 1946, 1.

Judd, Lawrence M. *Lawrence M. Judd and Hawaii: An Autobiography.* Tokyo: Charles E. Tuttle Company, Inc., 1971.

Kamai, Nancine "Missy," William H. Folk, and Hallett H. Hammatt. Final Archaeological Literature Review and Field Inspection Report for the Po'ipū Road Multi-Modal Improvements Project Kōloa and Weliweli Ahupua'a, Kōloa District, Kaua'i TMKs: multiple 34–36" (Kailua: Cultural Surveys Hawai'i, Inc., April 2021): 34–36.

Kashima, Tetsuden. *Judgement Without Trial: Japanese American Imprisonment during World War II.* Seattle: University of Washington Press, 2003.

Katoda, Tetsuei. *The Fiftieth Anniversary of the Establishment of the Shingon Sect Mission of Hawaii.* Honolulu: The Mission, 1966.

Kent, Noel J. *Hawaii, Islands Under the Influence.* New York: Monthly Review Press, 1983.

Kim, Heidi Kathleen, ed. *Taken from the Paradise Isle: The Hoshida Family Story.* Boulder: University Press of Colorado, 2015.

Kimura, Yukiko. "A Comparative Study of the Collective Adjustment of the Issei, the First Generation Japanese, in Hawaii and the Mainland United States Since Pearl Harbor." PhD diss., University of Chicago, 1952.

Kimura, Yukiko. *Issei: Japanese Immigrants in Hawaii.* Honolulu: University of Hawaiʻi Press, 1988.

Kimura, Yukiko. "Psychological Aspects of Japanese Immigration." *Social Process in Hawaii* 6 (July 1940): 10–22.

Kimura, Yukiko. "Rumor Among the Japanese." *Social Process in Hawaii* 11 (May 1947): 84–92.

Kimura, Yukiko. "A Sociological Analysis of Types of Social Readjustment of Alien Japanese in Hawaii Since the War." Master's thesis, University of Hawaiʻi at Mānoa, 1947.

Kimura, Yukiko. "Some Effects of the War Situation Upon the Alien Japanese in Hawaii." *Social Process in Hawaii* 8 (November 1943): 18–28.

Klass, Tim. *World War II on Kauai: Historical Research by Tim Klass.* Prepared for the Kauaʻi Historical Society by the Westland Foundation. Portland, OR: The Westland Foundation, 1970.

Klein, Christina. *Cold War Orientalism: Asia in the Middlebrow Imagination, 1945–1961.* Berkeley: University of California Press, 2004.

Kodama-Nishimoto, Michi, Warren S. Nishimoto, and Cynthia A. Oshiro, *Talking Hawaiʻi's Story: Oral Histories of an Island People.* Mānoa: Published for the Biographical Research Center by the University of Hawaiʻi Press, 2009.

Kotani, Roland. *The Japanese in Hawaii: A Century of Struggle.* Honolulu: The Hawaii Hochi, 1985.

Kuykendall, Ralph S. *The Hawaiian Kingdom,* vol. III: *1874–1893, The Kalakaua Dynasty.* Honolulu: University of Hawaiʻi Press, 1967.

La Violette, Forrest Emmanuel. *Americans of Japanese Ancestry, a Study of Assimilation in the American Community.* Toronto: Canadian Institute of International Affairs, 1945.

Lānaʻi Culture and Heritage Center. "2008 Lānaʻi City Hongwanji Excerpts."

Lim-Chong, Lily, and Harry V. Ball. *Opium and the Law: Hawaii, 1856–1900.* Honolulu: N.p., 1988.

Lind, Andrew W. "Assimilation in Rural Hawaii." *American Journal of Sociology* 45, no. 2 (Sept. 1939): 200–214.

Lind, Andrew W. *The Japanese in Hawaii Under Wartime Conditions.* Honolulu and New York: American Council, Institute of Pacific Relations, 1943.

Lind, Andrew W. "Some Problems of Veteran Adjustment in Hawaii." *Social Process in Hawaii* 12 (August 1948): 58–73.

"Looking Backward." *Honolulu Record,* 12 August 1948, 8.

"Luna's Abuse Provoked Workers." *Honolulu Record,* 16 October 1952, 8.

Lydon, Edward C. *The Anti-Chinese Movement in the Hawaiian Kingdom, 1852–1886.* San Francisco: R and E Research Associates, 1975.

MacCaughey, Vaughan. "Some Outstanding Educational Problems of Hawaii." *School and Society* 9 (January 1919): 100–101.

Mason Architects. *Historic Architecture Assessment of Four Buildings at the Police Station/ Courthouse/ Jail Complex in Lanai City.* Honolulu: N.p., 2006.

Matsuo, Dorothy. *Boyhood to War: History and Anecdotes of the 442nd RCT.* Korea: Mutual Publishing of Honolulu, 1992.

Maui Historical Society. *World War II's Impact on Maui County: A Social History.* Wailuku: Maui Historical Society, 1992.

Merry, Sally Engle. *Colonizing Hawai'i: The Cultural Power of Law.* Princeton, NJ: Princeton University Press, 2000.

Miyamoto, Kazuo. *Hawaii: End of the Rainbow.* Rutland, VT: Bridgeway Press [distributed by C.E. Tuttle], 1964.

Miyasaki, Gail. "Hole-Hole Bushi: The Only Song of the Japanese in Hawaii." *Hawaii Herald,* 2 February 1973, 5.

Moniz Nakamura, Jadelyn J. "Up in Arms! The Struggle to Preserve the Legacy of the National Park Service During Wartime." *Hawaiian Journal of History* 47 (2013): 179–209.

Moriyama, Alan Takeo. "Imingaisha: Japanese Emigration Companies and Hawaii, 1894–1908." PhD diss., University of California, Los Angeles, 1982.

Most Honorable Son. Documentary produced by KDN Films. Written and Directed by Bill Kubota. 2007. 57 min. http://www.pbs.org/mosthonorableson/.

Nakahodo, Masanori. "The POW Camp in Hawai'i: On the Yasuo Kayo 'Islands of captives,'/ ハワイの捕虜収容所—嘉陽安男「捕虜たちの島」をめぐって" *Bulletin of the Faculty of Law and Letters University of the Ryukyus/ 日本東洋文化論集琉球大学本文部紀要* (March 2014): 49.

Nakamura, Kelli Y. "Bishop Mitsumyo Tottori: Patriotism Through Buddhism During World War II." *Hawaiian Journal of History* 51 (2017): 115–145.

Nakamura, Kelli Y. "'Violence and Press Incendiarism': Media and Labor Conflicts in the 1909 Strike." *Hawaiian Journal of History* 45 (2011): 69–99.

Nelligan, Peter J., and Harry V. Ball. *Ethnic Juries in Hawai'i, 1825–1990.* Honolulu: The Friends of The Judiciary History Center, 1996.

Nellist, George F., ed. *The Story of Hawaii and Its Builders.* Territory of Hawaii: Honolulu Star-Bulletin, Ltd., 1925.

Nishigawa, Linda, and Ernest Oshiro. "Reviving the Lotus: Japanese Buddhism and World War II Internment," *Social Process in Hawai'i* 45 (2014): 173–198.

Odo, Franklin. *No Sword to Bury: Japanese Americans in Hawaii During World War II.* Philadelphia: Temple University Press, 2004.

Ogawa, Dennis M. *Jan Ken Po: The World of Hawaii's Japanese.* Honolulu: University of Hawai'i Press, 1973.

Ogawa, Dennis M. *Kodomo no tame ni: For the Sake of the Children, The Japanese American Experience in Hawaii.* Honolulu: University of Hawai'i Press, 1978.

Ogawa, Dennis M., and Evarts C. Fox Jr. "Japanese Internment and Relocation: The Hawaii Experience." Paper presented at the International Conference of Relocation and Redress: The Japanese-American Experience, March 1983.

Ogawa, Dennis M., and Christine Kitano. *Who You? Hawaii Issei.* Honolulu: Japanese Cultural Center of Hawai'i, 2018.

Okahata, James H., ed. *A History of the Japanese in Hawaii.* Honolulu: The United Japanese Society of Hawaii, 1971.

Okamura, Jonathan Y. "Race Relations in Hawai'i During World War II: The Non-internment of Japanese Americans." *Amerasia Journal* 26, no. 2 (2000): 117–141.

Okamura, Jonathan Y. *Raced to Death in 1920s Hawai'i: Injustice and Revenge in the Fukunaga Case.* Urbana: University of Illinois Press, 2019.

Okawa, Gail Y. *Remembering Our Grandfathers' Exile: US Imprisonment of Hawai'i's Japanese in World War II.* Honolulu: University of Hawai'i Press, 2020.

Okihiro, Gary Y. *Cane Fires: The Anti-Japanese Movement in Hawaii 1865–1945.* Philadelphia: Temple University Press, 1991.

Okihiro, Gary Y. *Encyclopedia of Japanese American Internment.* Santa Barbara, CA: Greenwood, an Imprint of ABC-CLIO, LLC, 2013.

"An Oral History with Ben Kuroki." Interviewed by Arthur A. Hansen, October 17, 1994, Ojai, California, pp. 46–51. Center for Oral and Public History, California State University, Fullerton, Japanese American Oral History Project, OH 2385. http://digitalcollections.archives.csudh.edu/digital/collection/p16855coll4/id/12092/rec/3.

Pioneer Mill Company: A Maui Sugar Plantation Legacy. Honolulu: Center for Oral History, Social Science Research Institute, University of Hawai'i at Mānoa, 2003.

Reinecke, John E. *Labor Disturbances in Hawaii, 1890–1925: A Summary.* Honolulu: N.p., 1966.

Robinson, Greg. *By Order of the President: FDR and the Internment of Japanese.* Cambridge, MA: Harvard University Press, 2001.

Robinson, Greg. *A Tragedy of Democracy: Japanese Confinement in North America.* New York: Columbia University Press, 2009.

Saiki, Patsy Sumie. *Ganbare!: An Example of Japanese Spirit.* Honolulu: Mutual Publishing, 2004.

Sakamoto, Pamela Rotner. *Midnight in Broad Daylight: A Japanese American Family Caught Between Two Worlds.* New York: HarperCollins, 2016.

"Sanji Abe, 87; First AJA in Isle Senate," Abe, Sanji. University of Hawai'i at Mānoa. Microfiche D98050 Biographical.

Saranillio, Dean Itsuji. *Unsustainable Empire: Alternative Histories of Hawai'i Statehood.* Durham, NC: Duke University Press, 2018.

Sato, Claire, and Violet Harada. *A Resilient Spirit: The Voice of Hawai'i's Internees.* Honolulu: Japanese Cultural Center of Hawai'i, 2018.

Scheiber, Harry N., and Jane L. Scheiber. *Bayonets in Paradise: Martial Law in Hawai'i During World War II Honolulu.* Honolulu: University of Hawai'i Press, 2016.

Scheiber, Harry N., and Jane L. Scheiber. "Constitutional Liberty in World War II: Army Rule and Martial Law in Hawaii: 1941–1946." *Western Legal History* 3, no. 2 (1990): 340–378.

Shiramizu, Shigehiko. "Ethnic Press and Its Society: A Case of Japanese Press in Hawaii." *KEIO Communication Review* 11 (1990): 49–71.

Slackman, Michael. "The Orange Race: George S. Patton, Jr.'s Japanese American Hostage Plan." *Biography: An Interdisciplinary Quarterly* 7, no. 1 (Winter 1984): 1–22.

Stannard, David E. *Honor Killing: Race, Rape, and Clarence Darrow's Spectacular Last Case.* New York: Penguin, 2006.

Stephan, John J. *Hawaii Under the Rising Sun: Japan's Plans for Conquest After Pearl Harbor.* Honolulu: University of Hawai'i Press, 1984.

Stephenson, Larry K., and Amy A. Miyashiro. "Rural-Urban Contrasts of *Kumiai's* in Hawaii." *Social Process in Hawaii* 27 (1979): 78–80.

Strazar, Marie D. *Moloka'i in History: A Guide to the Resources.* Honolulu: History and Humanities Program of the Hawai'i State Foundation on Culture and the Arts, 2000.

Sturken, Marita. *Tangled Memories: The Vietnam War, the Aids Epidemic, and the Politics of Remembering.* Berkeley: University of California Press, 1997.

Sullivan, Edward Dean. *The Snatch Racket.* New York: Vanguard Press, 1932.

Suzuki, Kei. "Sanji Abe." *Hawaii Herald,* 17 October 2008, B-3.

Takaki, Ronald. *Pau Hana: Plantation Life and Labor in Hawaii, 1835–1920.* Honolulu: University of Hawai'i Press, 1983.

Tamura, Eileen H. *Americanization, Acculturation, and Ethnic Identity: The Nisei Generation in Hawaii.* Urbana: University of Illinois Press, 1994.

Thomas, Dorothy S., Charles Kikuchi, and James Minoru Sakoda. *The Salvage.* Berkeley: University of California Press, 1975.

Thomas, Dorothy S., Richard Nishimoto, and Jacobus TenBroek. *The Spoilage: Japanese-American Evacuation and Resettlement During World War II.* Berkeley: University of California Press, 1946.

Thompson, Erwin N. *Pacific Ocean Engineers: History of the U.S. Army Corps of Engineers in the Pacific, 1905–1980.* Washington, DC: U.S. Government Printing Office, 1985.

Thompson, Richard Austin. *The Yellow Peril, 1890–1924.* New York: Arno Press, 1978.

University of Hawaiʻi at Mānoa. Center for Oral History. *Unspoken Memories: Oral Histories of Hawaiʻi Internees at Jerome, Arkansas.* Honolulu: Center for Oral History, Social Science Research Institute, University of Hawaiʻi at Mānoa, 2014.

Uyeda, Clifford, "International Implication of Internment: WWII Story of Japanese Hawaiians, Japanese Peruvians, Japanese Canadians, and Aleuts." *Nikkei Heritage* 4, no. 1 (Winter 1992).

Uyehara, Yukuo. "The Horehore-Bushi: A Type of Japanese Folksong Developed and Sung Among the Early Immigrants in Hawaii." *Social Process in Hawaii* 28 (1980–1981): 110–120.

Van Dyke, Jon M. *Who Owns the Crown Lands of Hawaiʻi.* Honolulu: University of Hawaiʻi Press, 2008.

Waiakea Town, or, "Yashijima Story": Home of the Waiakea Pirates. Hilo: N.p., 1994.

Wakukawa, Ernest. *A History of the Japanese People in Hawaii.* Honolulu: The Toyo Shoin, 1938.

Weglyn, Michi. *Years of Infamy: The Untold Story of America's Concentration Camps.* New York: Morrow Quill Paperbacks, 1976.

Wilcox, Carol. *Sugar Water: Hawaii's Plantation Ditches.* Honolulu: University of Hawaiʻi Press, 1996.

Williams, Duncan R. "Complex Loyalties: Issei Buddhist Ministers during the Wartime Incarceration." *Pacific World,* 3rd ser., no. 5 (Fall 2003): 255–274.

Yamamoto, Misako. "Cultural Conflicts and Accommodations of the First and Second Generation Japanese." *Social Process in Hawaii* 4 (May 1938): 40–48.

Index

About the Author

Kelli Y. Nakamura is a professor at Kapiʻolani Community College. Her research interests focus on Japanese and Japanese American history. She has published articles in the *Journal of World History*, *Amerasia*, the *Historian*, the *Pacific Historical Review*, and the *Hawaiian Journal of History*, where she currently serves as a co-editor. She also teaches at the Ethnic Studies and History Department at the University of Hawaiʻi at Mānoa.